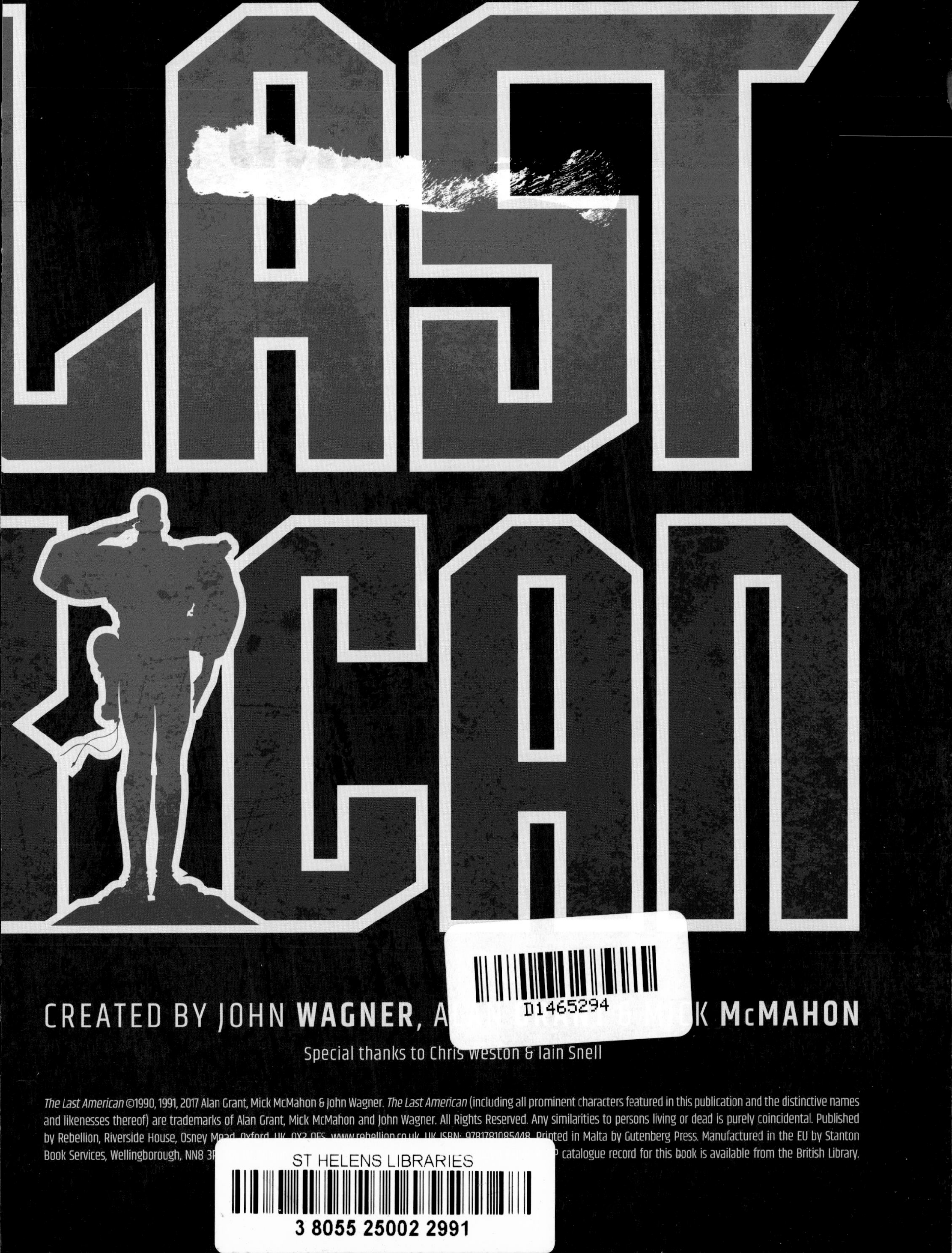
LAST
CAN

CREATED BY JOHN **WAGNER**, A… K **McMAHON**

Special thanks to Chris Weston & Iain Snell

 Published by Rebellion, Riverside House, Osney Mead, Oxford, UK, OX2 0ES. www.rebellion.co.uk. UK ISBN: 9781781085448. Printed in Malta by Gutenberg Press. Manufactured in the EU by Stanton Book Services, Wellingborough, NN8 3P… P catalogue record for this book is available from the British Library.

THE LAST AMERICAN, THE BOMB, AND ME.

I grew up during the height of the Cold War. The fear of sudden personal annihilation in the inevitable nuclear attack has stayed with me to this day. You just had to put it to the back of your mind so that you could get on with your life.

One of my clearest childhood memories is of being sporadically woken in the morning by a vague and distant tremor, a tremor generated in a dream, that would convince me that a nuclear attack had just started. I would creep to my bedroom window terrified that I would see the mushroom cloud.

Very scary stuff for the over imaginative young me, but understandable given that I can also clearly remember seeing Soviet Premier Nikita Khrushchev ranting on TV and being really frightened by him (and not just because he looked like Tor Johnson). I think this would have been during the 1962 Cuban Missile Crisis, when I was nine years old.

And just to add to the gaiety of nations, my school organised a showing of Peter Watkins BBC film 'The War Game', a highly disturbing depiction of a nuclear attack on Britain, so disturbing in fact that it was banned from public exhibition. I think I was twelve when I watched it.

Conceived four years before the fall of the Berlin Wall, The Last American is our attempt to depict the reality of nuclear war, or at least the aftermath. Gathering reference material for the book, I came across John Hersey's 'Hiroshima', a compelling article about six victims of the atomic attack. The experiences of these six individuals made a great impression on me, so that as well as brooding over dying in a nuclear war, I am now just as aware of the ghastliness of surviving.

Happy days!

Mick McMahon

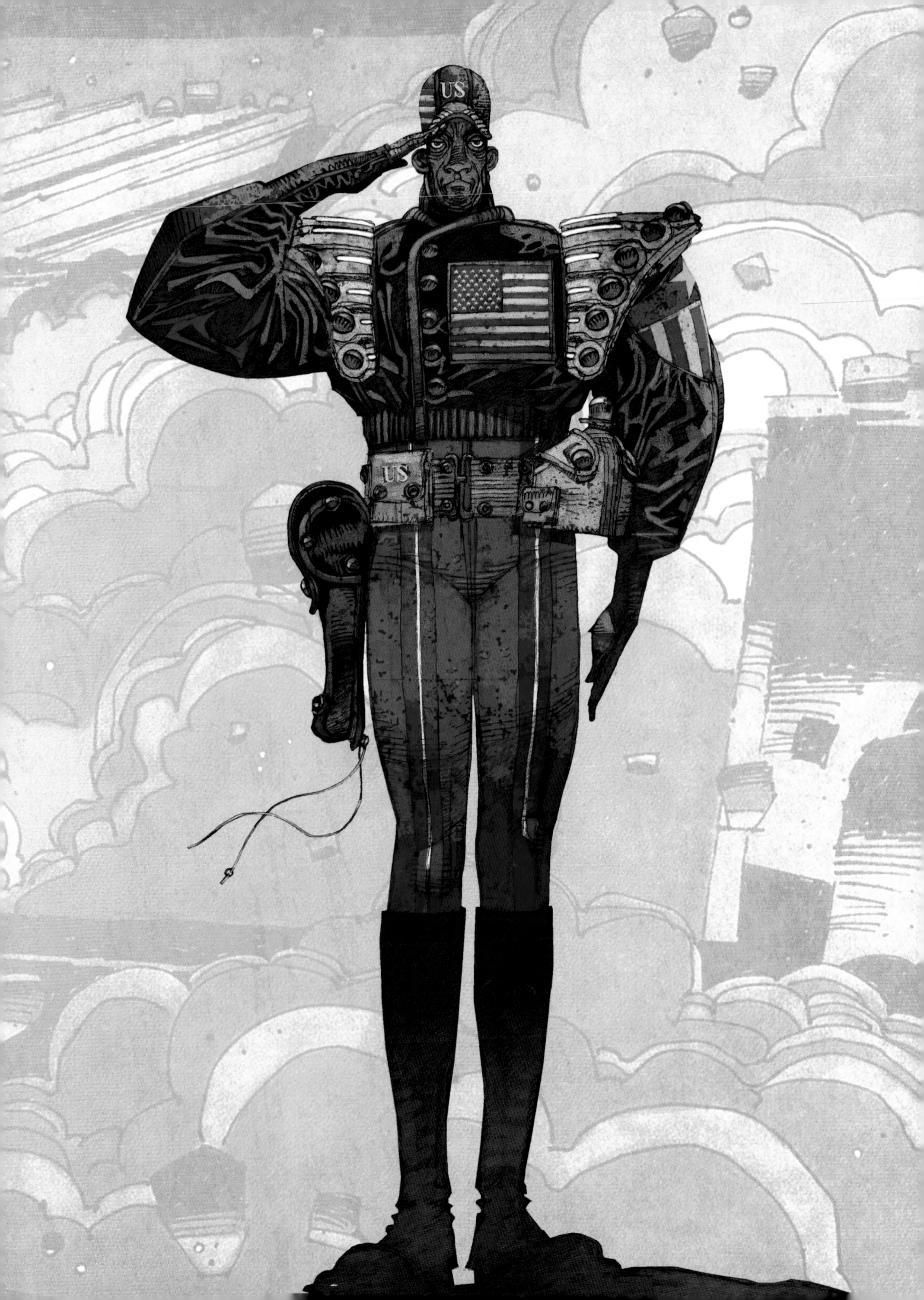
US
US

THE LAST AMERICAN

Script
John Wagner & Alan Grant

Art
Mick McMahon

Letters
Phil Felix

Originally published as a four-part series by Epic Comics

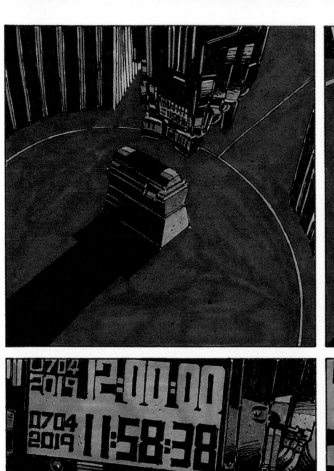

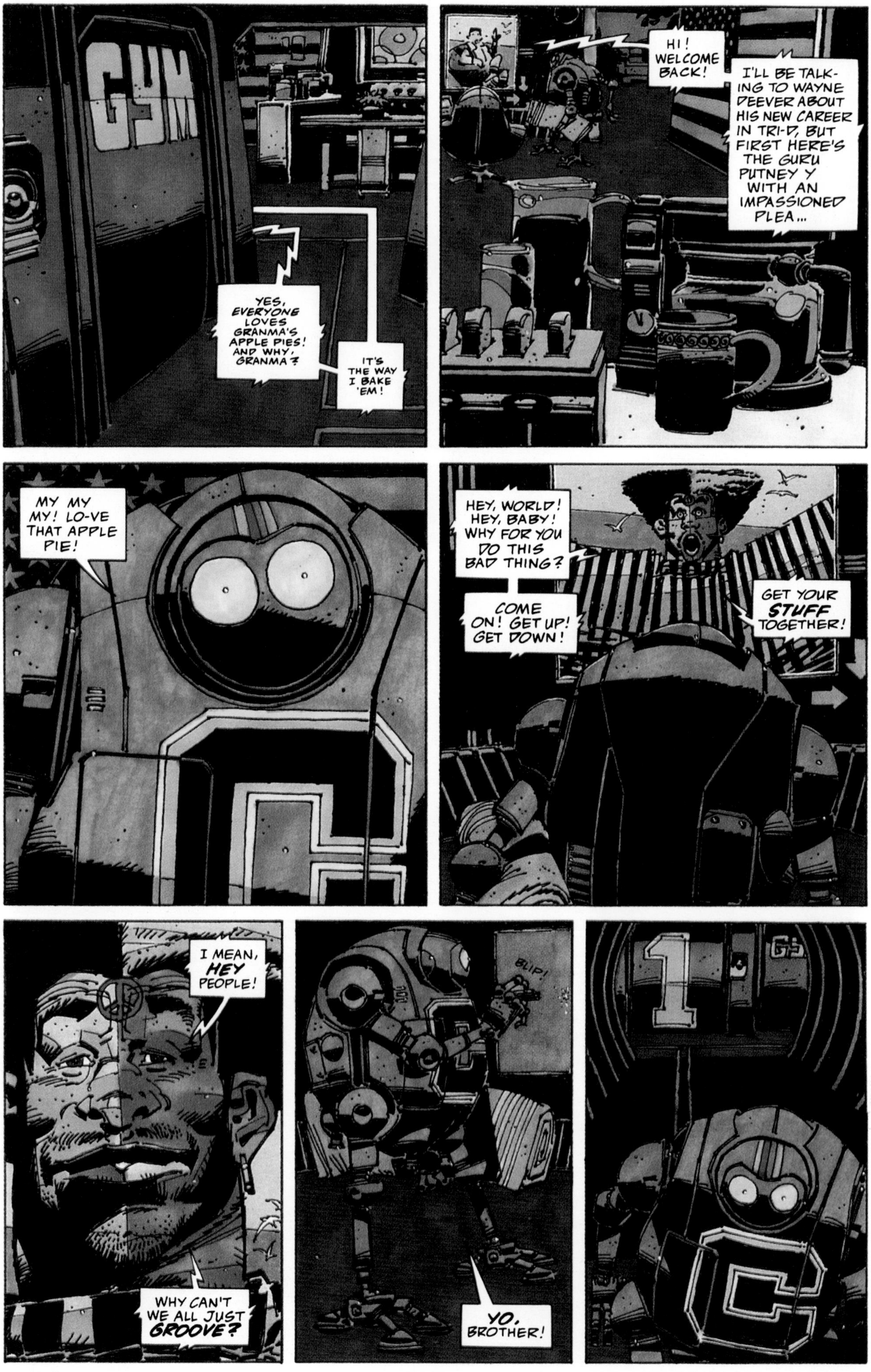
YES, EVERYONE LOVES GRANMA'S APPLE PIES! AND WHY, GRANMA?
IT'S THE WAY I BAKE 'EM!
HI! WELCOME BACK!
I'LL BE TALKING TO WAYNE DEEVER ABOUT HIS NEW CAREER IN TRI-D, BUT FIRST HERE'S THE GURU PUTNEY Y WITH AN IMPASSIONED PLEA...
MY MY MY! LO-VE THAT APPLE PIE!
HEY, WORLD! HEY, BABY! WHY FOR YOU DO THIS BAD THING?
COME ON! GET UP! GET DOWN!
GET YOUR STUFF TOGETHER!
I MEAN, HEY PEOPLE!
WHY CAN'T WE ALL JUST GROOVE?
BLIP!
YO, BROTHER!

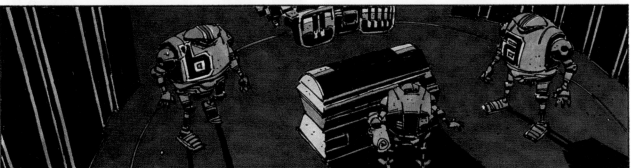

STAND BY.

TEMPERATURE'S RISING.

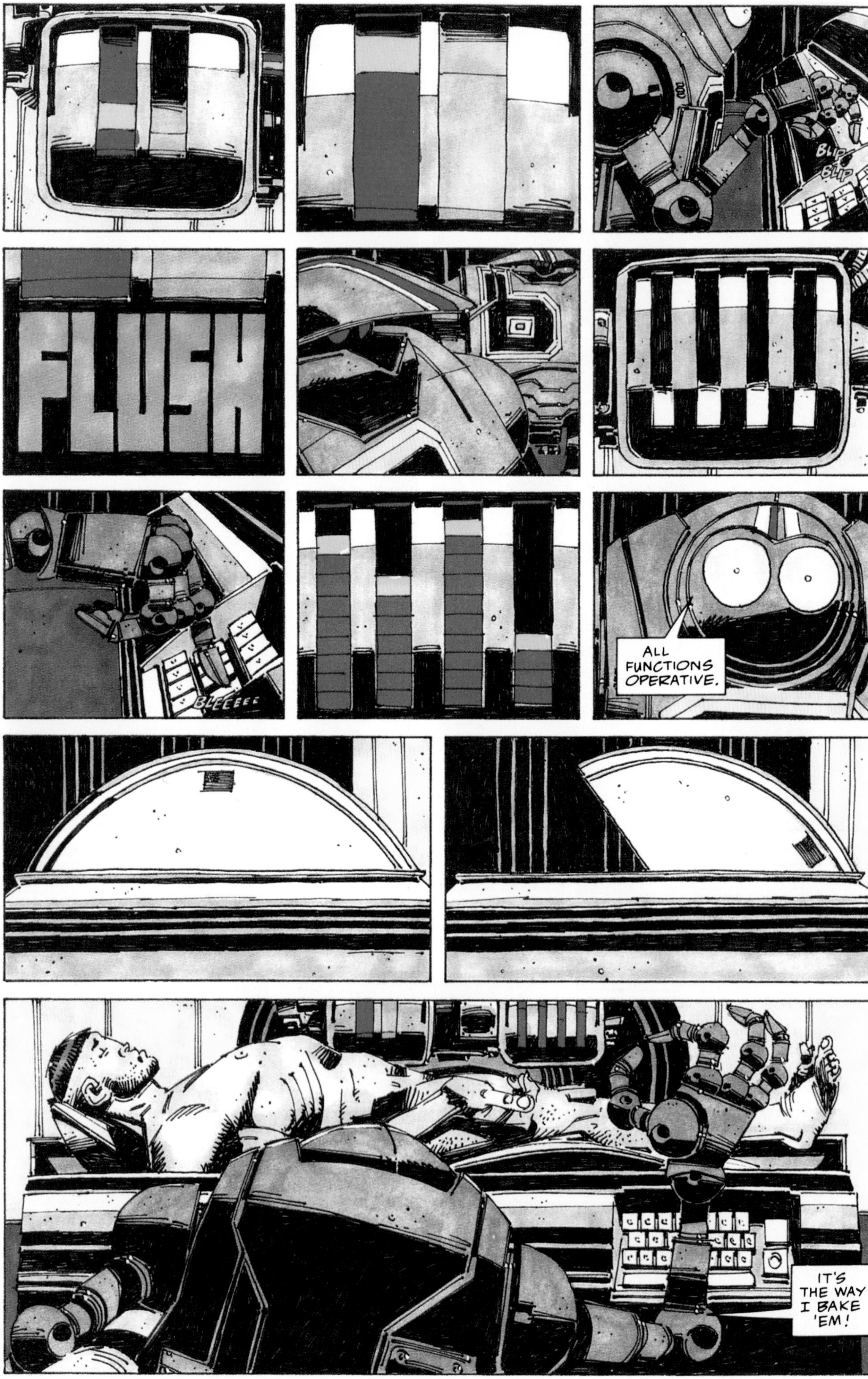
BLIP
BLIP
FLUSH
BLEEEEE
ALL FUNCTIONS OPERATIVE.
IT'S THE WAY I BAKE 'EM!

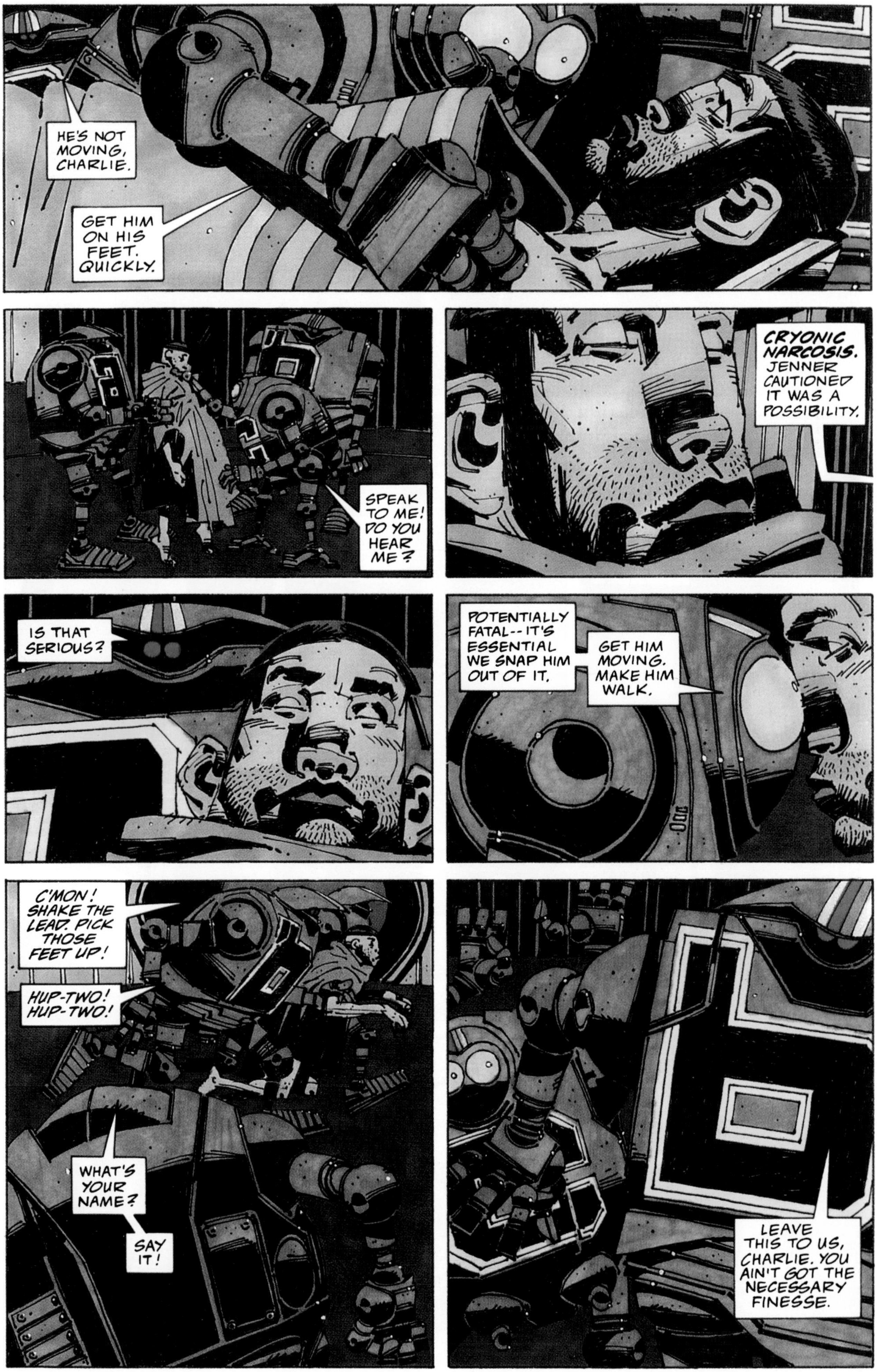
HE'S NOT MOVING, CHARLIE.
GET HIM ON HIS FEET. QUICKLY.
SPEAK TO ME! DO YOU HEAR ME?
CRYONIC NARCOSIS. JENNER CAUTIONED IT WAS A POSSIBILITY.
IS THAT SERIOUS?
POTENTIALLY FATAL--IT'S ESSENTIAL WE SNAP HIM OUT OF IT.
GET HIM MOVING. MAKE HIM WALK.
C'MON! SHAKE THE LEAD. PICK THOSE FEET UP!
HUP-TWO! HUP-TWO!
WHAT'S YOUR NAME?
SAY IT!
LEAVE THIS TO US, CHARLIE. YOU AIN'T GOT THE NECESSARY FINESSE.

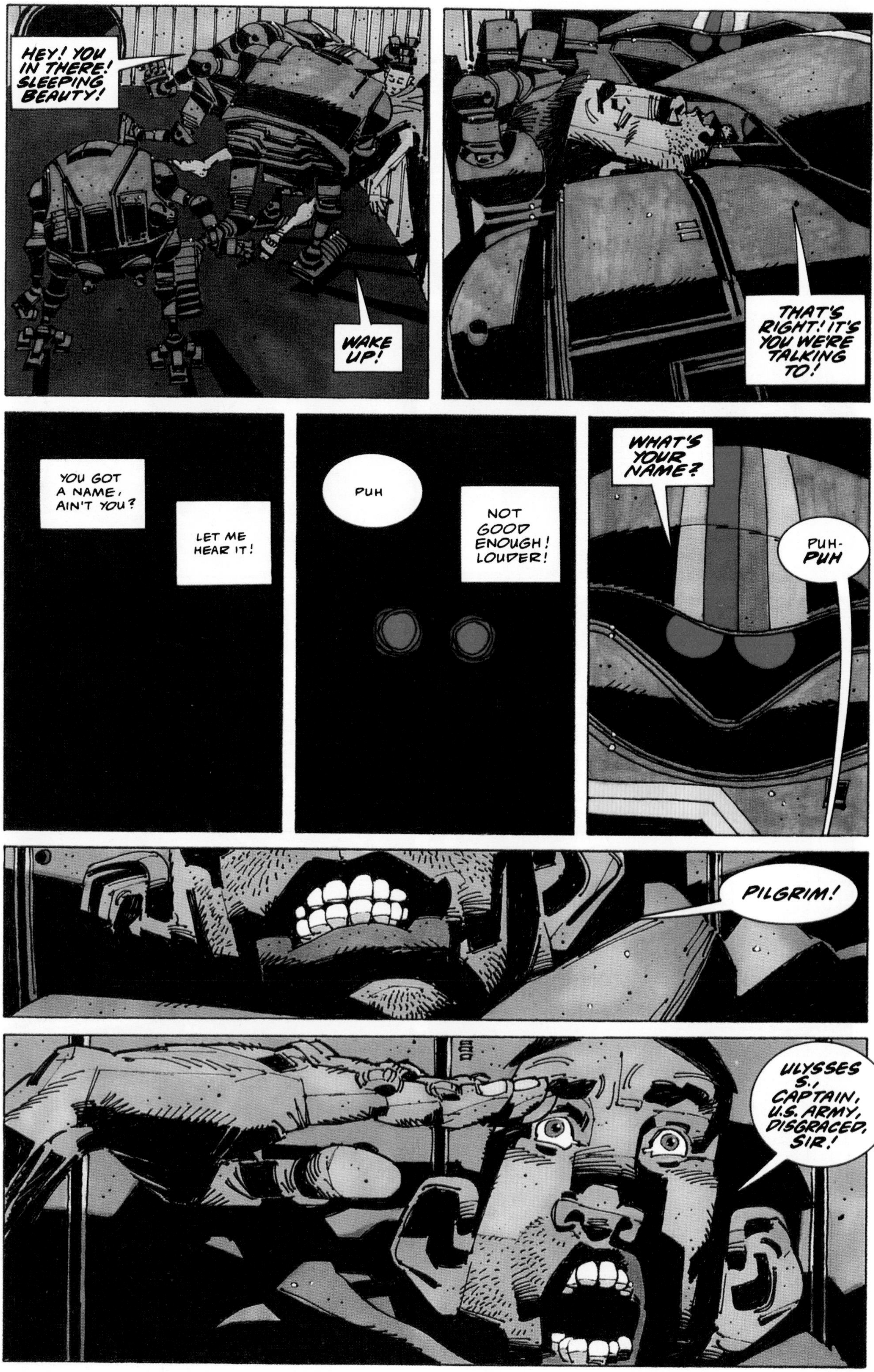
HEY! YOU IN THERE! SLEEPING BEAUTY!
WAKE UP!
THAT'S RIGHT! IT'S YOU WE'RE TALKING TO!
YOU GOT A NAME, AIN'T YOU?
LET ME HEAR IT!
PUH
NOT GOOD ENOUGH! LOUDER!
WHAT'S YOUR NAME?
PUH-PUH
PILGRIM!
ULYSSES S., CAPTAIN, U.S. ARMY, DISGRACED, SIR!

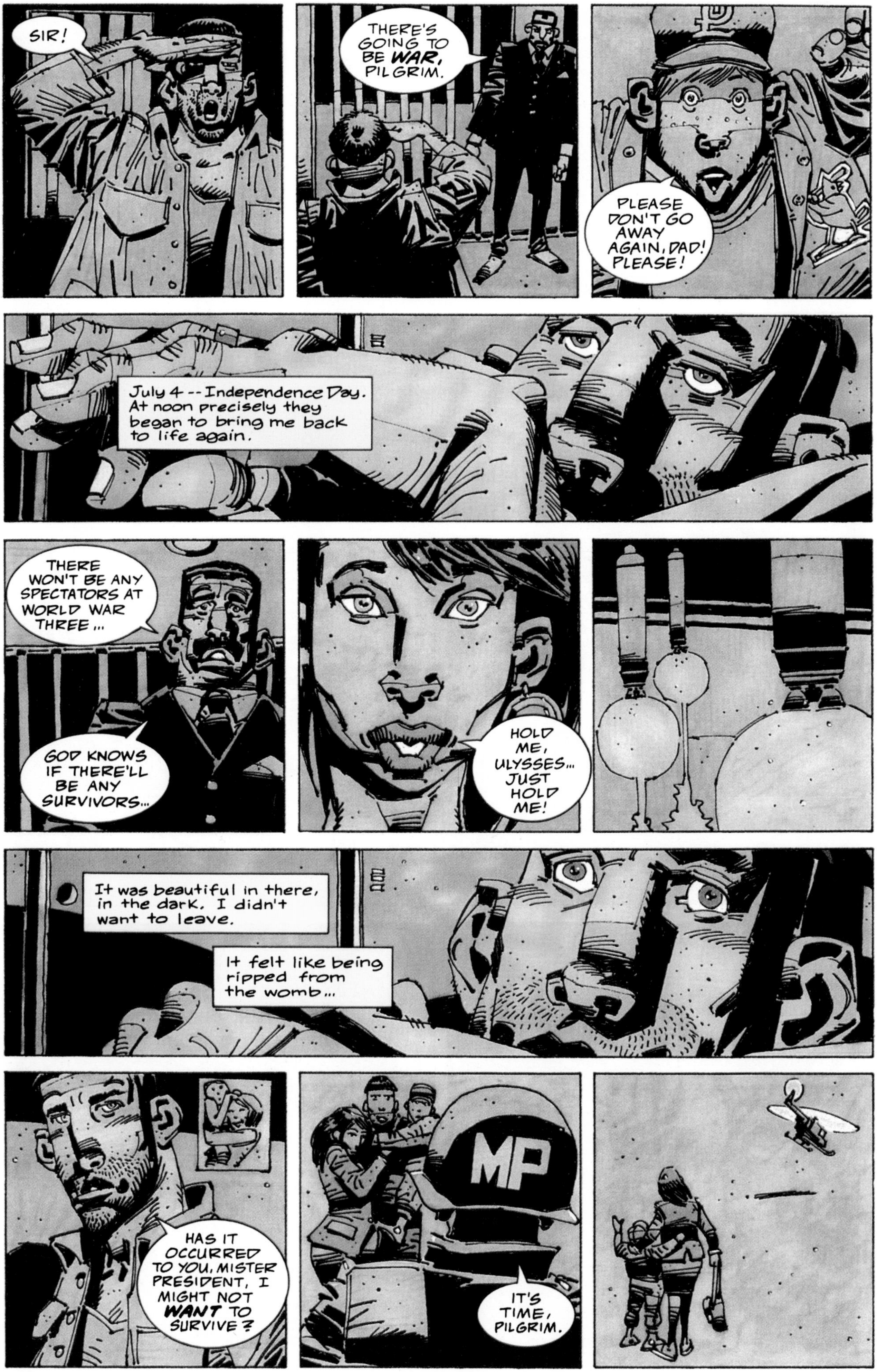
SIR!
THERE'S GOING TO BE WAR, PILGRIM.
PLEASE DON'T GO AWAY AGAIN, DAD! PLEASE!
July 4 -- Independence Day. At noon precisely they began to bring me back to life again.
THERE WON'T BE ANY SPECTATORS AT WORLD WAR THREE...
GOD KNOWS IF THERE'LL BE ANY SURVIVORS...
HOLD ME, ULYSSES... JUST HOLD ME!
It was beautiful in there, in the dark. I didn't want to leave.
It felt like being ripped from the womb...
HAS IT OCCURRED TO YOU, MISTER PRESIDENT, I MIGHT NOT WANT TO SURVIVE?
MP
IT'S TIME, PILGRIM.

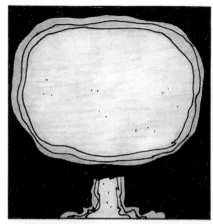
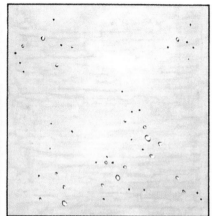

THE WAR... IS IT...

IT'S BEEN OVER TWENTY YEARS, BOSS.

TWENTY YEARS...

WHO WON...?

Dumb question.

COLD, CHARLIE... REAL COLD...

A SIDE EFFECT OF THE PROCESS. IT WILL PASS.

I'VE GOT CLOTHES AND HOT COFFEE WAITING.

MM-MM! THAT REAL COFFEE TASTE -- AT A PRICE YOU CAN AFFORD!

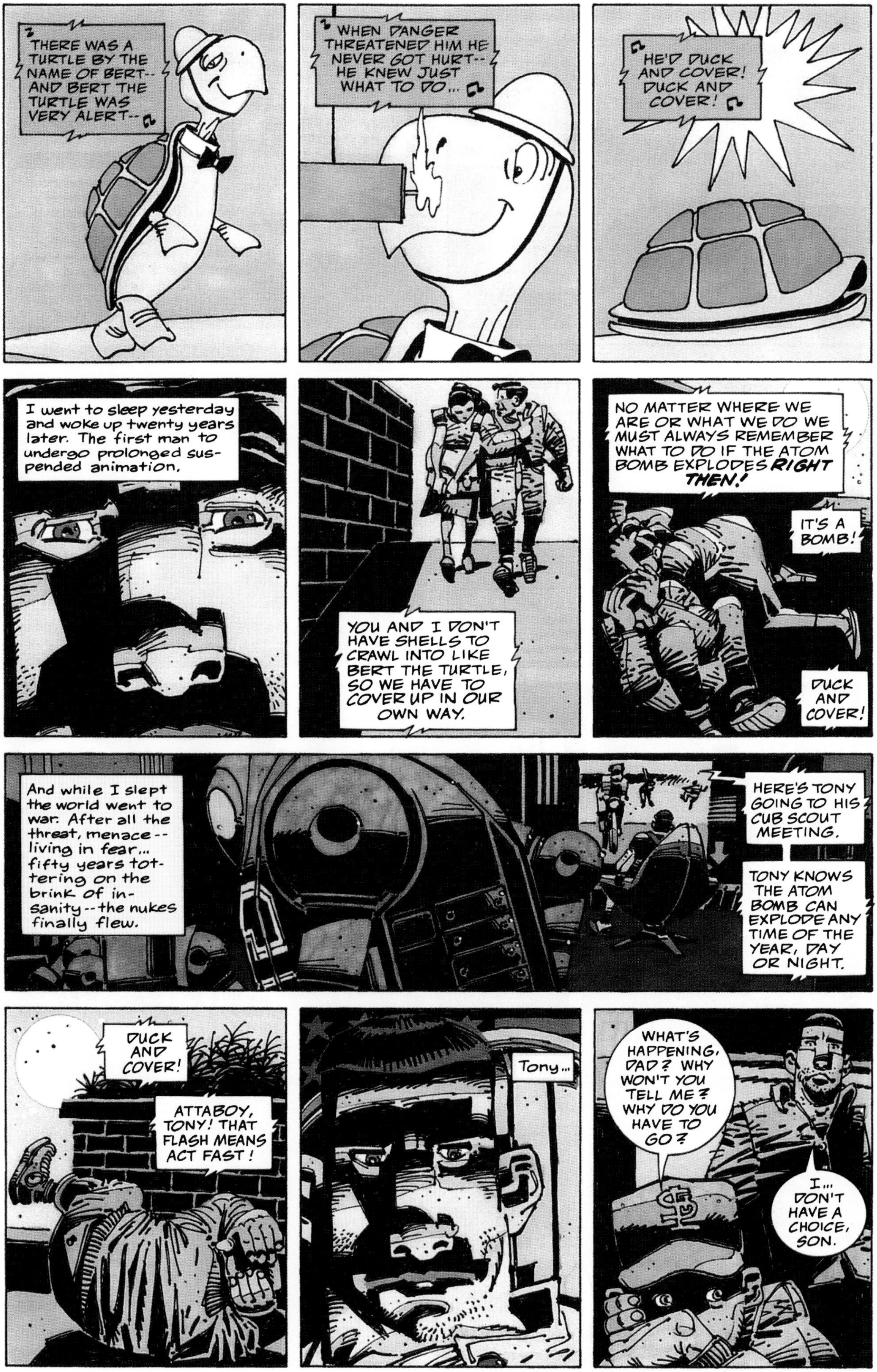
THERE WAS A TURTLE BY THE NAME OF BERT-- AND BERT THE TURTLE WAS VERY ALERT--
WHEN DANGER THREATENED HIM HE NEVER GOT HURT-- HE KNEW JUST WHAT TO DO...
HE'D DUCK AND COVER! DUCK AND COVER!
I went to sleep yesterday and woke up twenty years later. The first man to undergo prolonged suspended animation.
YOU AND I DON'T HAVE SHELLS TO CRAWL INTO LIKE BERT THE TURTLE, SO WE HAVE TO COVER UP IN OUR OWN WAY.
NO MATTER WHERE WE ARE OR WHAT WE DO WE MUST ALWAYS REMEMBER WHAT TO DO IF THE ATOM BOMB EXPLODES RIGHT THEN!
IT'S A BOMB!
DUCK AND COVER!
And while I slept the world went to war. After all the threat, menace -- living in fear... fifty years tottering on the brink of insanity -- the nukes finally flew.
HERE'S TONY GOING TO HIS CUB SCOUT MEETING.
TONY KNOWS THE ATOM BOMB CAN EXPLODE ANY TIME OF THE YEAR, DAY OR NIGHT.
DUCK AND COVER!
ATTABOY, TONY! THAT FLASH MEANS ACT FAST!
Tony...
WHAT'S HAPPENING, DAD? WHY WON'T YOU TELL ME? WHY DO YOU HAVE TO GO?
I... DON'T HAVE A CHOICE, SON.

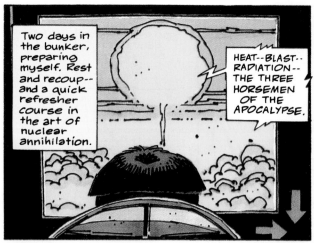

Two days in the bunker, preparing myself. Rest and recoup-- and a quick refresher course in the art of nuclear annihilation.

HEAT--BLAST--RADIATION-- THE THREE HORSEMEN OF THE APOCALYPSE.

IN A TYPICAL TEN THOUSAND MEGATON STRIKE OVER TWO BILLION WILL DIE IMMEDIATELY--OR WITHIN THE FIRST FEW DAYS.

I don't know how bad things are up there. Charlie's been monitoring since the beginning.

No radio traffic. That's the worrying thing. Background radiation varies between five and seven times normal. But that figure could be anomalous to this locale. There's no way of telling.

...AND THE FOURTH HORSEMAN IS WINTER.

Temperature levels since the big bang indicate a period of nuclear winter lasting over two years.

If that's the case, can anyone have survived?

Am I the last American?

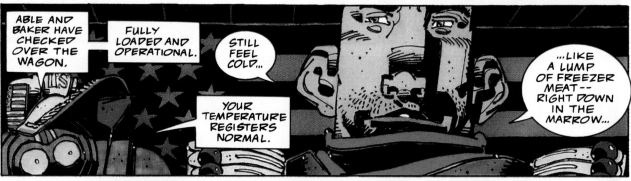

ABLE AND BAKER HAVE CHECKED OVER THE WAGON.

FULLY LOADED AND OPERATIONAL.

STILL FEEL COLD...

YOUR TEMPERATURE REGISTERS NORMAL.

...LIKE A LUMP OF FREEZER MEAT-- RIGHT DOWN IN THE MARROW...

MARROWBONE! THE MEATY GOODNESS THAT SETS THE DOGS BARKING!

※ARF! ARF!※

WHAT GIVES WITH YOU CHARLIE. YOU SOME KIND OF T.V. JUNKIE?

THE LIBRARY HAS A VAST QUANTITY OF RECORDED OUTPUT. I FIND IT MOST INTERESTING.

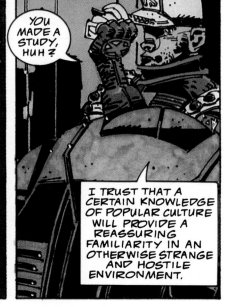

YOU MADE A STUDY, HUH?

I TRUST THAT A CERTAIN KNOWLEDGE OF POPULAR CULTURE WILL PROVIDE A REASSURING FAMILIARITY IN AN OTHERWISE STRANGE AND HOSTILE ENVIRONMENT.

Crazy robot. But the real madness, that's up there...

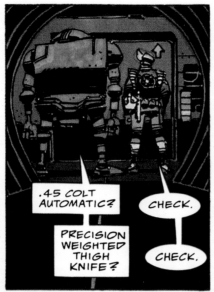

.45 COLT AUTOMATIC?

CHECK.

PRECISION WEIGHTED THIGH KNIFE?

CHECK.

M393 REGULATOR SUBMACHINE GUN?

CHECK.

FRAG GRENADES?

IS ALL THIS HARDWARE NECESSARY?

LIKE THE BOY SCOUTS USED TO SAY, CAPTAIN--BE PREPARED.

I try to picture it, try to imagine a world without people--but the chill rushes up through my veins and turns my brain to ice. The prospect is too terrible to contemplate.

There must be hope. There must be.

GOING UP!

HEY, HEY, HEY, HEY, PEOPLE--!

LET'S BE CAREFUL OUT THERE!

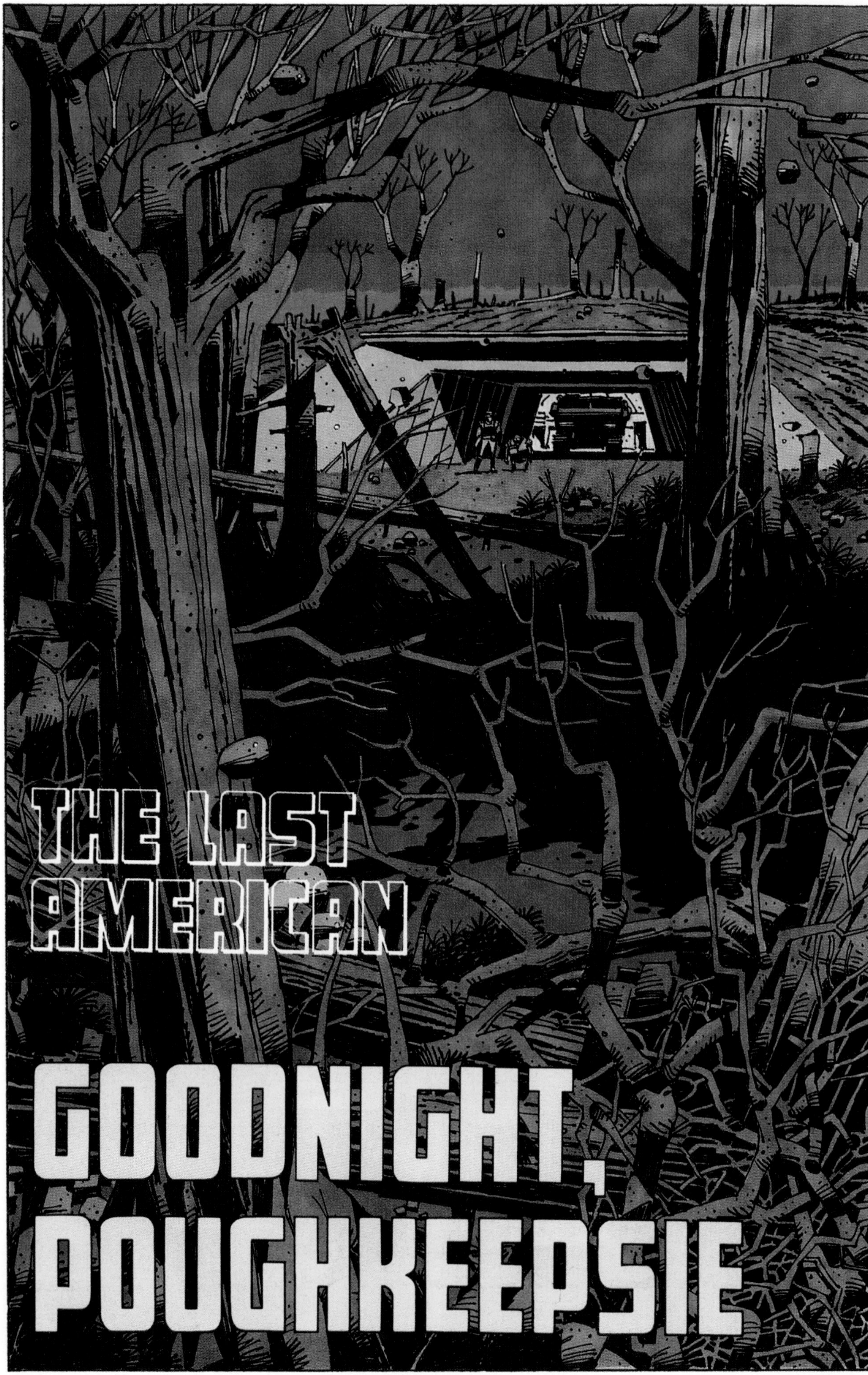
THE LAST
AMERICAN
GOODNIGHT,
POUGHKEEPSIE

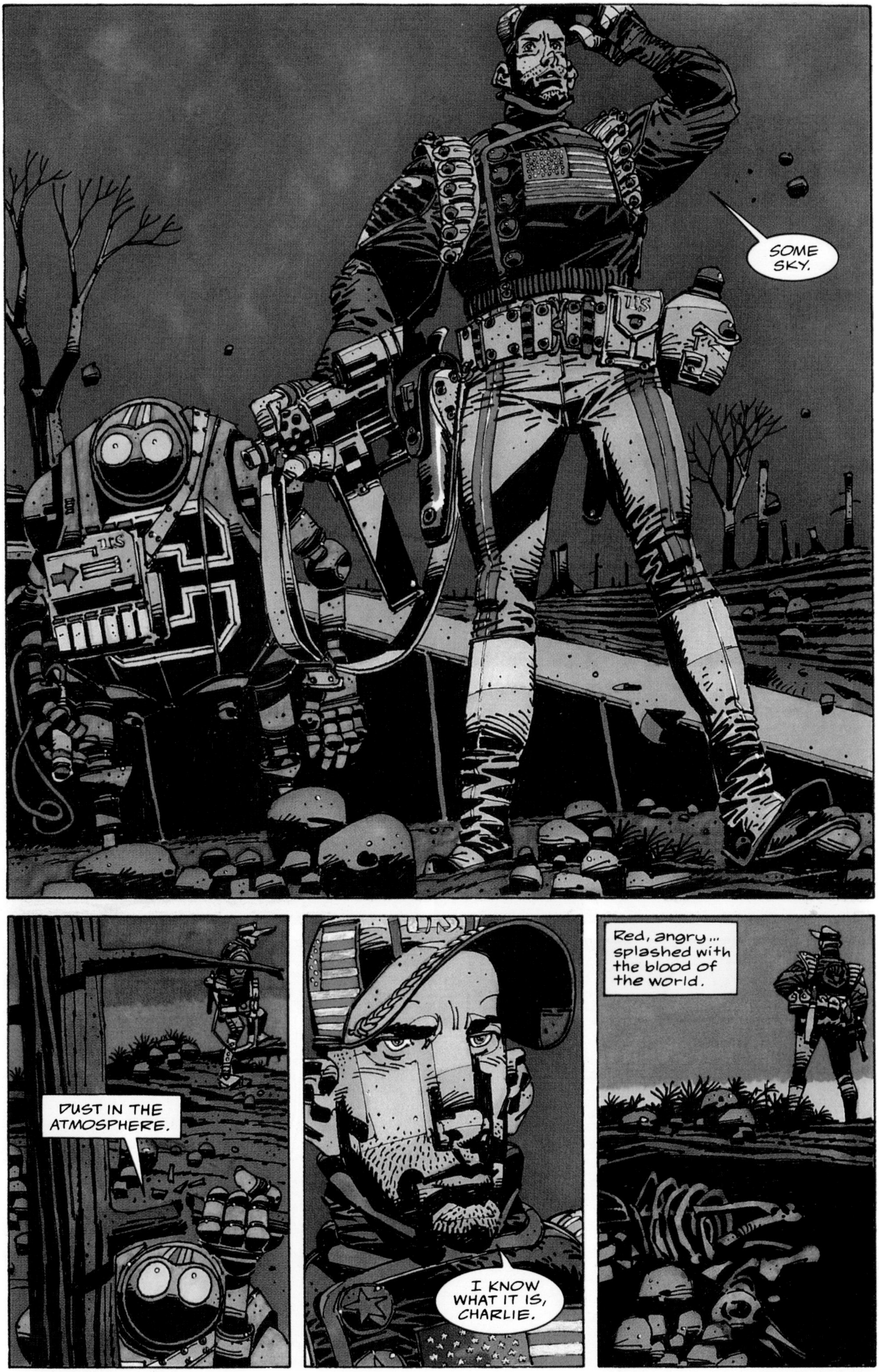
SOME SKY.
DUST IN THE ATMOSPHERE.
I KNOW WHAT IT IS, CHARLIE.
Red, angry... splashed with the blood of the world.

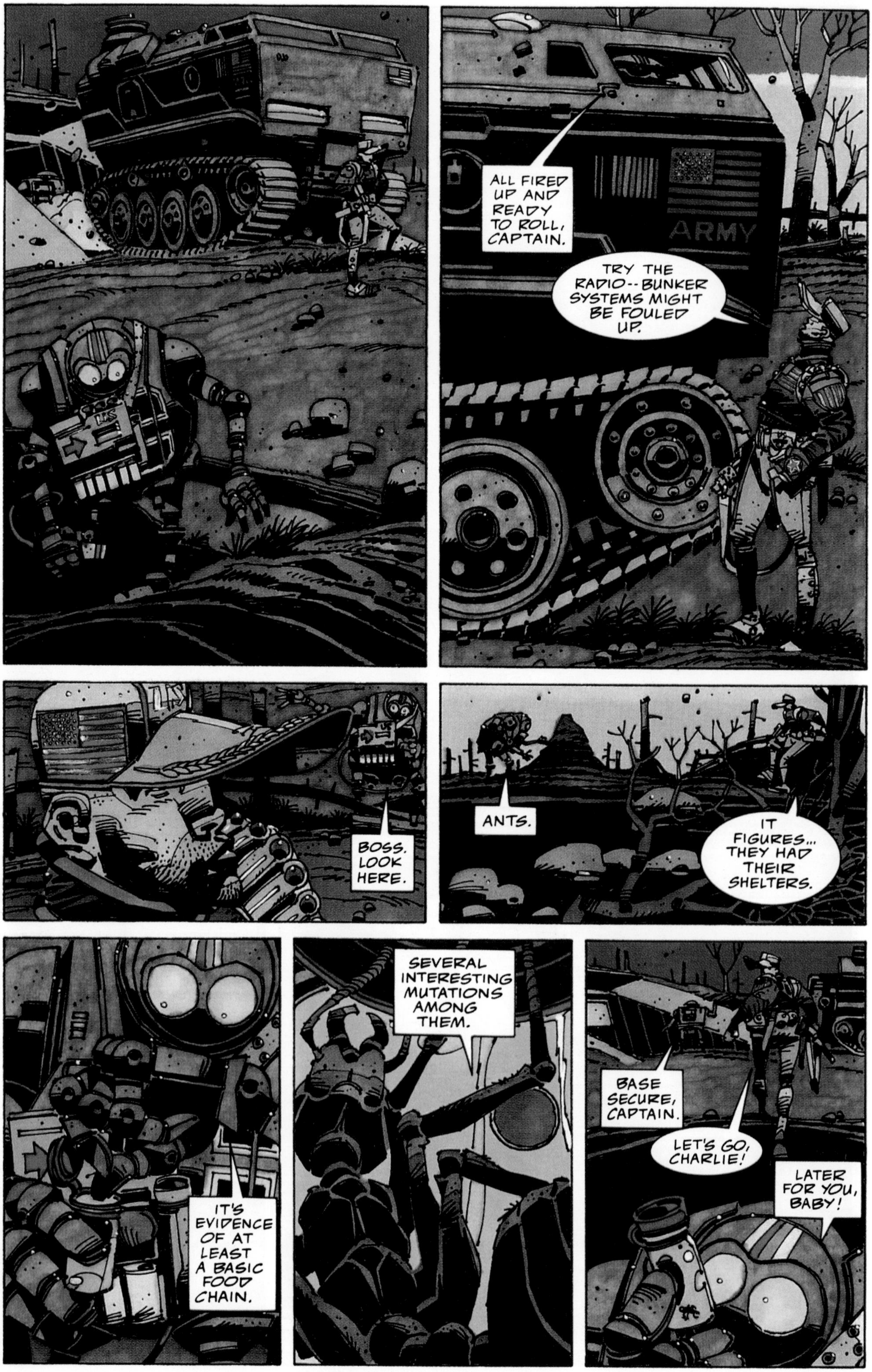
ALL FIRED UP AND READY TO ROLL, CAPTAIN.
ARMY
TRY THE RADIO-- BUNKER SYSTEMS MIGHT BE FOULED UP.
BOSS. LOOK HERE.
ANTS.
IT FIGURES... THEY HAD THEIR SHELTERS.
IT'S EVIDENCE OF AT LEAST A BASIC FOOD CHAIN.
SEVERAL INTERESTING MUTATIONS AMONG THEM.
BASE SECURE, CAPTAIN.
LET'S GO, CHARLIE!
LATER FOR YOU, BABY!

THERE'S A GREAT DEAL WE CAN ACCOMPLISH RIGHT HERE.

MAY I SUGGEST WE MAKE A PRELIMINARY BIOLOGICAL STUDY BEFORE PROCEEDING?

I'VE WAITED TWENTY YEARS FOR THIS.

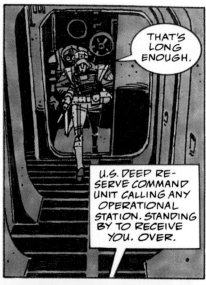

THAT'S LONG ENOUGH.

U.S. DEEP RE-SERVE COMMAND UNIT CALLING ANY OPERATIONAL STATION. STANDING BY TO RECEIVE YOU. OVER.

ANYTHING?

NOTHING BUT STATIC.

CONDITIONS MIGHT BE BETTER ONCE WE GET OUT OF THESE HILLS.

'KAY, KEEP TRYING.

WHEN YOU'RE READY.

ROLL UP! ROLL UP FOR THE MYSTERY TOUR!

THE MAGICAL MYSTERY TOUR IS WAITING TO TAKE YOU AWAY...

...WAITING TO TAKE YOU AWAY...

...EXPLOSIONS WILL CARRY AN IMMENSE AMOUNT OF DUST AND SOOT INTO THE UPPER ATMOSPHERE, BLOTTING OUT THE SUN.

FOR MORE THAN A WEEK IT MAY BE TOO DARK TO SEE.

CITIES WILL CONTINUE TO BURN FOR DAYS, ADDING TO THE PALL.

FIRESTORMS WILL RAGE UNCHECKED THROUGH AFFORESTED AREAS.

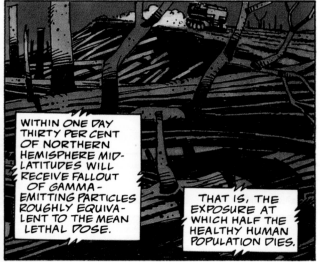

WITHIN ONE DAY THIRTY PER CENT OF NORTHERN HEMISPHERE MID-LATITUDES WILL RECEIVE FALLOUT OF GAMMA-EMITTING PARTICLES ROUGHLY EQUIVALENT TO THE MEAN LETHAL DOSE.

THAT IS, THE EXPOSURE AT WHICH HALF THE HEALTHY HUMAN POPULATION DIES.

ON LATEST CALCULATIONS SURFACE TEMPERATURES IN THE NUCLEAR GLOOM WILL FALL RAPIDLY TO AS LOW AS FORTY BELOW ZERO AND MAY REMAIN THERE FOR MANY MONTHS.

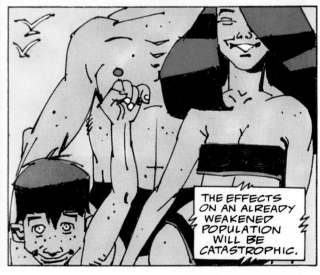

THE EFFECTS ON AN ALREADY WEAKENED POPULATION WILL BE CATASTROPHIC.

HOLD IT HERE!

DRESSED FOR WINTER, ANYWAY.

NOTHIN' ON HIM!

INTERESTING.

TAKES A LICKING-- KEEPS ON TICKING!

IN THE WAGON, CHARLIE.

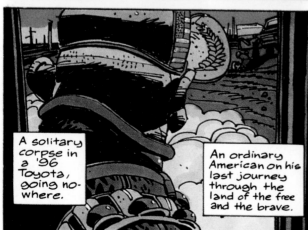

A solitary corpse in a '96 Toyota, going nowhere.

An ordinary American on his last journey through the land of the free and the brave.

He was the first. I knew he wouldn't be the last.

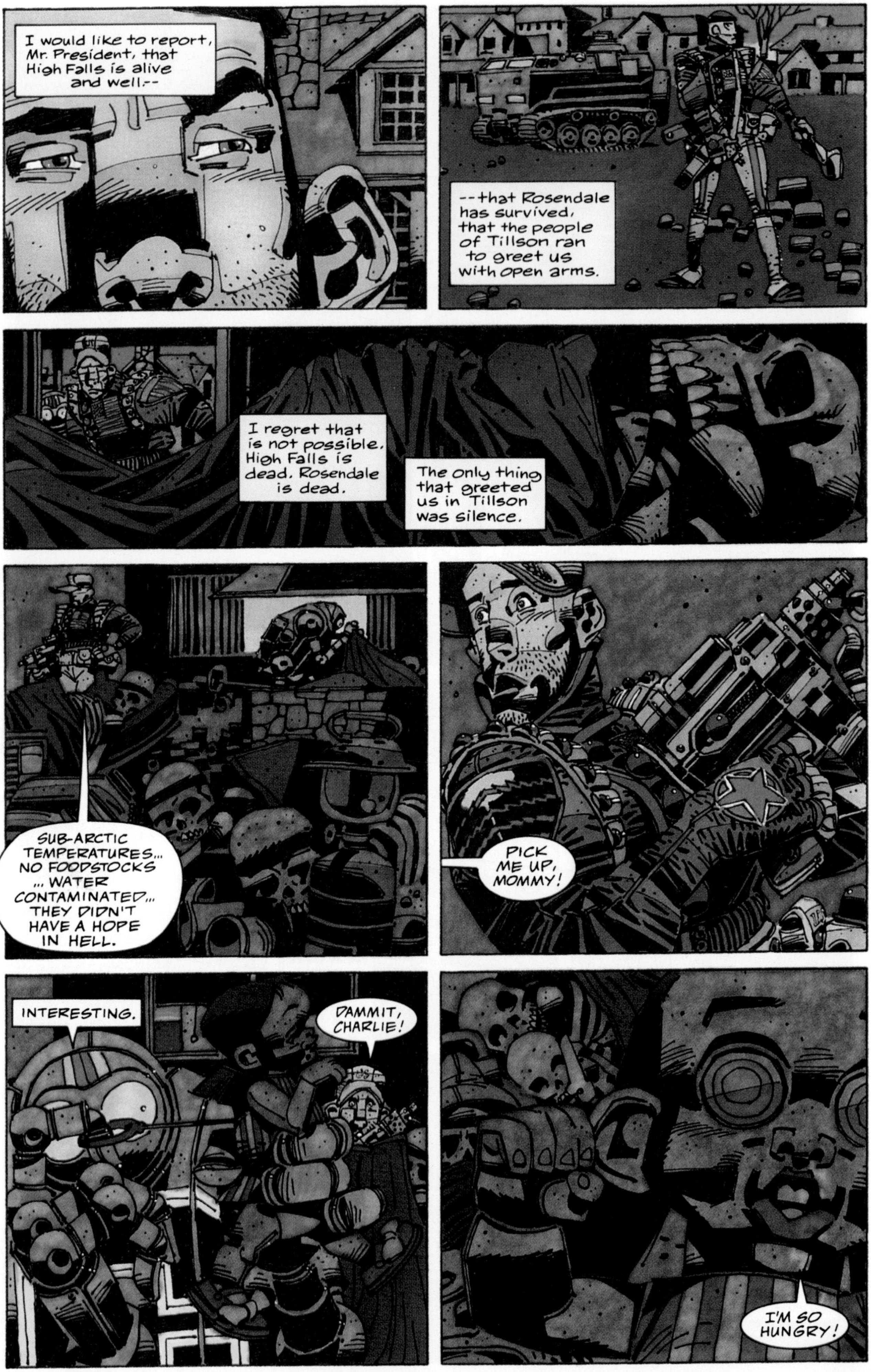
I would like to report, Mr. President, that High Falls is alive and well.--
--that Rosendale has survived, that the people of Tillson ran to greet us with open arms.
I regret that is not possible. High Falls is dead. Rosendale is dead.
The only thing that greeted us in Tillson was silence.
SUB-ARCTIC TEMPERATURES... NO FOODSTOCKS ... WATER CONTAMINATED... THEY DIDN'T HAVE A HOPE IN HELL.
PICK ME UP, MOMMY!
INTERESTING.
DAMMIT, CHARLIE!
I'M SO HUNGRY!

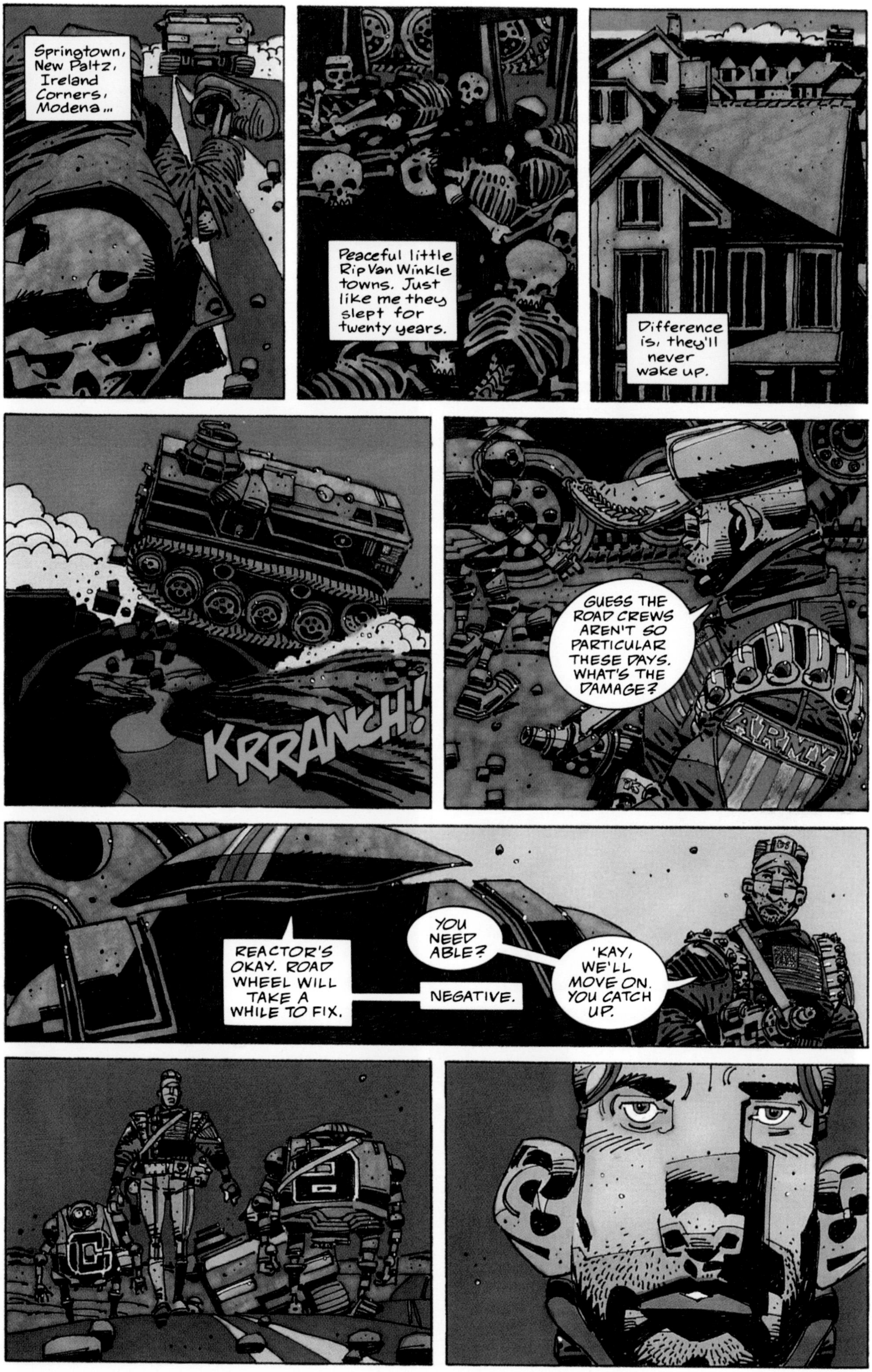

Springtown, New Paltz, Ireland Corners, Modena...
Peaceful little Rip Van Winkle towns. Just like me they slept for twenty years.
Difference is, they'll never wake up.
KRRANCH!
GUESS THE ROAD CREWS AREN'T SO PARTICULAR THESE DAYS. WHAT'S THE DAMAGE?
ARMY
REACTOR'S OKAY. ROAD WHEEL WILL TAKE A WHILE TO FIX.
YOU NEED ABLE?
NEGATIVE.
'KAY, WE'LL MOVE ON. YOU CATCH UP.

Interstate 87... a crumbling asphalt cemetery, littered with the rusting gravestones of America.

Silent as a tomb.

The ice was creeping through me again, and a strange sense of unreality-- as if I wasn't really part of this-- it wasn't happening...

...If I just kept moving I'd walk right on out of it, back into the real world.

THAT'S A ROJ.

HEADING EAST ON 299. TELL YOUR BUDDY.

POOR BASTARDS. WHERE'D THEY THINK THERE WAS TO RUN TO?

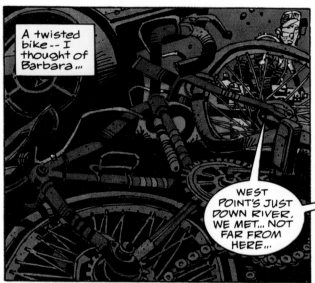

A twisted bike -- I thought of Barbara...

WEST POINT'S JUST DOWN RIVER, WE MET... NOT FAR FROM HERE...

...A ONE WAY STREET IN POUGHKEEPSIE...

SHE WAS SOMETHING... ALL THAT RED HAIR FLYING.

Are you still out there, Barbara, somewhere? What color is your hair now -- old and gray? Or is it burnt and crisp... just so much dust floating in the stratosphere?

BACKGROUND RADIATION IS UP FOUR POINTS. WE SHOULD PROCEED WITH CAUTION.

POUGHKEEPSIE, BOSS.

BRING BACK ANY HAPPY MEMORIES?

JESUS...

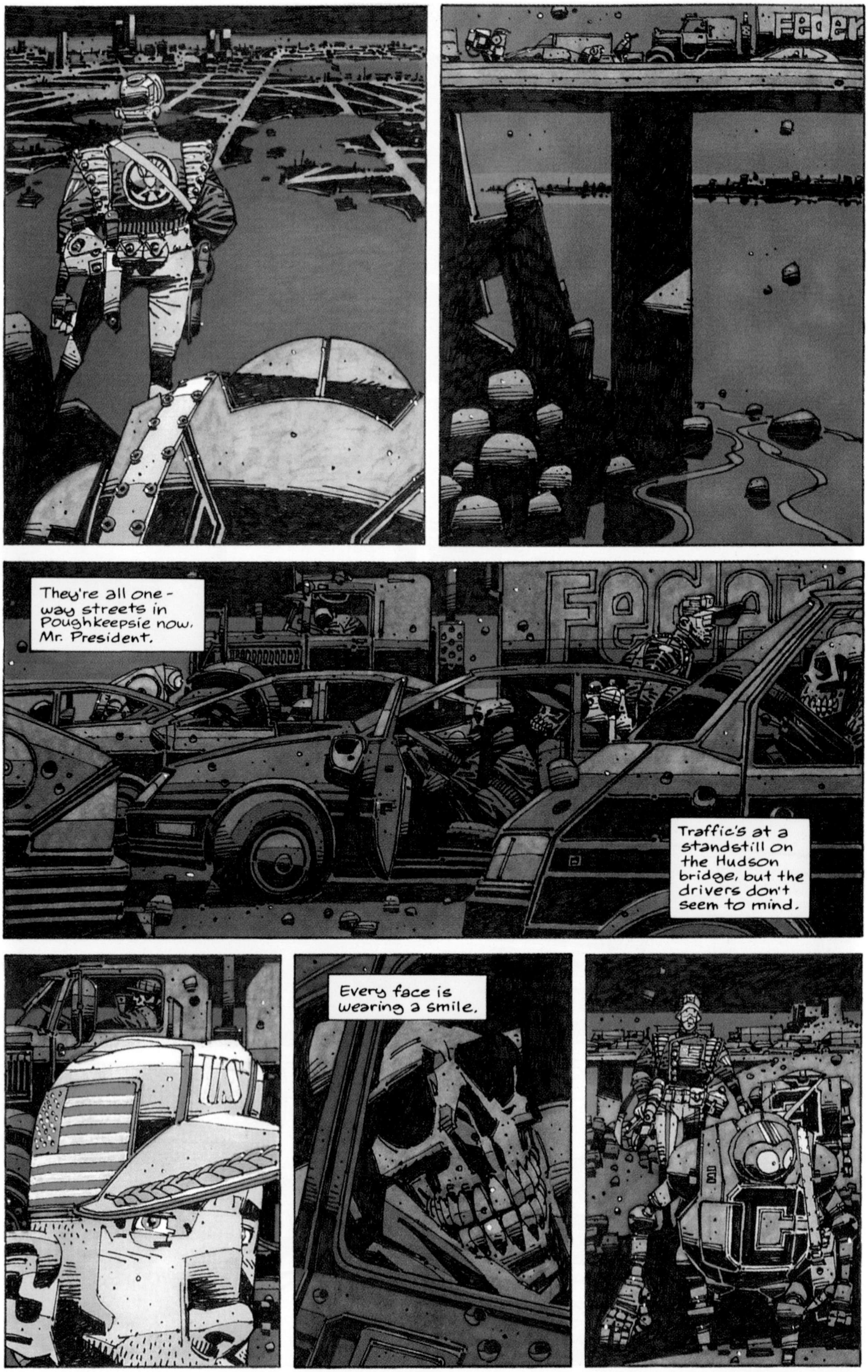
They're all one-way streets in Poughkeepsie now, Mr. President.
Traffic's at a standstill on the Hudson bridge, but the drivers don't seem to mind.
Every face is wearing a smile.

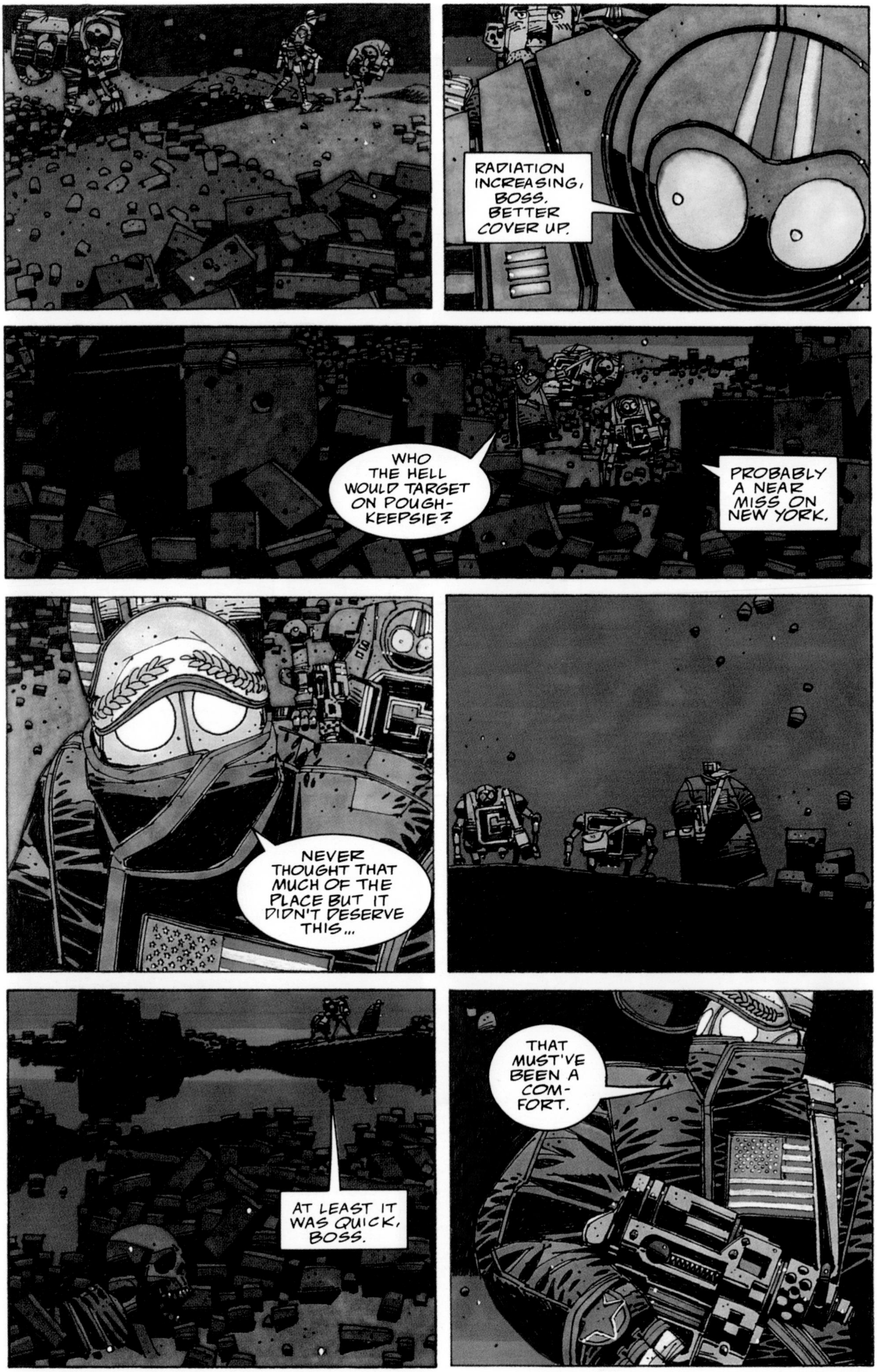

RADIATION INCREASING, BOSS. BETTER COVER UP.
WHO THE HELL WOULD TARGET ON POUGH-KEEPSIE?
PROBABLY A NEAR MISS ON NEW YORK.
NEVER THOUGHT THAT MUCH OF THE PLACE BUT IT DIDN'T DESERVE THIS...
AT LEAST IT WAS QUICK, BOSS.
THAT MUST'VE BEEN A COM-FORT.

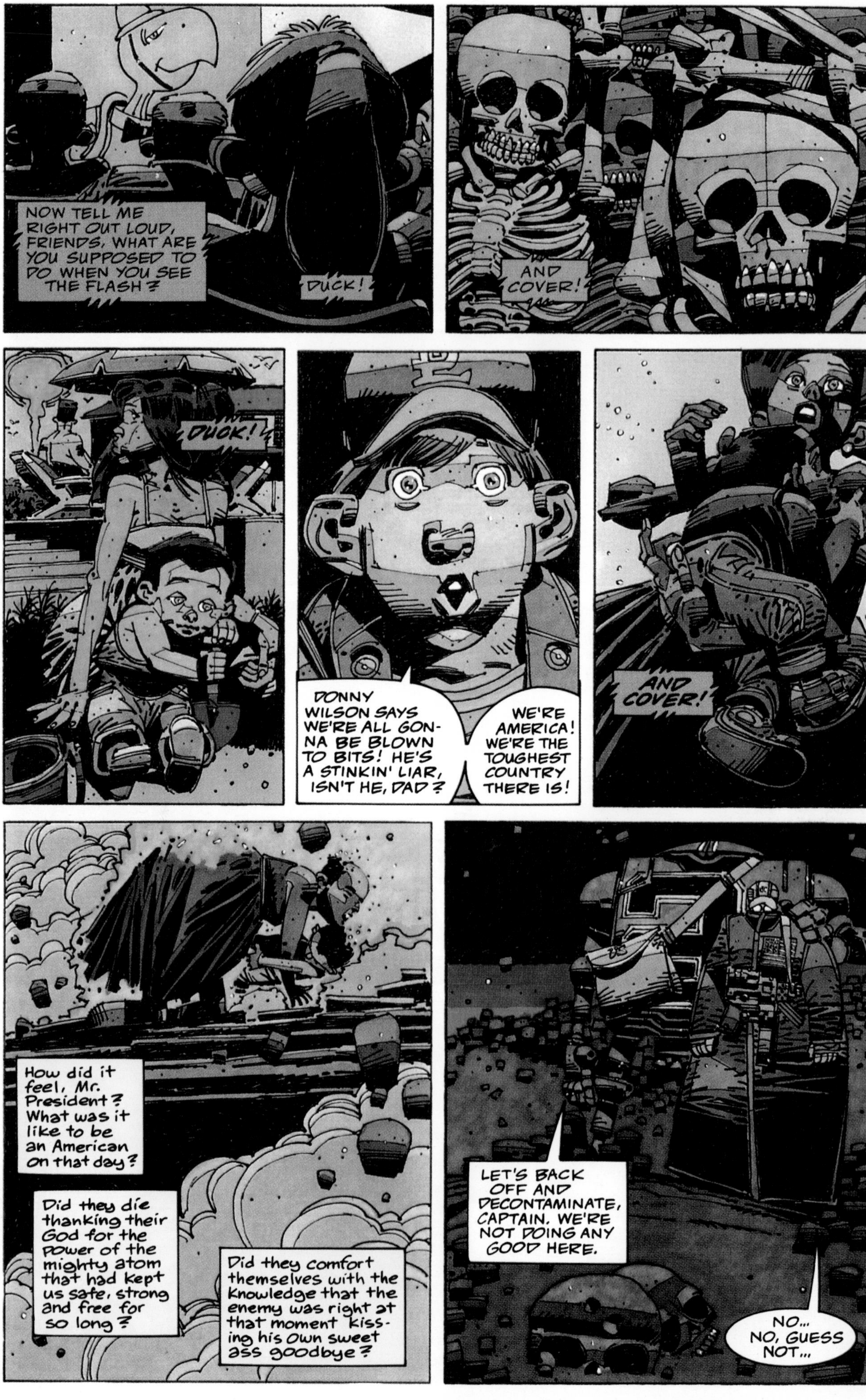
NOW TELL ME RIGHT OUT LOUD, FRIENDS, WHAT ARE YOU SUPPOSED TO DO WHEN YOU SEE THE FLASH?
DUCK!
AND COVER!
DUCK!
DONNY WILSON SAYS WE'RE ALL GONNA BE BLOWN TO BITS! HE'S A STINKIN' LIAR, ISN'T HE, DAD?
WE'RE AMERICA! WE'RE THE TOUGHEST COUNTRY THERE IS!
AND COVER!
How did it feel, Mr. President? What was it like to be an American on that day?
Did they die thanking their God for the power of the mighty atom that had kept us safe, strong and free for so long?
Did they comfort themselves with the knowledge that the enemy was right at that moment kissing his own sweet ass goodbye?
LET'S BACK OFF AND DECONTAMINATE, CAPTAIN. WE'RE NOT DOING ANY GOOD HERE.
NO... NO, GUESS NOT...

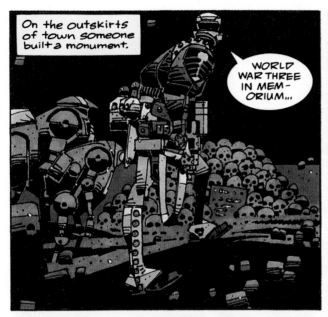

On the outskirts of town someone built a monument.

WORLD WAR THREE IN MEMORIUM...

THAT'S ONE WAY TO BEAT THE FOOD SHORTAGE.

LOOK AT THE DATE, THAT'S MORE THAN A YEAR, BOSS.

I KILLED NO ONE I AM INNOCENT GOD FORGIVE ME
JOE JOHNSON CANNIBAL (2001)

SO WHERE IS HE NOW?

HELLO?

WILL THE MAN WHO ATE POUGHKEEPSIE PLEASE STAND UP!

FRESH MEAT!

COME AND GET IT, BUDDY!

ALL GONE, CHARLIE... EVEN THE CANNIBALS ARE DEAD!

SNIK!

YOU LOOK LIKE YOU COULD USE A SHOT A' RED EYE, PARDNER!

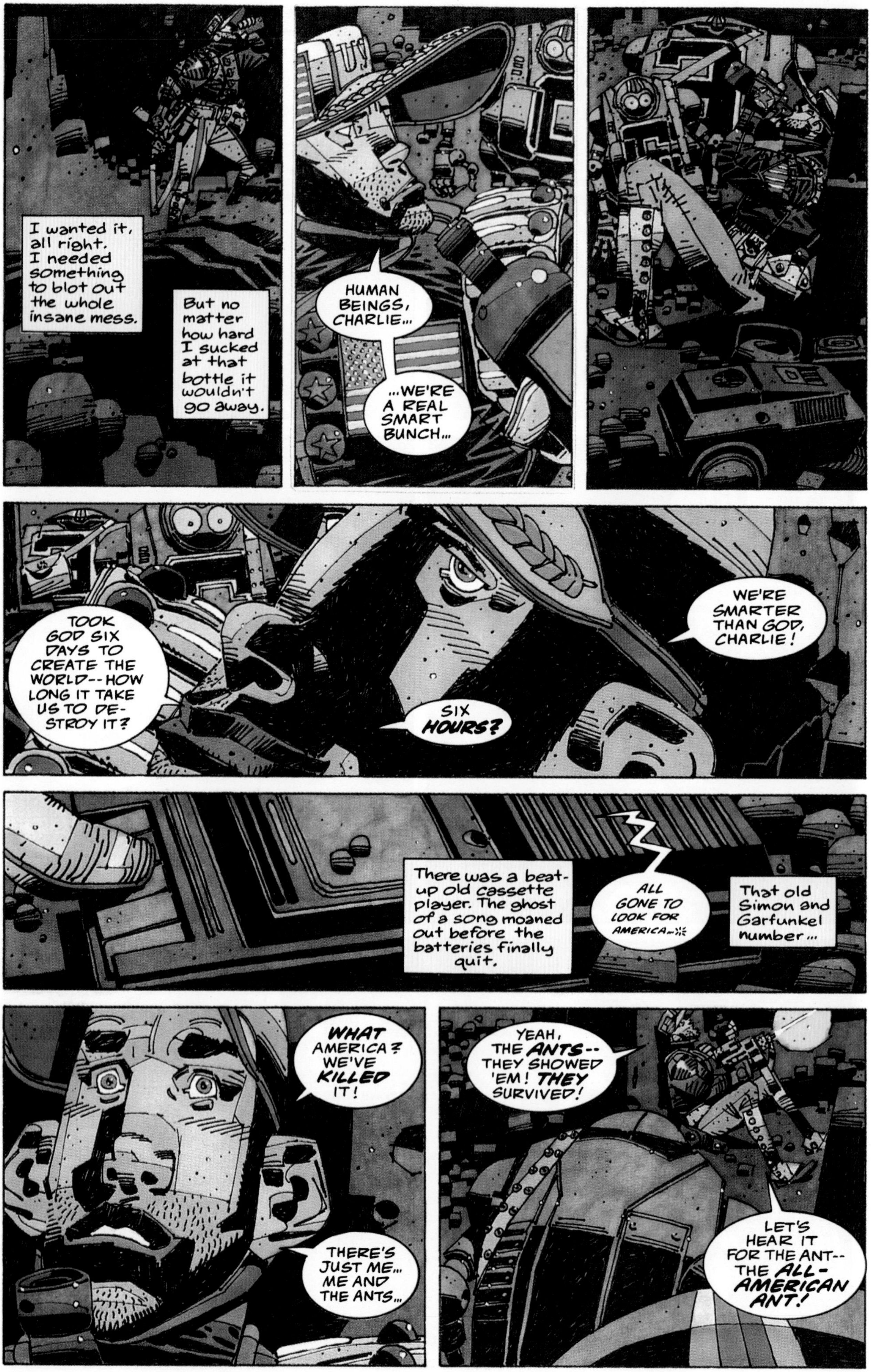

I wanted it, all right. I needed something to blot out the whole insane mess.
But no matter how hard I sucked at that bottle it wouldn't go away.
HUMAN BEINGS, CHARLIE...
...WE'RE A REAL SMART BUNCH...
TOOK GOD SIX DAYS TO CREATE THE WORLD--HOW LONG IT TAKE US TO DE-STROY IT?
SIX HOURS?
WE'RE SMARTER THAN GOD, CHARLIE!
There was a beat-up old cassette player. The ghost of a song moaned out before the batteries finally quit.
ALL GONE TO LOOK FOR AMERICA...
That old Simon and Garfunkel number...
WHAT AMERICA? WE'VE KILLED IT!
THERE'S JUST ME... ME AND THE ANTS...
YEAH, THE ANTS--THEY SHOWED 'EM! THEY SURVIVED!
LET'S HEAR IT FOR THE ANT--THE ALL-AMERICAN ANT!

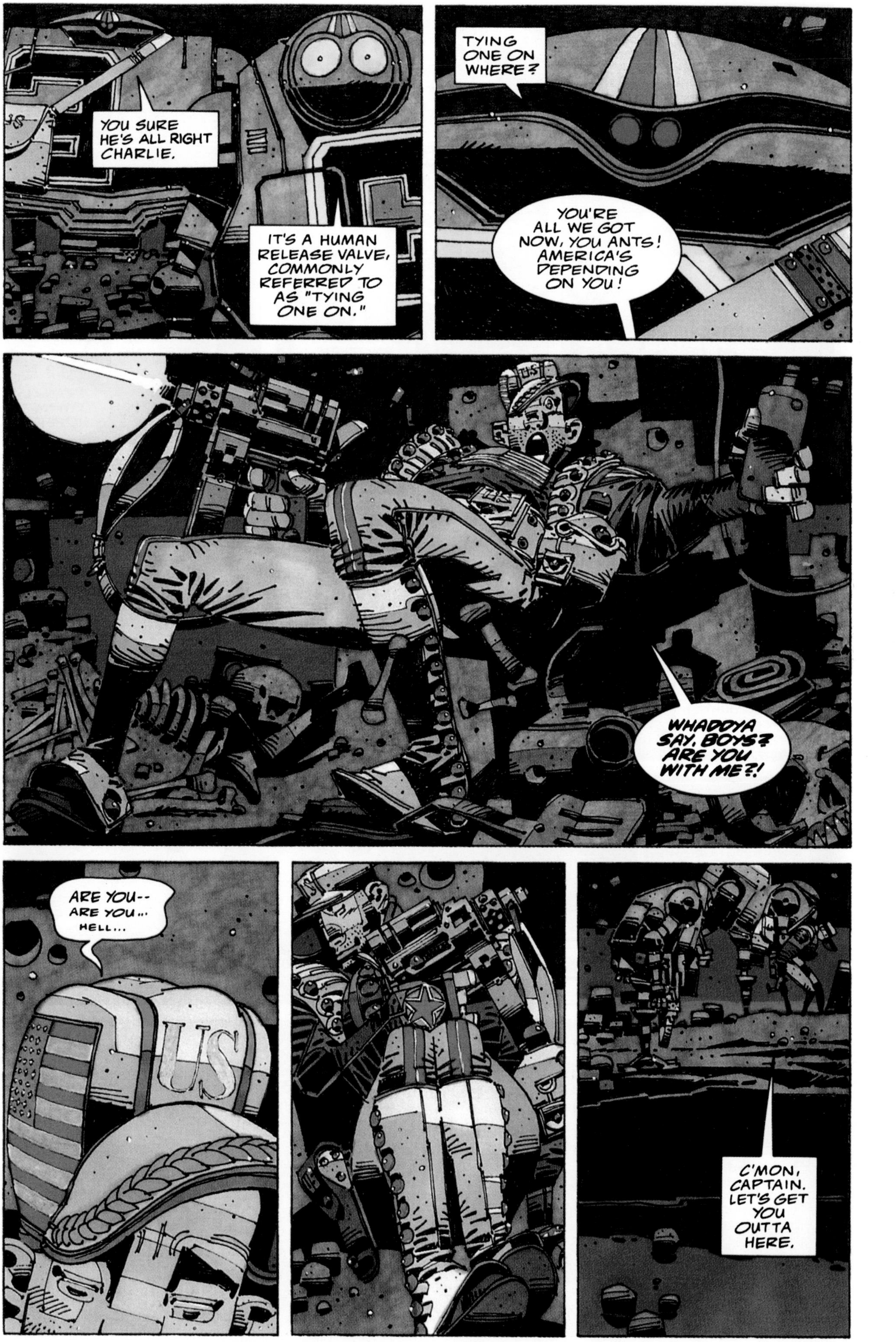
YOU SURE HE'S ALL RIGHT CHARLIE.
IT'S A HUMAN RELEASE VALVE, COMMONLY REFERRED TO AS "TYING ONE ON."
TYING ONE ON WHERE?
YOU'RE ALL WE GOT NOW, YOU ANTS! AMERICA'S DEPENDING ON YOU!
WHADDOYA SAY, BOYS? ARE YOU WITH ME?!
ARE YOU-- ARE YOU... HELL...
C'MON, CAPTAIN. LET'S GET YOU OUTTA HERE.

When I came to I felt like I'd been nuked. And that damned song was still running through my head...

WHERE'S BAKER?

HE RECKONS ANOTHER TWO HOURS, CAPTAIN. HE'LL FOLLOW ON.

LISTEN, BOSS. I KNOW THINGS LOOK BAD, BUT THIS IS A BIG COUNTRY--

--THERE'S GOT TO BE SOMETHING LEFT.

YOU THINK SO?

FRANKLY, I'M NOT HOPEFUL.

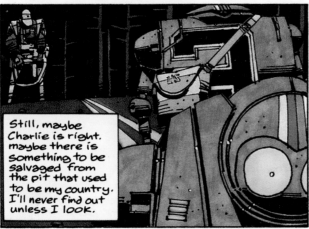

Still, maybe Charlie is right. maybe there is something to be salvaged from the pit that used to be my country. I'll never find out unless I look.

YOURS IS THE HARDEST TASK I COULD WISH ON ANY MAN, PILGRIM. YOU MUST SURVIVE.

So I took my submachine gun, my Colt .45, my precision-weighted thigh knife and my frag grenades--

--and I walked off to look for America.

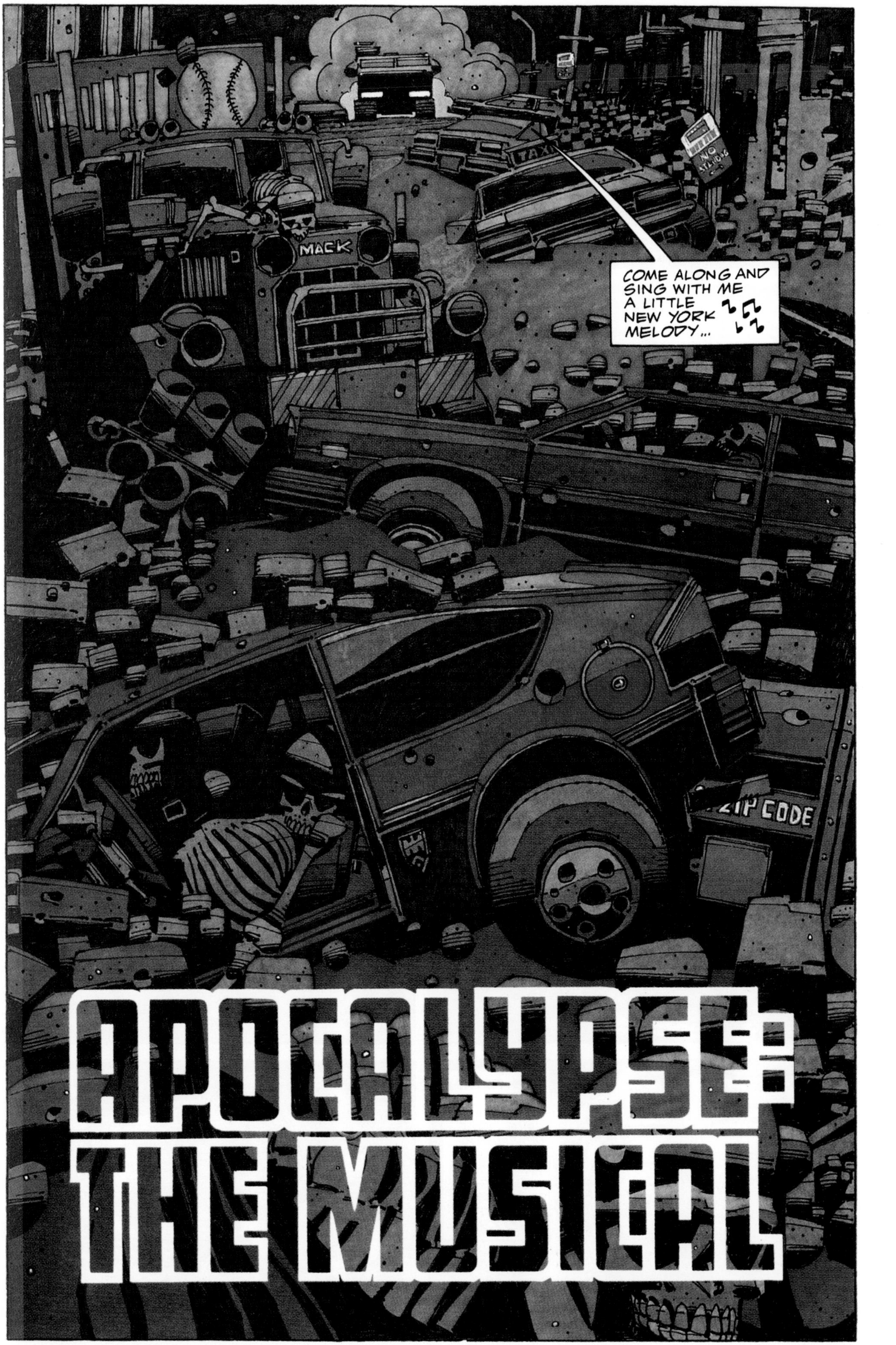

COME ALONG AND SING WITH ME A LITTLE NEW YORK MELODY...
MACK
TAXI
NO STANDING
ZIP CODE
APOCALYPSE: THE MUSICAL

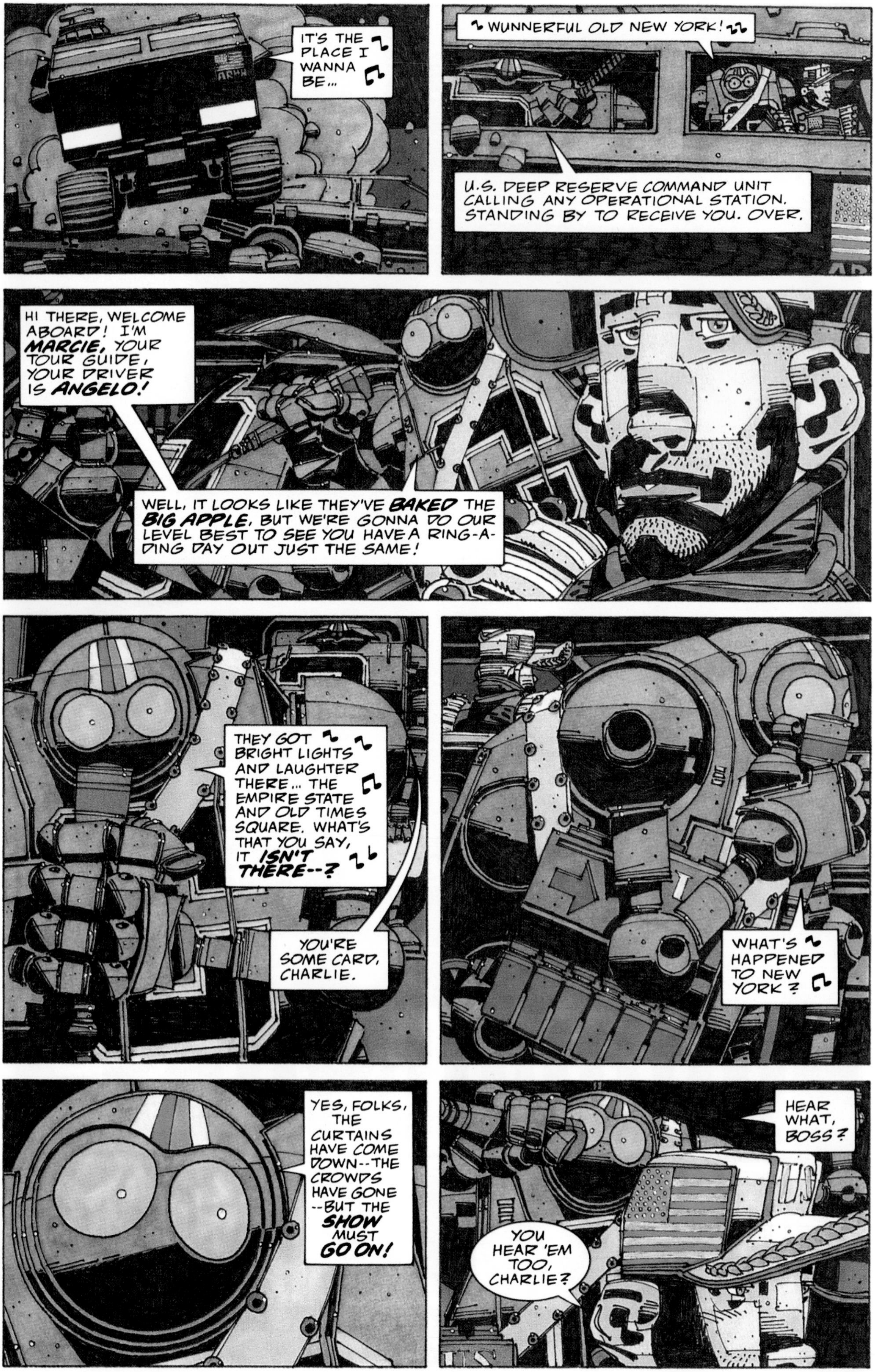

IT'S THE PLACE I WANNA BE...
WUNNERFUL OLD NEW YORK!
U.S. DEEP RESERVE COMMAND UNIT CALLING ANY OPERATIONAL STATION. STANDING BY TO RECEIVE YOU. OVER.
HI THERE, WELCOME ABOARD! I'M MARCIE, YOUR TOUR GUIDE, YOUR DRIVER IS ANGELO!
WELL, IT LOOKS LIKE THEY'VE BAKED THE BIG APPLE, BUT WE'RE GONNA DO OUR LEVEL BEST TO SEE YOU HAVE A RING-A-DING DAY OUT JUST THE SAME!
THEY GOT BRIGHT LIGHTS AND LAUGHTER THERE... THE EMPIRE STATE AND OLD TIMES SQUARE. WHAT'S THAT YOU SAY, IT ISN'T THERE--?
YOU'RE SOME CARD, CHARLIE.
WHAT'S HAPPENED TO NEW YORK?
YES, FOLKS, THE CURTAINS HAVE COME DOWN--THE CROWDS HAVE GONE --BUT THE SHOW MUST GO ON!
HEAR WHAT, BOSS?
YOU HEAR 'EM TOO, CHARLIE?

THE VOICES...

THEY'RE SINGING TO ME.

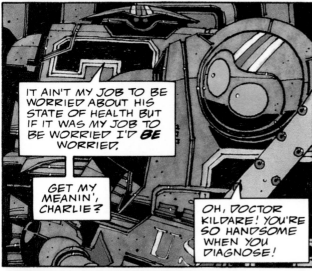

IT AIN'T MY JOB TO BE WORRIED ABOUT HIS STATE OF HEALTH BUT IF IT WAS MY JOB TO BE WORRIED I'D **BE** WORRIED.

GET MY MEANIN', CHARLIE?

OH, DOCTOR KILDARE! YOU'RE SO HANDSOME WHEN YOU DIAGNOSE!

COME TO THAT, I'D BE WORRIED ABOUT **YOUR** STATE OF HEALTH.

I hear them sighing on the wind, rising above the rattle of our tracks.

I hear the drums throb and the trombones blare and the tap tap tap of dancing feet. Far away, like an echo from the past.

The ghosts of New York are playing their song ...

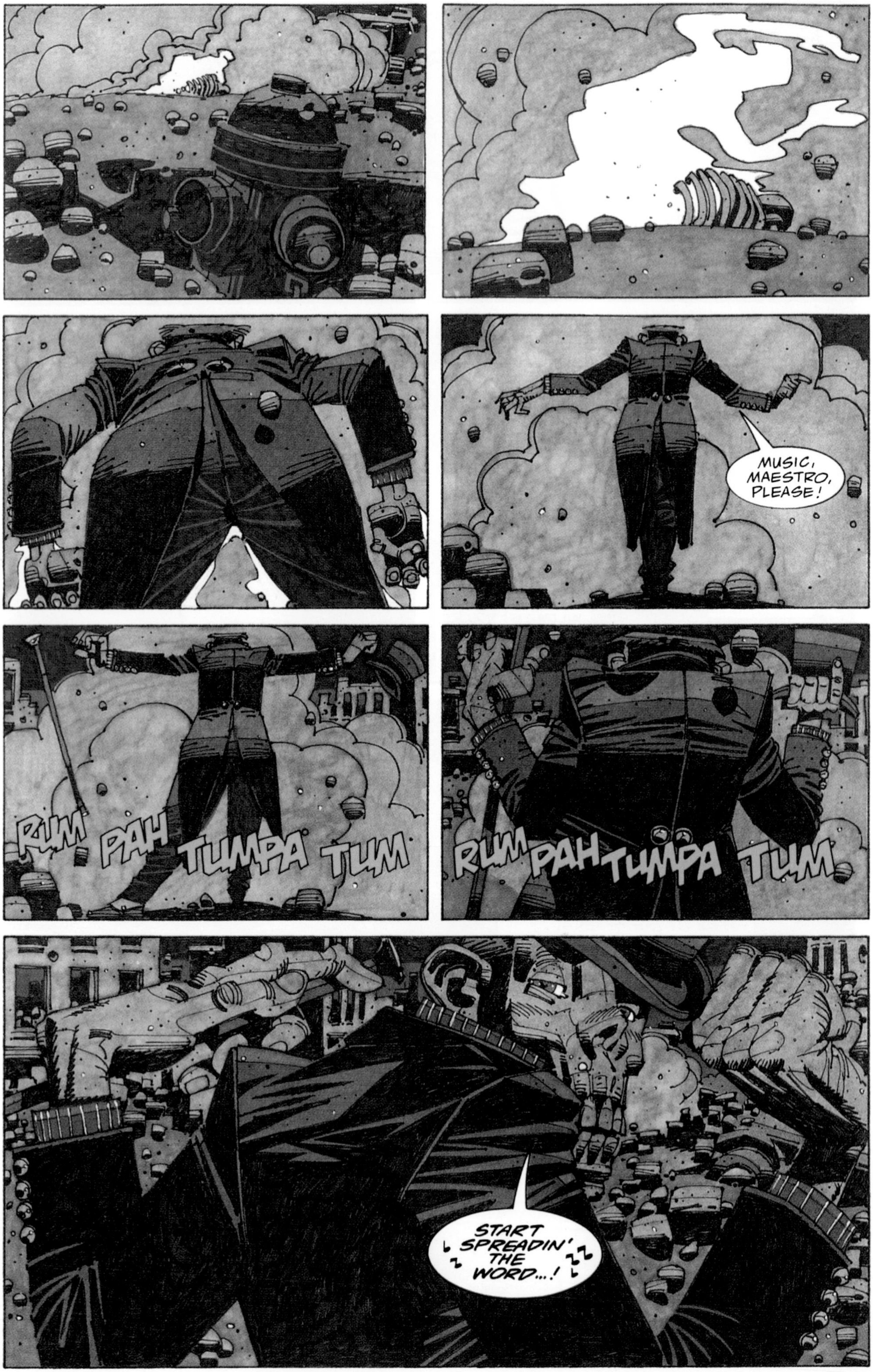
MUSIC, MAESTRO, PLEASE!
RUM PAH TUMPA TUM
RUM PAH TUMPA TUM
START SPREADIN' THE WORD...!

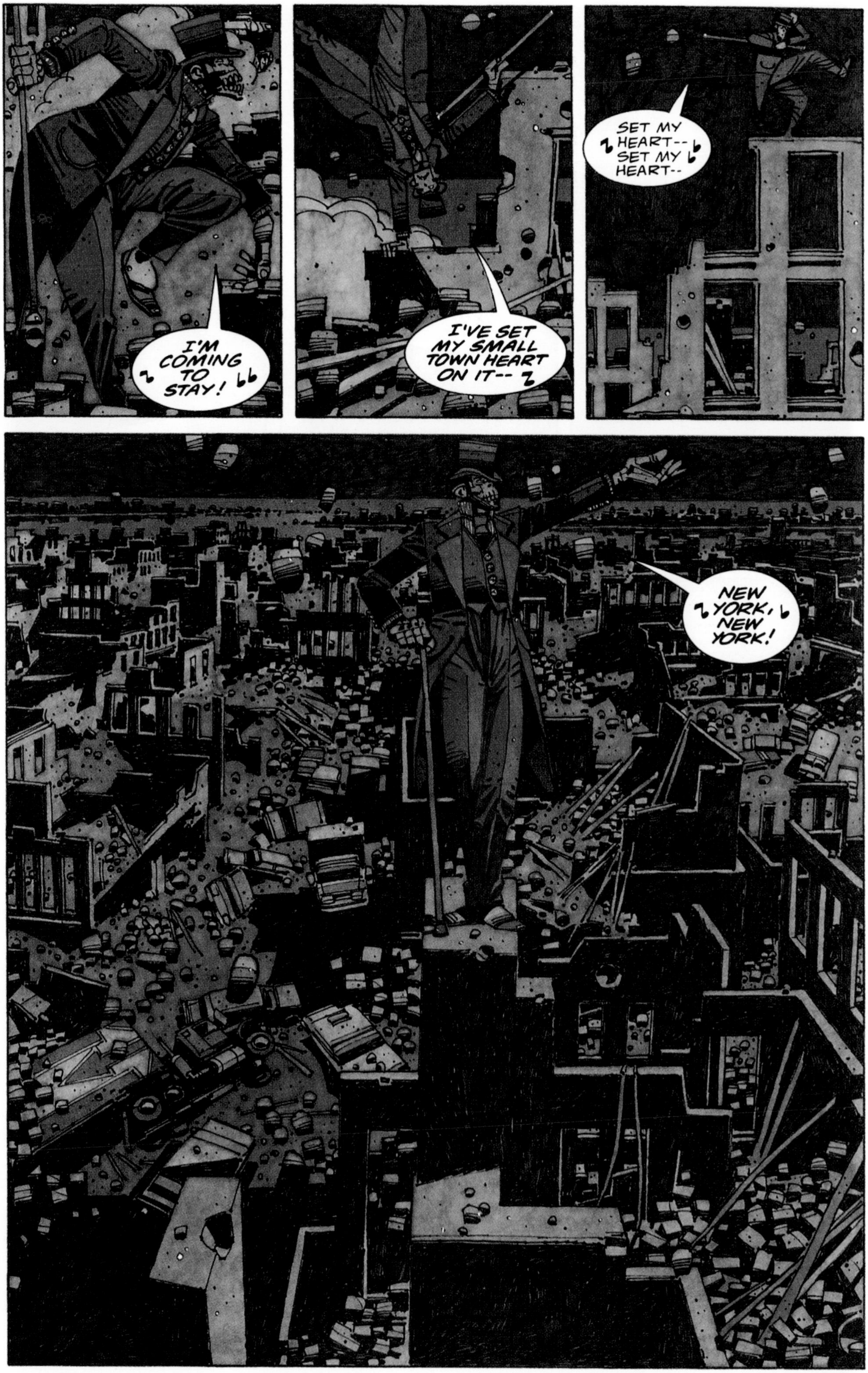
I'M COMING TO STAY!
I'VE SET MY SMALL TOWN HEART ON IT--
SET MY HEART-- SET MY HEART--
NEW YORK, NEW YORK!

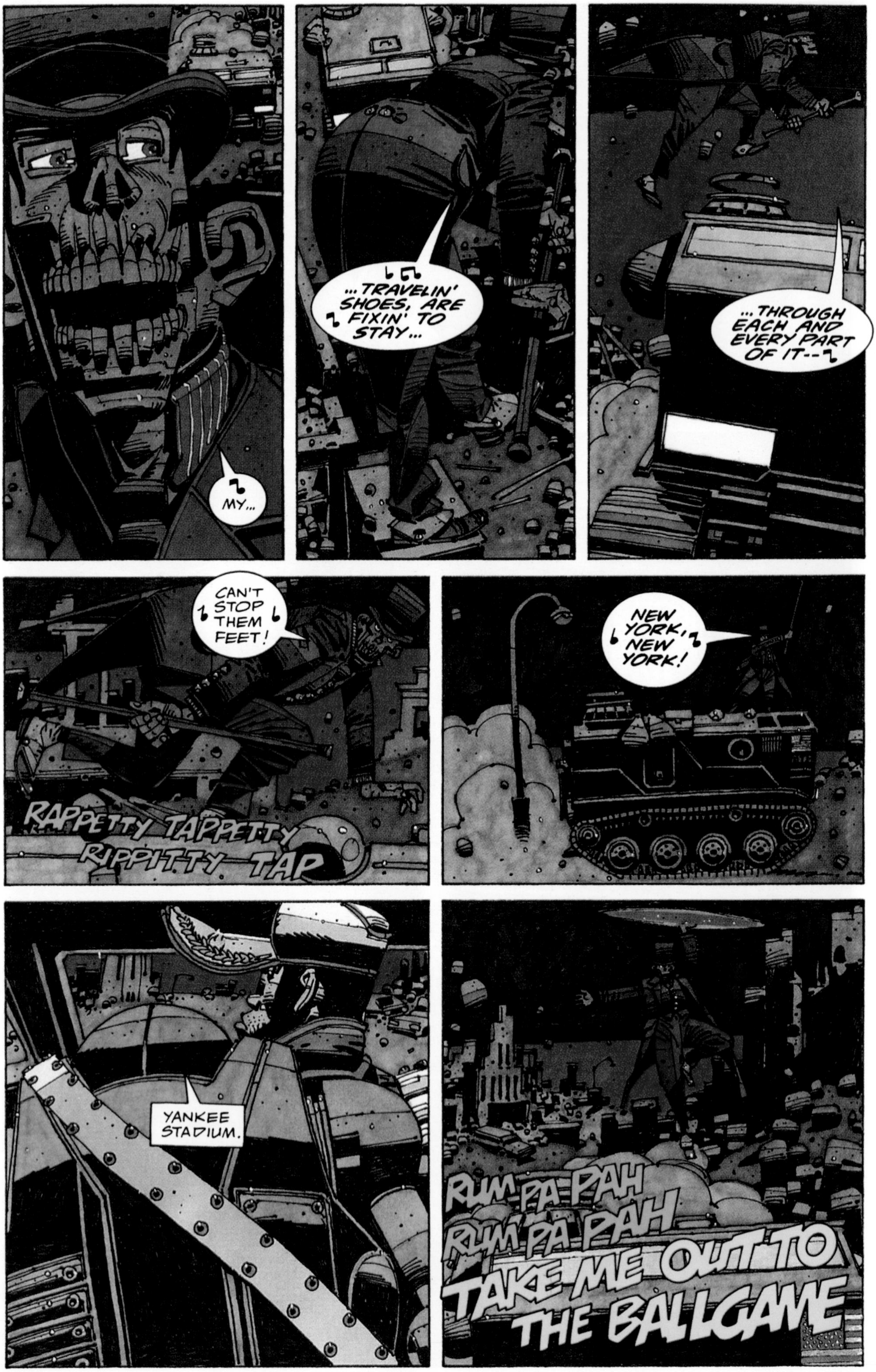
MY...
...TRAVELIN' SHOES, ARE FIXIN' TO STAY...
...THROUGH EACH AND EVERY PART OF IT--
CAN'T STOP THEM FEET!
RAPPETTY TAPPETTY RIPPITTY TAP
NEW YORK, NEW YORK!
YANKEE STADIUM.
RUM PA PAH
RUM PA PAH
TAKE ME OUT TO THE BALLGAME

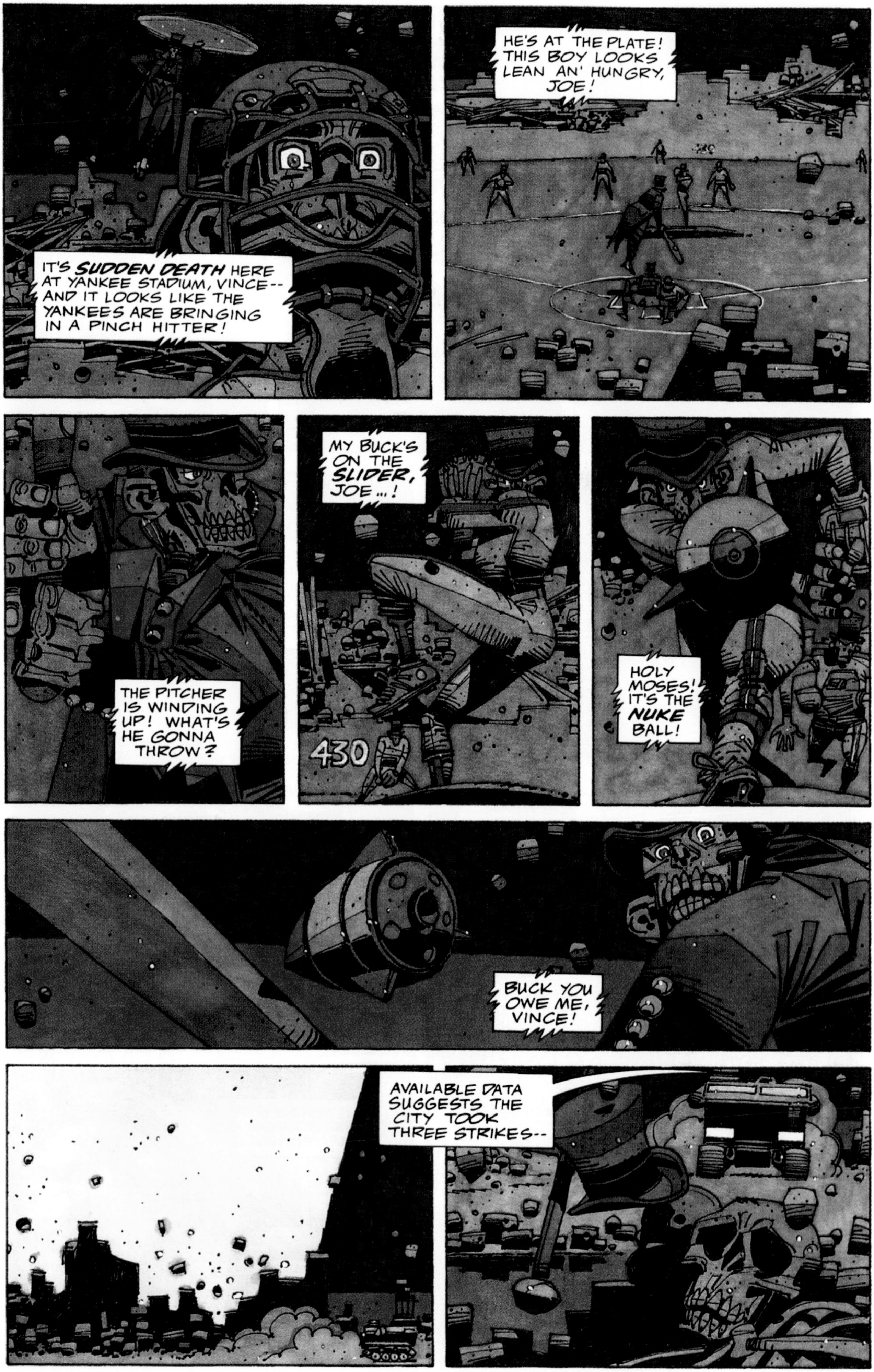
IT'S SUDDEN DEATH HERE AT YANKEE STADIUM, VINCE-- AND IT LOOKS LIKE THE YANKEES ARE BRINGING IN A PINCH HITTER!
HE'S AT THE PLATE! THIS BOY LOOKS LEAN AN' HUNGRY, JOE!
THE PITCHER IS WINDING UP! WHAT'S HE GONNA THROW?
MY BUCK'S ON THE SLIDER, JOE...!
430
HOLY MOSES! IT'S THE NUKE BALL!
BUCK YOU OWE ME, VINCE!
AVAILABLE DATA SUGGESTS THE CITY TOOK THREE STRIKES--

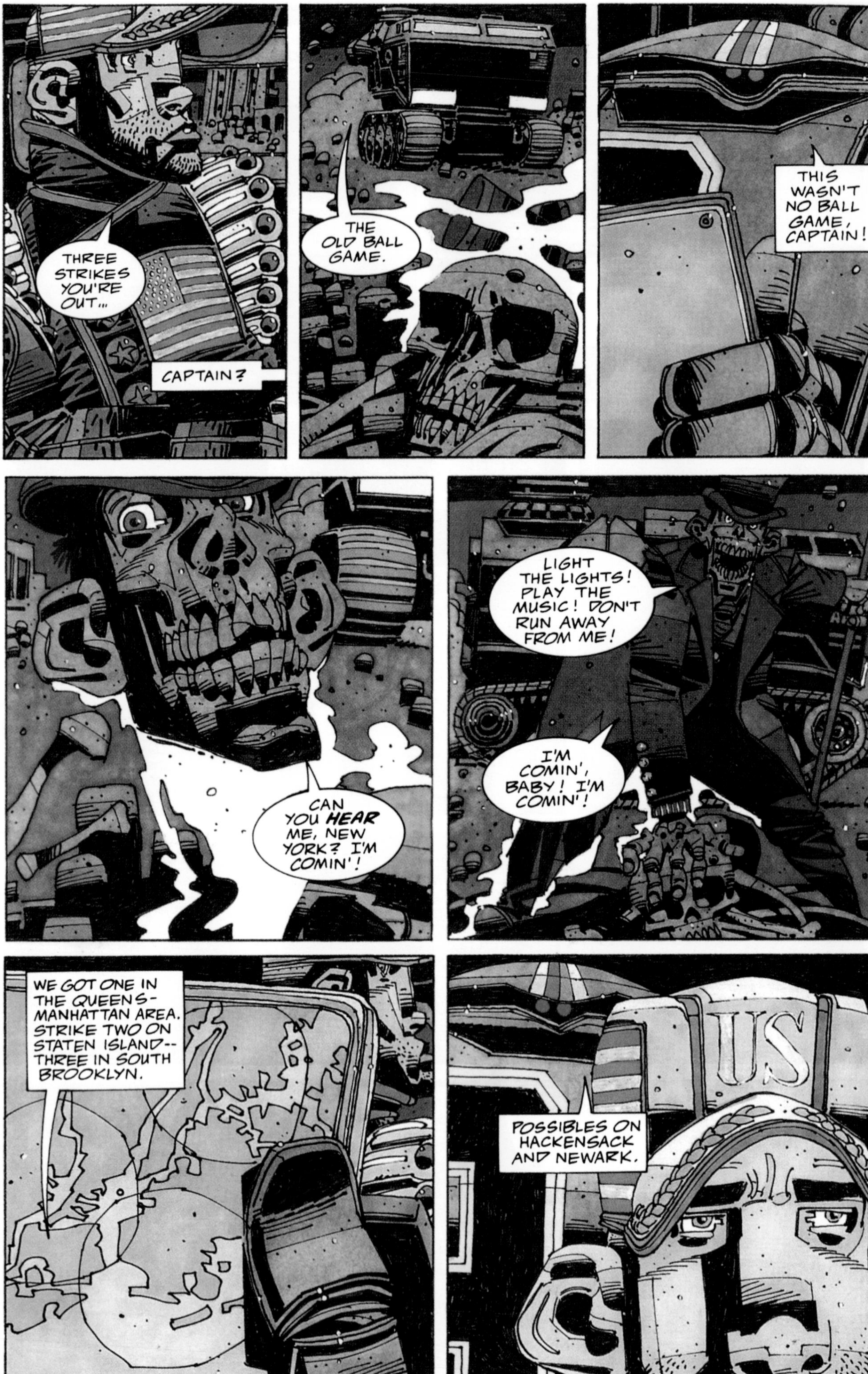

THREE STRIKES YOU'RE OUT...
CAPTAIN?
THE OLD BALL GAME.
THIS WASN'T NO BALL GAME, CAPTAIN!
CAN YOU HEAR ME, NEW YORK? I'M COMIN'!
LIGHT THE LIGHTS! PLAY THE MUSIC! DON'T RUN AWAY FROM ME!
I'M COMIN', BABY! I'M COMIN'!
WE GOT ONE IN THE QUEENS-MANHATTAN AREA. STRIKE TWO ON STATEN ISLAND-- THREE IN SOUTH BROOKLYN.
US
POSSIBLES ON HACKENSACK AND NEWARK.

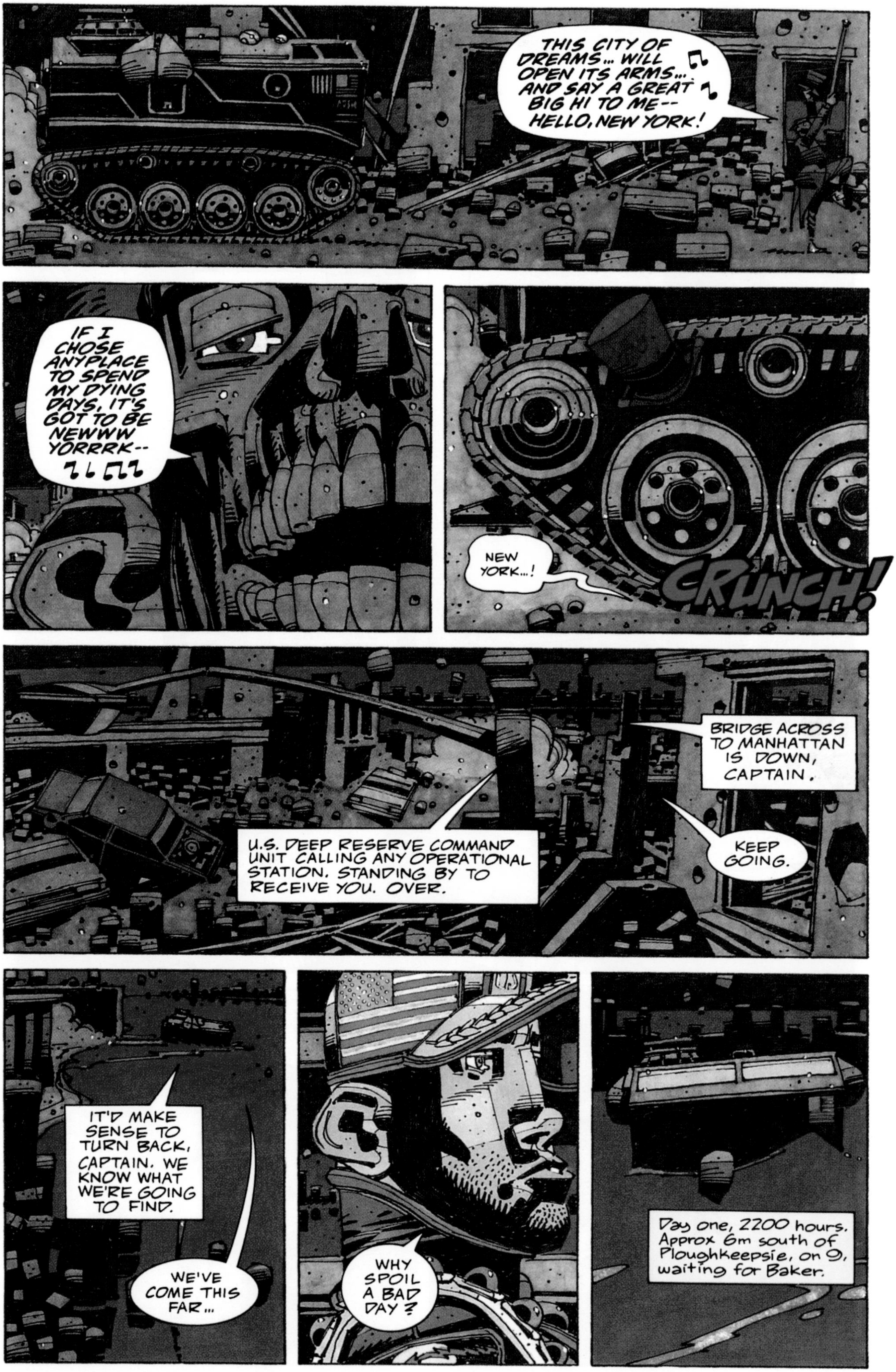
THIS CITY OF DREAMS... WILL OPEN ITS ARMS... AND SAY A GREAT BIG HI TO ME-- HELLO, NEW YORK!
IF I CHOSE ANYPLACE TO SPEND MY DYING DAYS, IT'S GOT TO BE NEWWW YORRRK--
NEW YORK...!
CRUNCH!
U.S. DEEP RESERVE COMMAND UNIT CALLING ANY OPERATIONAL STATION. STANDING BY TO RECEIVE YOU. OVER.
BRIDGE ACROSS TO MANHATTAN IS DOWN, CAPTAIN.
KEEP GOING.
IT'D MAKE SENSE TO TURN BACK, CAPTAIN. WE KNOW WHAT WE'RE GOING TO FIND.
WE'VE COME THIS FAR...
WHY SPOIL A BAD DAY?
Day one, 2200 hours. Approx 6m south of Ploughkeepsie, on 9, waiting for Baker.

For a change the sky has broken through and all the stars are out. It's almost possible to imagine the world has never changed...

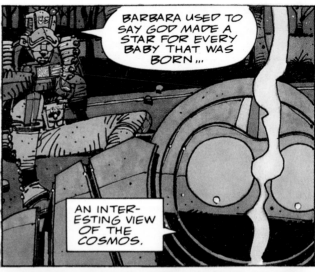

BARBARA USED TO SAY GOD MADE A STAR FOR EVERY BABY THAT WAS BORN...

AN INTER-ESTING VIEW OF THE COSMOS.

WHAT WAS THAT?

YOU HEAR THAT? SOUNDED LIKE A CRY--

JUST THE WIND, BOSS. RELAX.

YOU WERE SAYING--ABOUT YOUR WIFE?

OH YEAH... THE FIRST STAR YOU EVER SAW,... THAT WAS YOUR STAR... IT LOOKED AFTER YOU ALL YOUR LIFE, WHEN YOU DIED, IT DIED...

SHE GOT THAT WRONG ANYWAY, THE STARS ARE STILL THERE...

THERE IT IS AGAIN, DAMMIT!

SOMEONE'S CALLING OUT THERE! ABLE! WORK ROUND TO THE RIGHT--!

HELLO!

WE'RE WASTING OUR TIME. THERE'S NO ONE HERE.

I CAN STILL HEAR IT! DOWNWIND NOW--

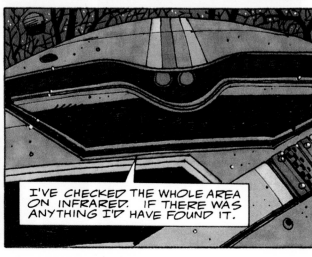

I'VE CHECKED THE WHOLE AREA ON INFRARED. IF THERE WAS ANYTHING I'D HAVE FOUND IT.

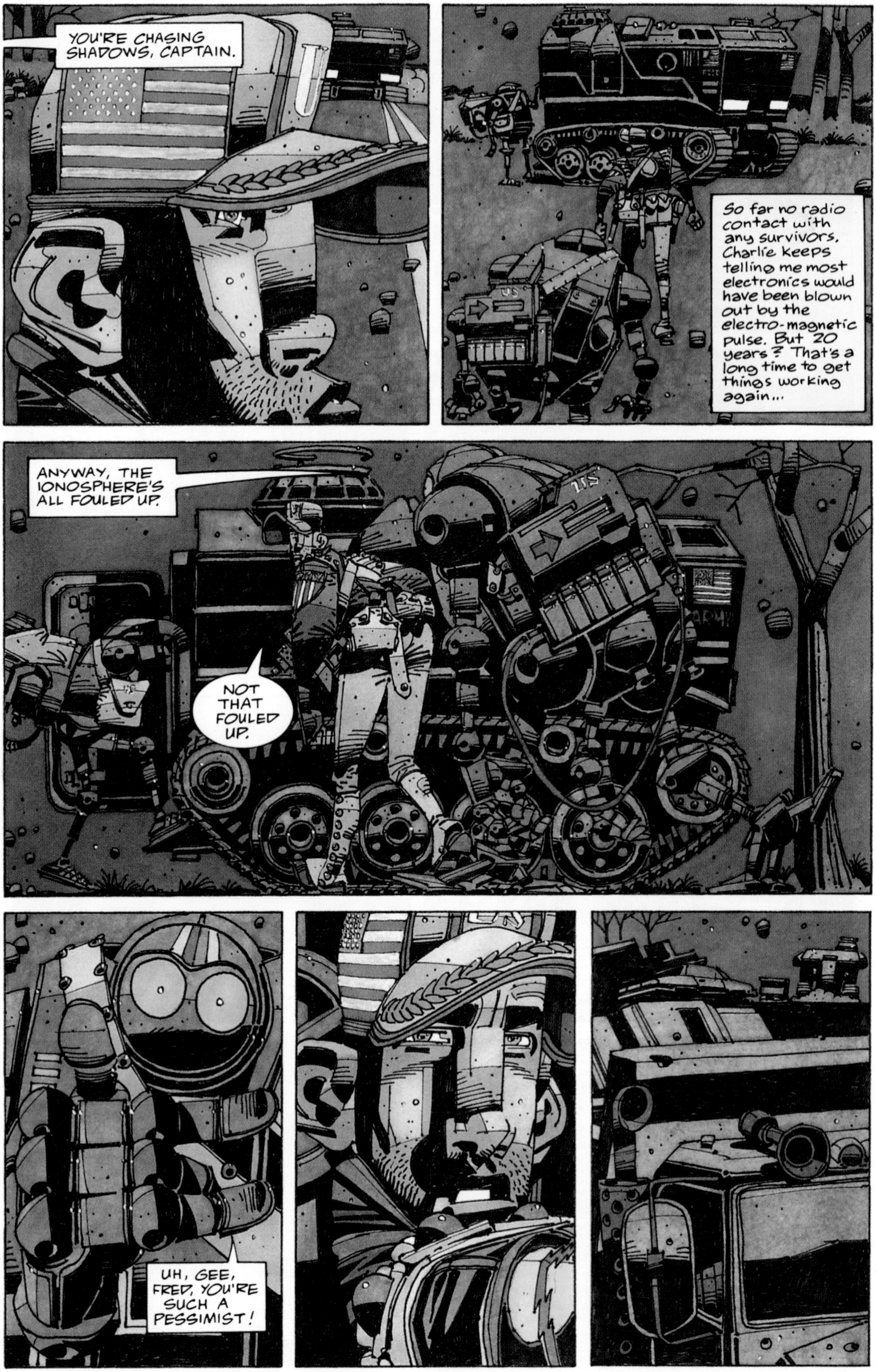
YOU'RE CHASING SHADOWS, CAPTAIN.
So far no radio contact with any survivors. Charlie keeps telling me most electronics would have been blown out by the electro-magnetic pulse. But 20 years? That's a long time to get things working again...
ANYWAY, THE IONOSPHERE'S ALL FOULED UP.
NOT THAT FOULED UP.
UH, GEE, FRED, YOU'RE SUCH A PESSIMIST!

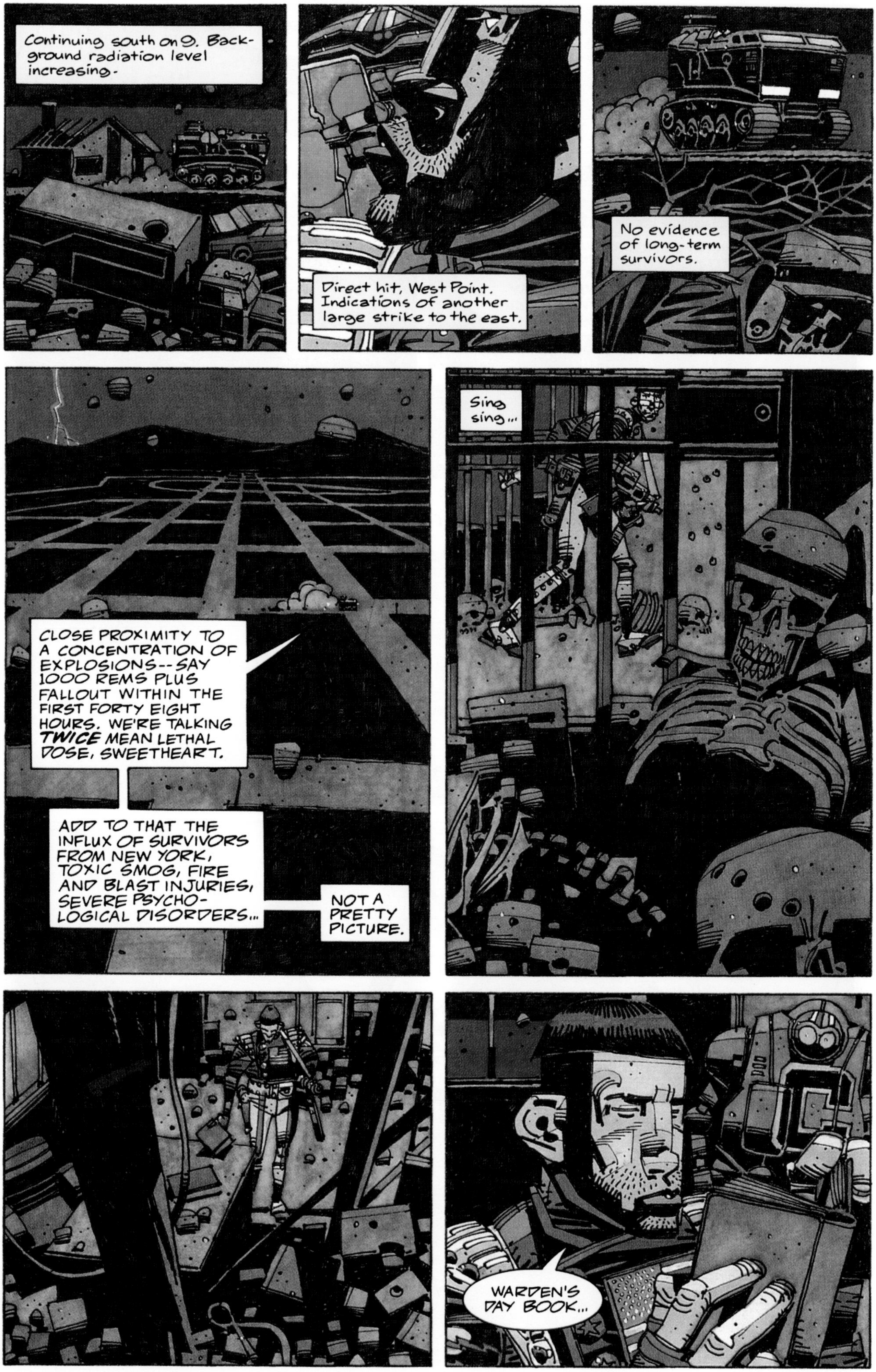
Continuing south on 9. Background radiation level increasing.
Direct hit, West Point. Indications of another large strike to the east.
No evidence of long-term survivors.
CLOSE PROXIMITY TO A CONCENTRATION OF EXPLOSIONS--SAY 1000 REMS PLUS FALLOUT WITHIN THE FIRST FORTY EIGHT HOURS. WE'RE TALKING TWICE MEAN LETHAL DOSE, SWEETHEART.
ADD TO THAT THE INFLUX OF SURVIVORS FROM NEW YORK, TOXIC SMOG, FIRE AND BLAST INJURIES, SEVERE PSYCHOLOGICAL DISORDERS...
NOT A PRETTY PICTURE.
Sing sing...
WARDEN'S DAY BOOK...

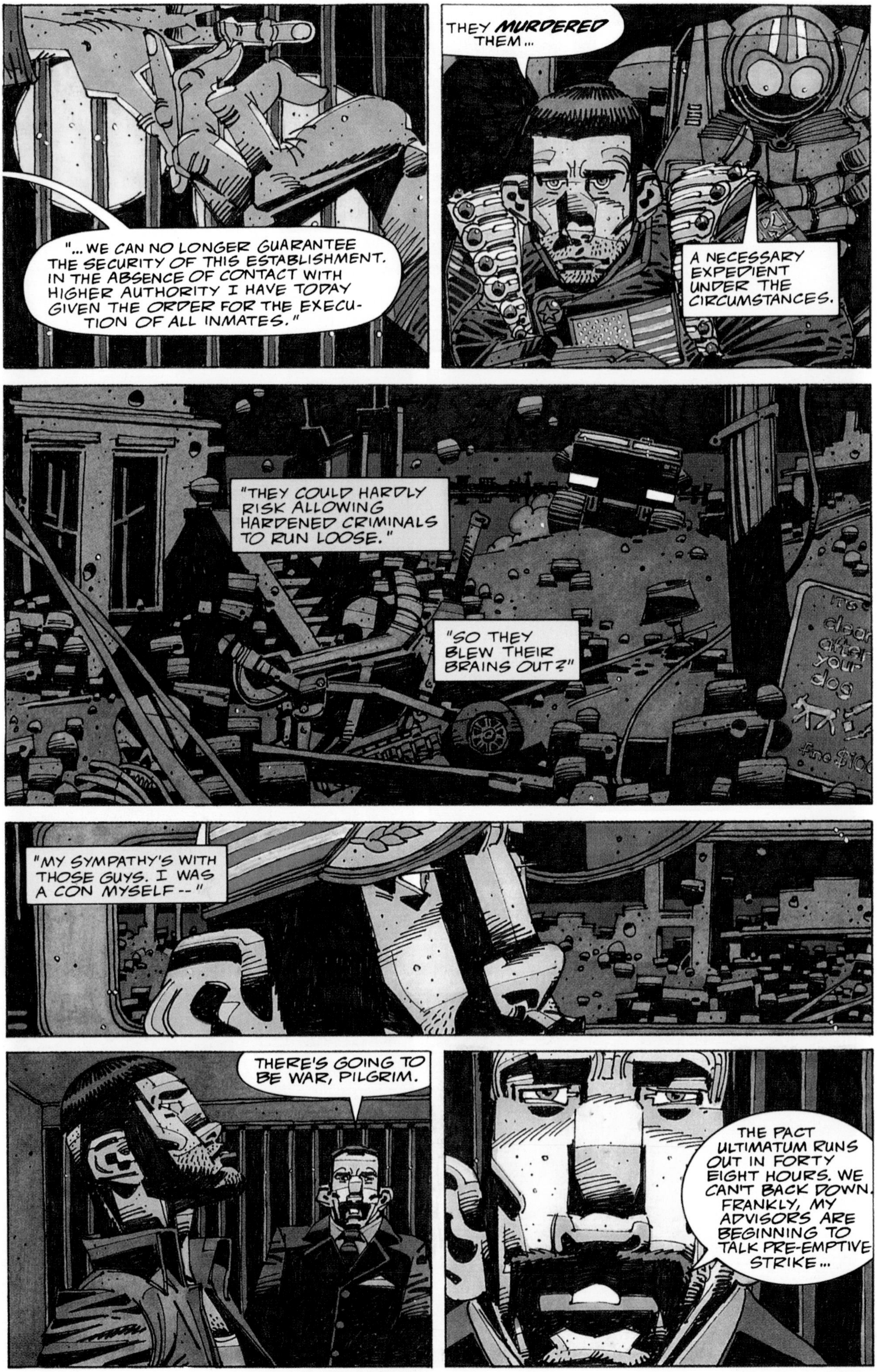
"...WE CAN NO LONGER GUARANTEE THE SECURITY OF THIS ESTABLISHMENT. IN THE ABSENCE OF CONTACT WITH HIGHER AUTHORITY I HAVE TODAY GIVEN THE ORDER FOR THE EXECUTION OF ALL INMATES."
THEY MURDERED THEM...
A NECESSARY EXPEDIENT UNDER THE CIRCUMSTANCES.
"THEY COULD HARDLY RISK ALLOWING HARDENED CRIMINALS TO RUN LOOSE."
"SO THEY BLEW THEIR BRAINS OUT?"
clean after your dog
"MY SYMPATHY'S WITH THOSE GUYS. I WAS A CON MYSELF --"
THERE'S GOING TO BE WAR, PILGRIM.
THE PACT ULTIMATUM RUNS OUT IN FORTY EIGHT HOURS. WE CAN'T BACK DOWN. FRANKLY, MY ADVISORS ARE BEGINNING TO TALK PRE-EMPTIVE STRIKE...

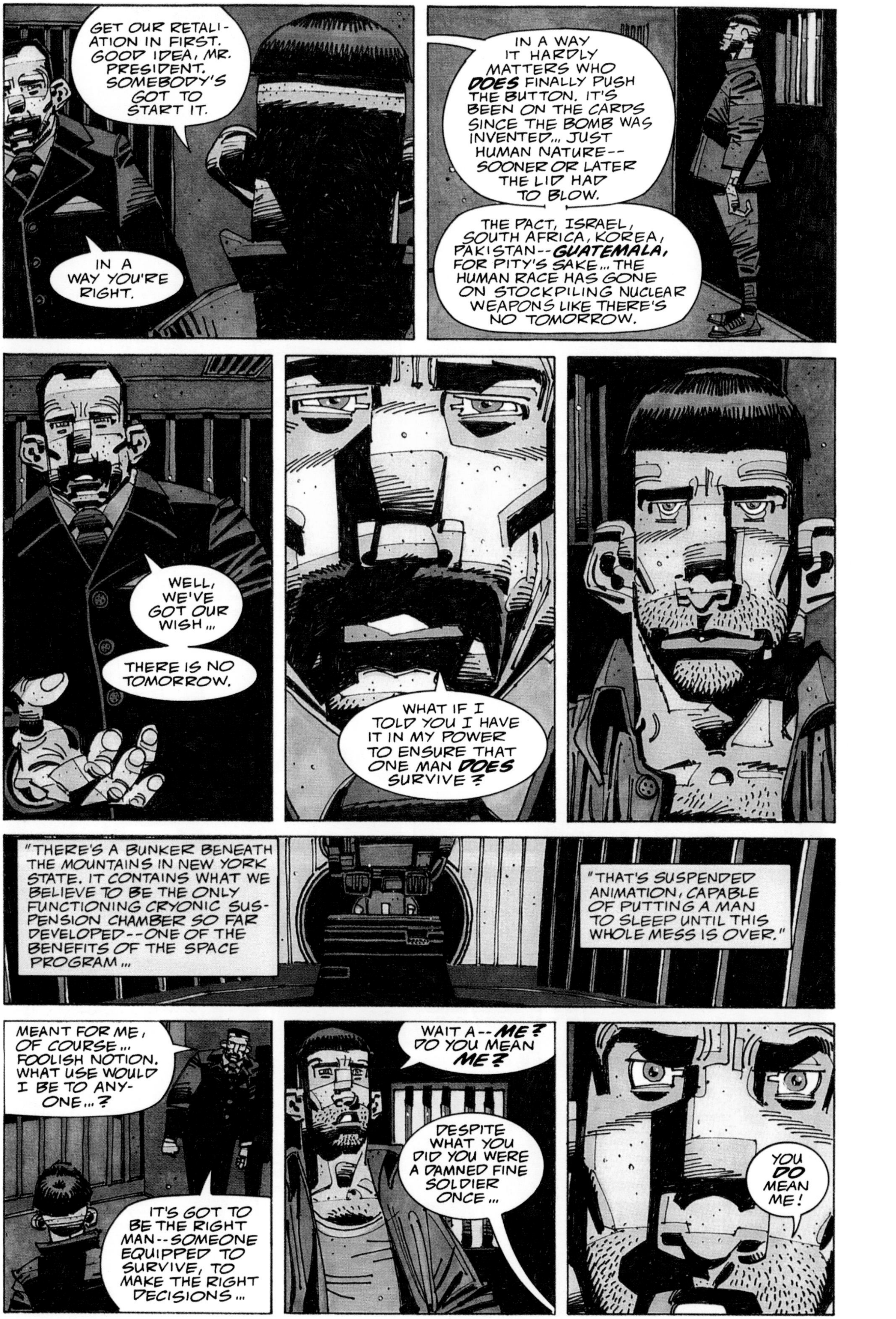
GET OUR RETALIATION IN FIRST. GOOD IDEA, MR. PRESIDENT. SOMEBODY'S GOT TO START IT.
IN A WAY YOU'RE RIGHT.
IN A WAY IT HARDLY MATTERS WHO **DOES** FINALLY PUSH THE BUTTON. IT'S BEEN ON THE CARDS SINCE THE BOMB WAS INVENTED... JUST HUMAN NATURE-- SOONER OR LATER THE LID HAD TO BLOW.
THE PACT, ISRAEL, SOUTH AFRICA, KOREA, PAKISTAN--**GUATEMALA,** FOR PITY'S SAKE... THE HUMAN RACE HAS GONE ON STOCKPILING NUCLEAR WEAPONS LIKE THERE'S NO TOMORROW.
WELL, WE'VE GOT OUR WISH...
THERE IS NO TOMORROW.
WHAT IF I TOLD YOU I HAVE IT IN MY POWER TO ENSURE THAT ONE MAN **DOES** SURVIVE?
"THERE'S A BUNKER BENEATH THE MOUNTAINS IN NEW YORK STATE. IT CONTAINS WHAT WE BELIEVE TO BE THE ONLY FUNCTIONING CRYONIC SUSPENSION CHAMBER SO FAR DEVELOPED--ONE OF THE BENEFITS OF THE SPACE PROGRAM...
"THAT'S SUSPENDED ANIMATION, CAPABLE OF PUTTING A MAN TO SLEEP UNTIL THIS WHOLE MESS IS OVER."
MEANT FOR ME, OF COURSE... FOOLISH NOTION. WHAT USE WOULD I BE TO ANYONE...?
IT'S GOT TO BE THE RIGHT MAN--SOMEONE EQUIPPED TO SURVIVE, TO MAKE THE RIGHT DECISIONS...
WAIT A--**ME?** DO YOU MEAN **ME?**
DESPITE WHAT YOU DID YOU WERE A DAMNED FINE SOLDIER ONCE...
YOU **DO** MEAN ME!

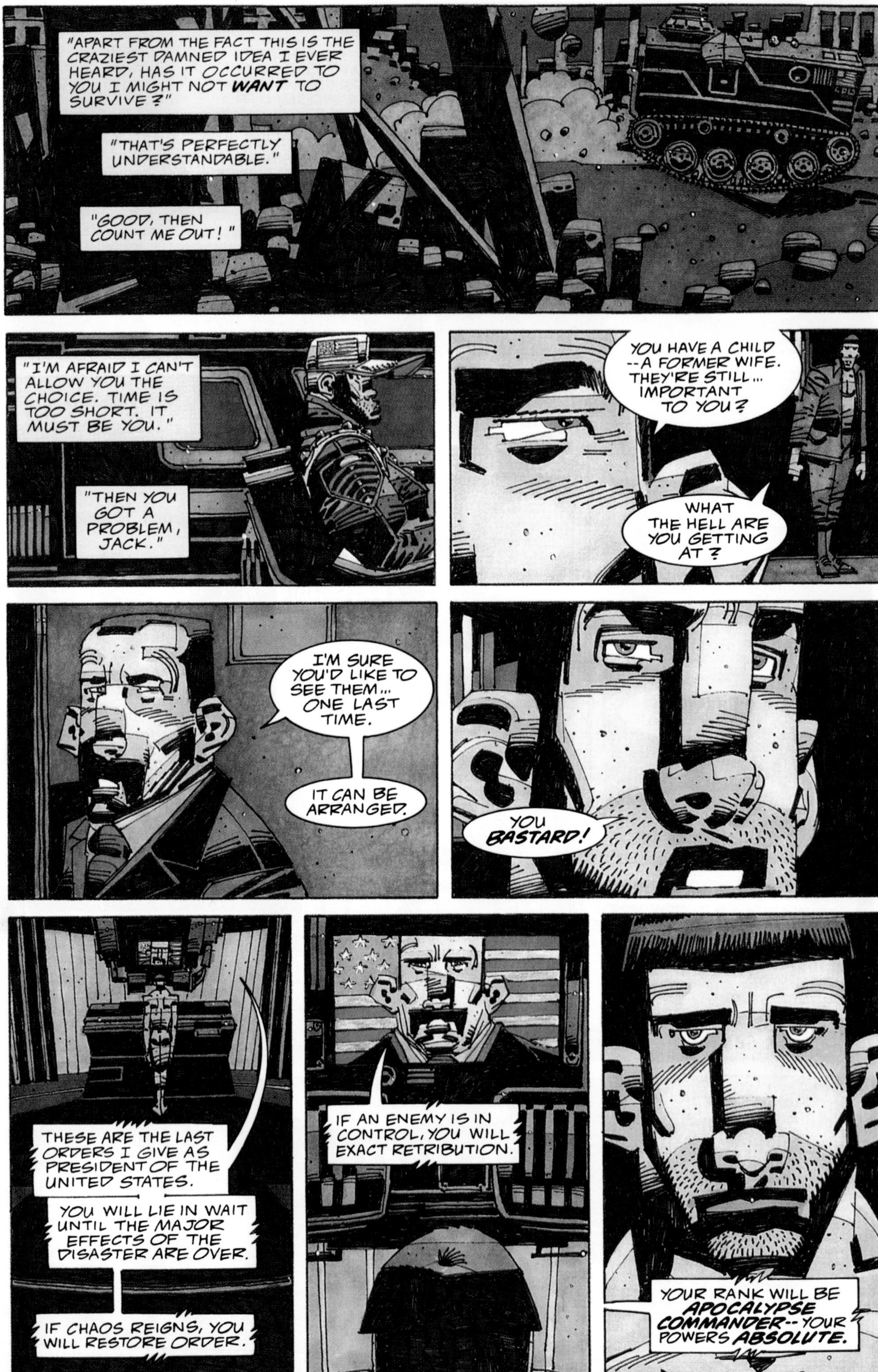
"APART FROM THE FACT THIS IS THE CRAZIEST DAMNED IDEA I EVER HEARD, HAS IT OCCURRED TO YOU I MIGHT NOT WANT TO SURVIVE?"
"THAT'S PERFECTLY UNDERSTANDABLE."
"GOOD, THEN COUNT ME OUT!"
"I'M AFRAID I CAN'T ALLOW YOU THE CHOICE. TIME IS TOO SHORT. IT MUST BE YOU."
"THEN YOU GOT A PROBLEM, JACK."
YOU HAVE A CHILD --A FORMER WIFE. THEY'RE STILL... IMPORTANT TO YOU?
WHAT THE HELL ARE YOU GETTING AT?
I'M SURE YOU'D LIKE TO SEE THEM... ONE LAST TIME.
IT CAN BE ARRANGED.
YOU BASTARD!
THESE ARE THE LAST ORDERS I GIVE AS PRESIDENT OF THE UNITED STATES.
YOU WILL LIE IN WAIT UNTIL THE MAJOR EFFECTS OF THE DISASTER ARE OVER.
IF CHAOS REIGNS, YOU WILL RESTORE ORDER.
IF AN ENEMY IS IN CONTROL, YOU WILL EXACT RETRIBUTION.
YOUR RANK WILL BE APOCALYPSE COMMANDER-- YOUR POWERS ABSOLUTE.

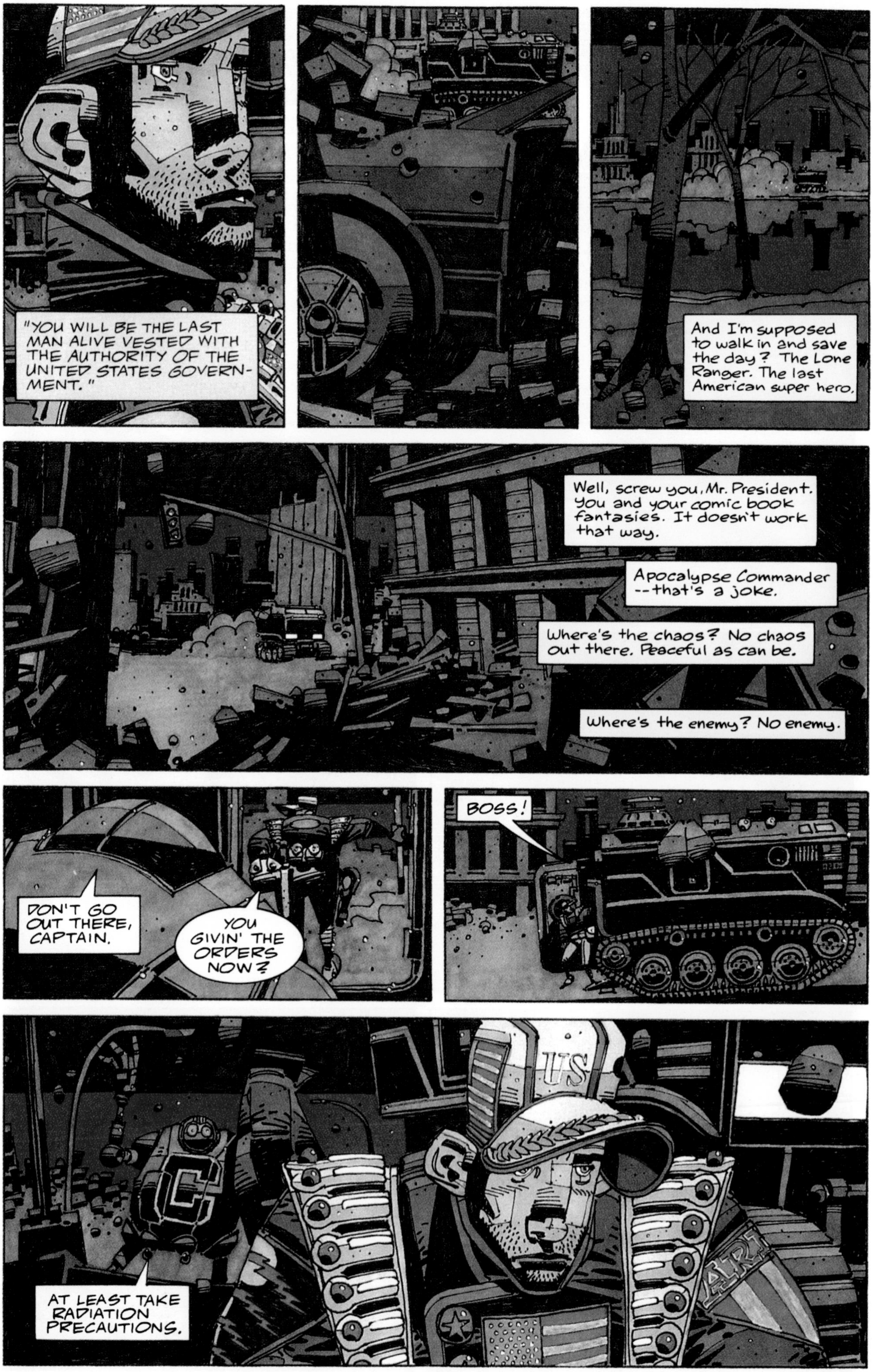
"YOU WILL BE THE LAST MAN ALIVE VESTED WITH THE AUTHORITY OF THE UNITED STATES GOVERNMENT."
And I'm supposed to walk in and save the day? The Lone Ranger. The last American super hero.
Well, screw you, Mr. President. You and your comic book fantasies. It doesn't work that way.
Apocalypse Commander --that's a joke.
Where's the chaos? No chaos out there. Peaceful as can be.
Where's the enemy? No enemy.
DON'T GO OUT THERE, CAPTAIN.
YOU GIVIN' THE ORDERS NOW?
BOSS!
US
AT LEAST TAKE RADIATION PRECAUTIONS.

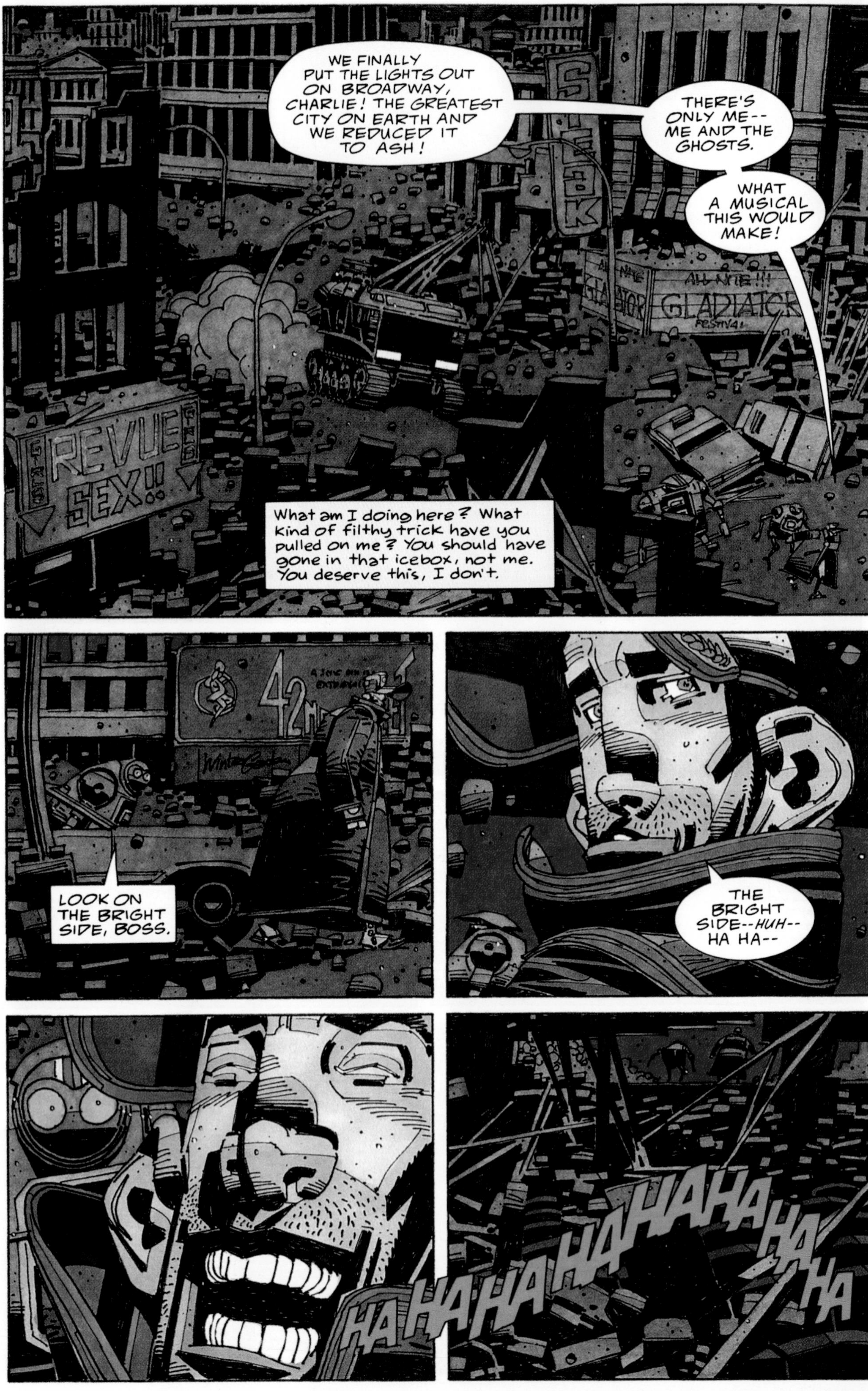

WE FINALLY PUT THE LIGHTS OUT ON BROADWAY, CHARLIE! THE GREATEST CITY ON EARTH AND WE REDUCED IT TO ASH!
THERE'S ONLY ME-- ME AND THE GHOSTS.
WHAT A MUSICAL THIS WOULD MAKE!
ALL NITE!!! GLADIATOR FESTIVAL
REVUE
SEX!!
What am I doing here? What kind of filthy trick have you pulled on me? You should have gone in that icebox, not me. You deserve this, I don't.
LOOK ON THE BRIGHT SIDE, BOSS.
THE BRIGHT SIDE--*HUH*-- HA HA--
HAHAHAHAHAHAHAHAHA

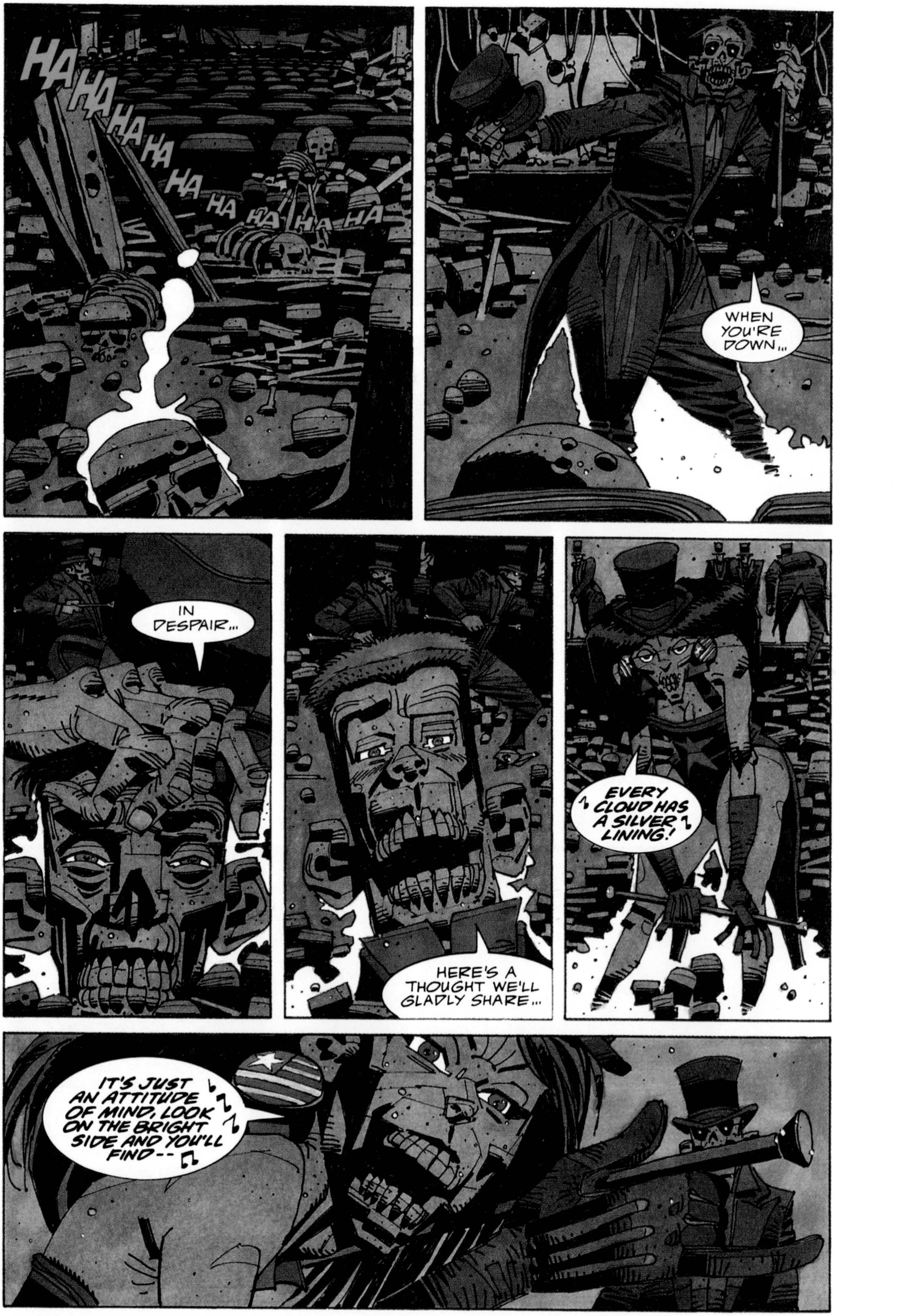
HA HA HA HA HA HA HA HA HA HA HA
WHEN YOU'RE DOWN...
IN DESPAIR...
HERE'S A THOUGHT WE'LL GLADLY SHARE...
EVERY CLOUD HAS A SILVER LINING!
IT'S JUST AN ATTITUDE OF MIND, LOOK ON THE BRIGHT SIDE AND YOU'LL FIND--

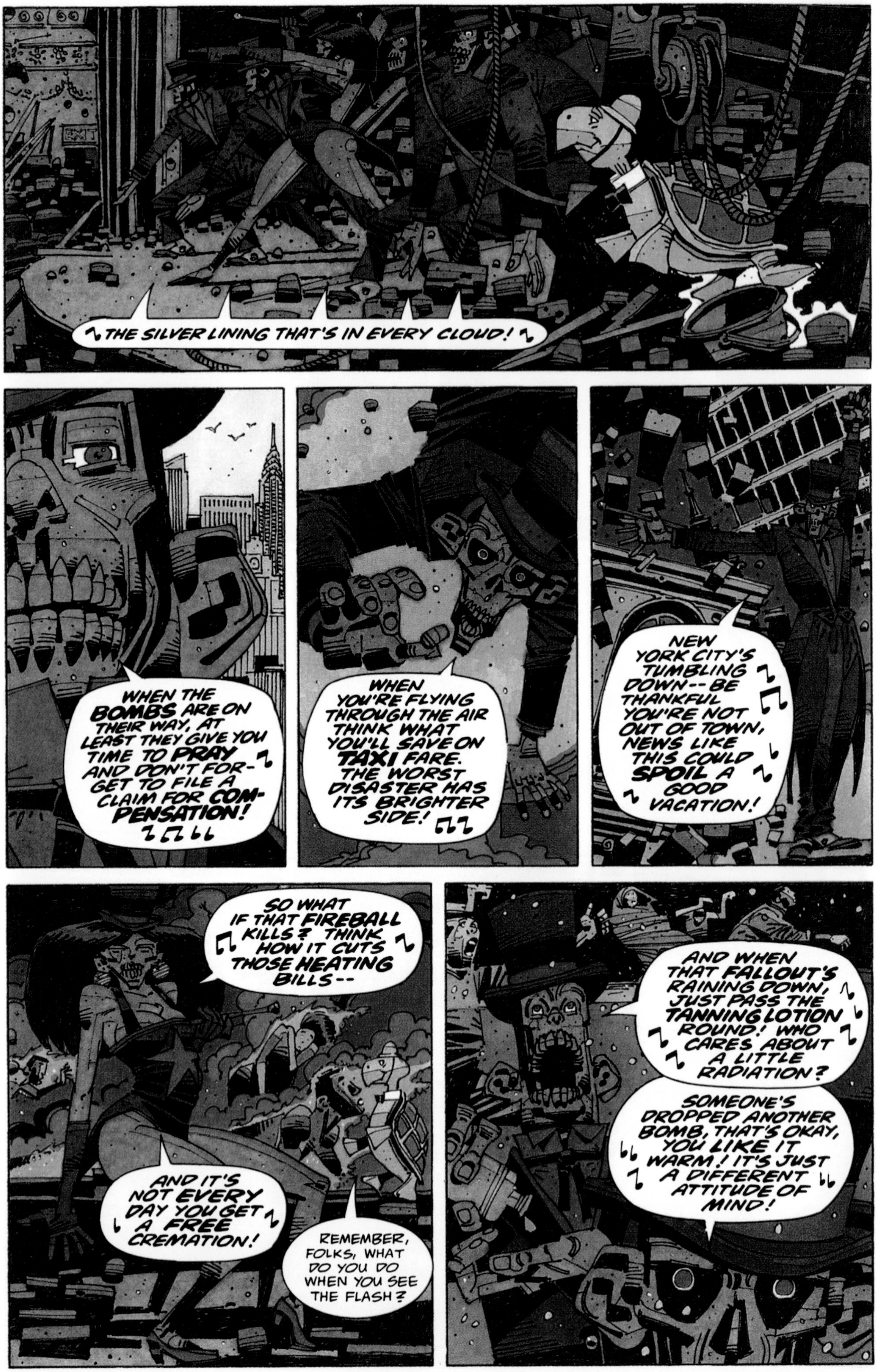
THE SILVER LINING THAT'S IN EVERY CLOUD!
WHEN THE BOMBS ARE ON THEIR WAY, AT LEAST THEY GIVE YOU TIME TO PRAY AND DON'T FORGET TO FILE A CLAIM FOR COMPENSATION!
WHEN YOU'RE FLYING THROUGH THE AIR THINK WHAT YOU'LL SAVE ON TAXI FARE. THE WORST DISASTER HAS ITS BRIGHTER SIDE!
NEW YORK CITY'S TUMBLING DOWN-- BE THANKFUL YOU'RE NOT OUT OF TOWN, NEWS LIKE THIS COULD SPOIL A GOOD VACATION!
SO WHAT IF THAT FIREBALL KILLS? THINK HOW IT CUTS THOSE HEATING BILLS--
AND IT'S NOT EVERY DAY YOU GET A FREE CREMATION!
REMEMBER, FOLKS, WHAT DO YOU DO WHEN YOU SEE THE FLASH?
AND WHEN THAT FALLOUT'S RAINING DOWN, JUST PASS THE TANNING LOTION ROUND! WHO CARES ABOUT A LITTLE RADIATION?
SOMEONE'S DROPPED ANOTHER BOMB, THAT'S OKAY, YOU LIKE IT WARM! IT'S JUST A DIFFERENT ATTITUDE OF MIND!

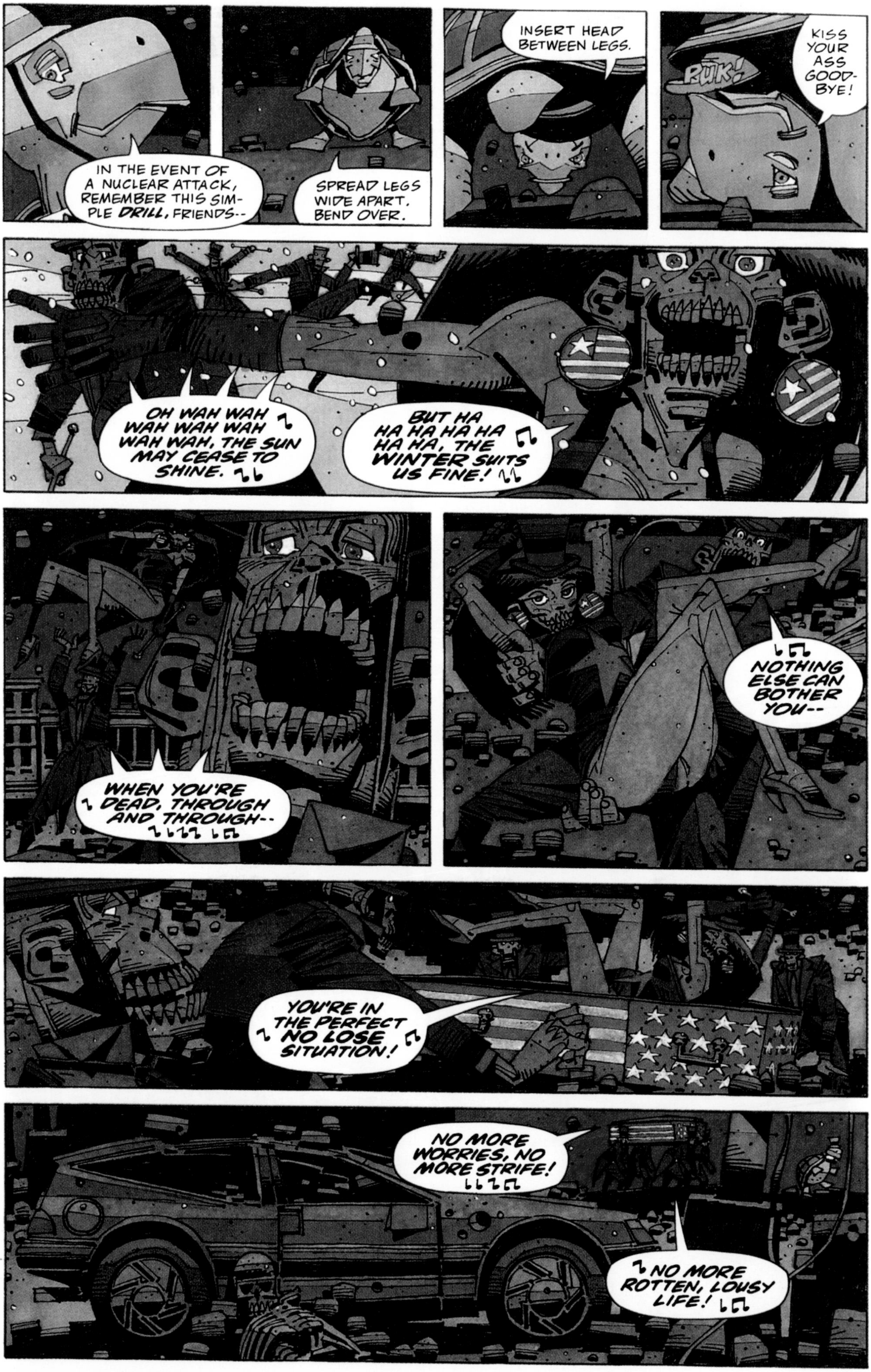
IN THE EVENT OF A NUCLEAR ATTACK, REMEMBER THIS SIMPLE DRILL, FRIENDS--
SPREAD LEGS WIDE APART. BEND OVER.
INSERT HEAD BETWEEN LEGS.
PUK!
KISS YOUR ASS GOOD-BYE!
OH WAH WAH WAH WAH WAH WAH WAH, THE SUN MAY CEASE TO SHINE.
BUT HA HA HA HA HA HA, THE WINTER SUITS US FINE!
WHEN YOU'RE DEAD, THROUGH AND THROUGH--
NOTHING ELSE CAN BOTHER YOU--
YOU'RE IN THE PERFECT NO LOSE SITUATION!
NO MORE WORRIES, NO MORE STRIFE!
NO MORE ROTTEN, LOUSY LIFE!

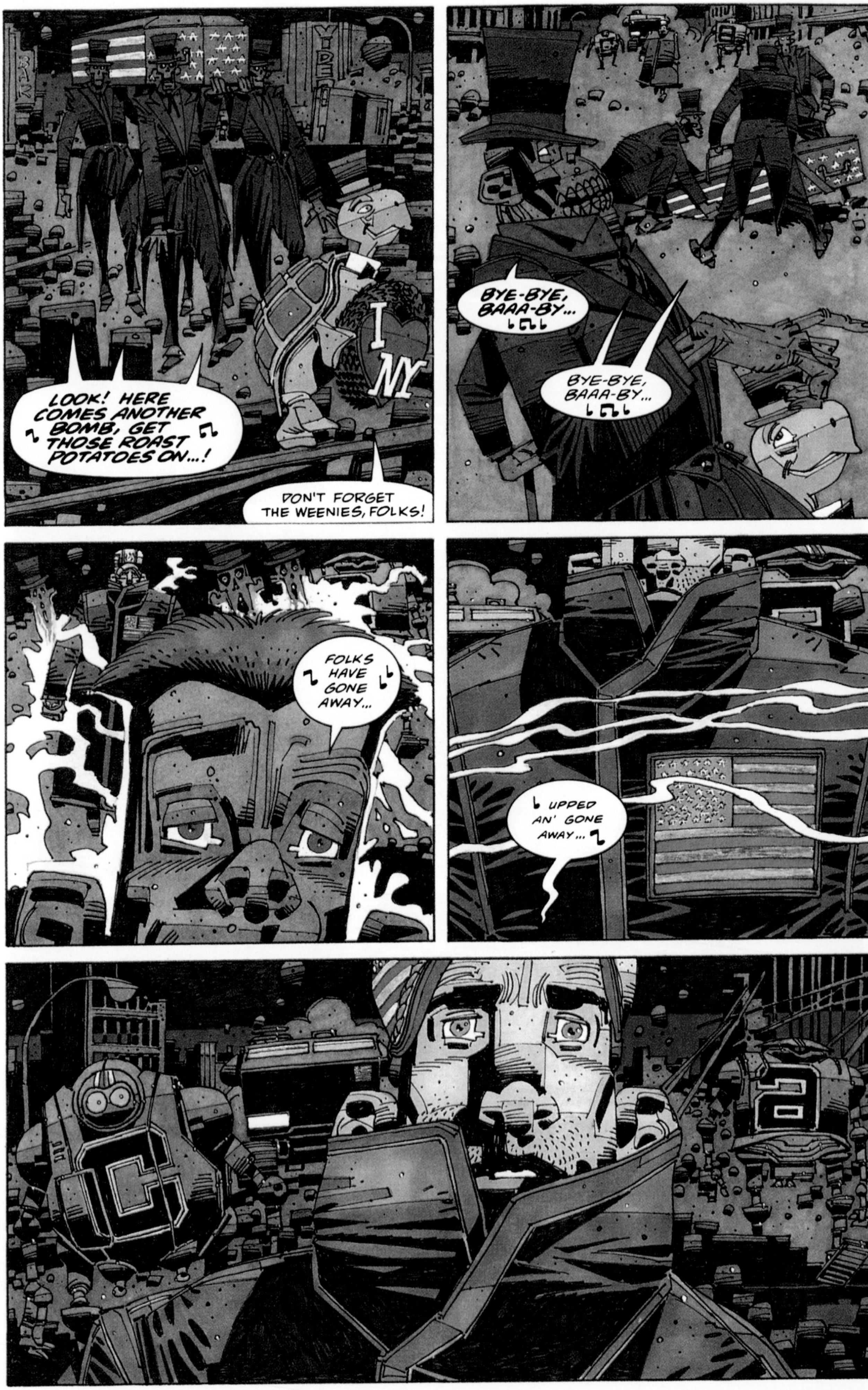

LOOK! HERE COMES ANOTHER BOMB, GET THOSE ROAST POTATOES ON...!
DON'T FORGET THE WEENIES, FOLKS!
BYE-BYE, BAAA-BY...
BYE-BYE, BAAA-BY...
FOLKS HAVE GONE AWAY...
UPPED AN' GONE AWAY...

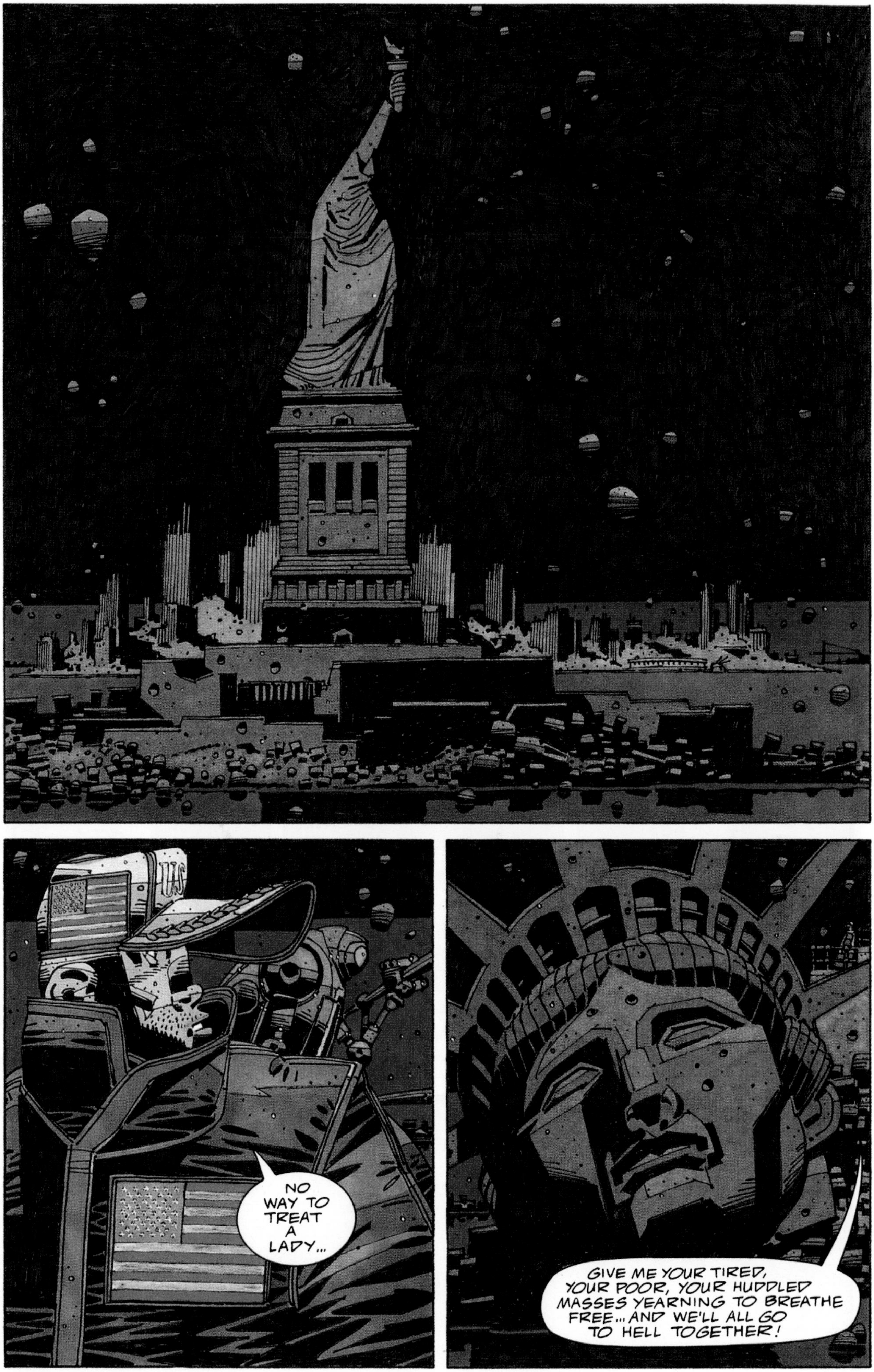
NO WAY TO TREAT A LADY...
GIVE ME YOUR TIRED, YOUR POOR, YOUR HUDDLED MASSES YEARNING TO BREATHE FREE... AND WE'LL ALL GO TO HELL TOGETHER!

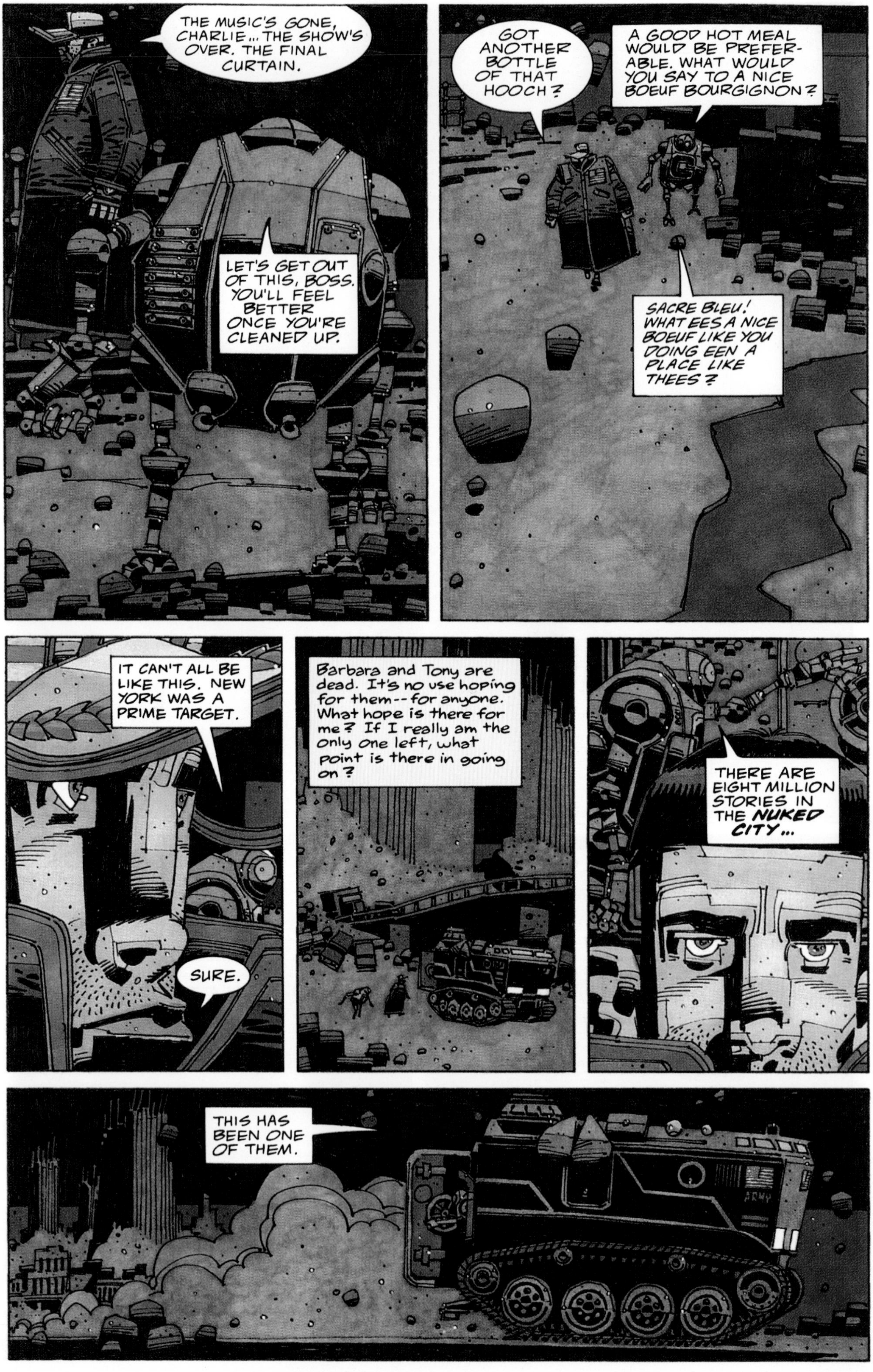

THE MUSIC'S GONE, CHARLIE... THE SHOW'S OVER. THE FINAL CURTAIN.
LET'S GET OUT OF THIS, BOSS. YOU'LL FEEL BETTER ONCE YOU'RE CLEANED UP.
GOT ANOTHER BOTTLE OF THAT HOOCH?
A GOOD HOT MEAL WOULD BE PREFERABLE. WHAT WOULD YOU SAY TO A NICE BOEUF BOURGIGNON?
SACRE BLEU! WHAT EES A NICE BOEUF LIKE YOU DOING EEN A PLACE LIKE THEES?
IT CAN'T ALL BE LIKE THIS. NEW YORK WAS A PRIME TARGET.
SURE.
Barbara and Tony are dead. It's no use hoping for them--for anyone. What hope is there for me? If I really am the only one left, what point is there in going on?
THERE ARE EIGHT MILLION STORIES IN THE ***NUKED CITY***...
THIS HAS BEEN ONE OF THEM.
ARMY

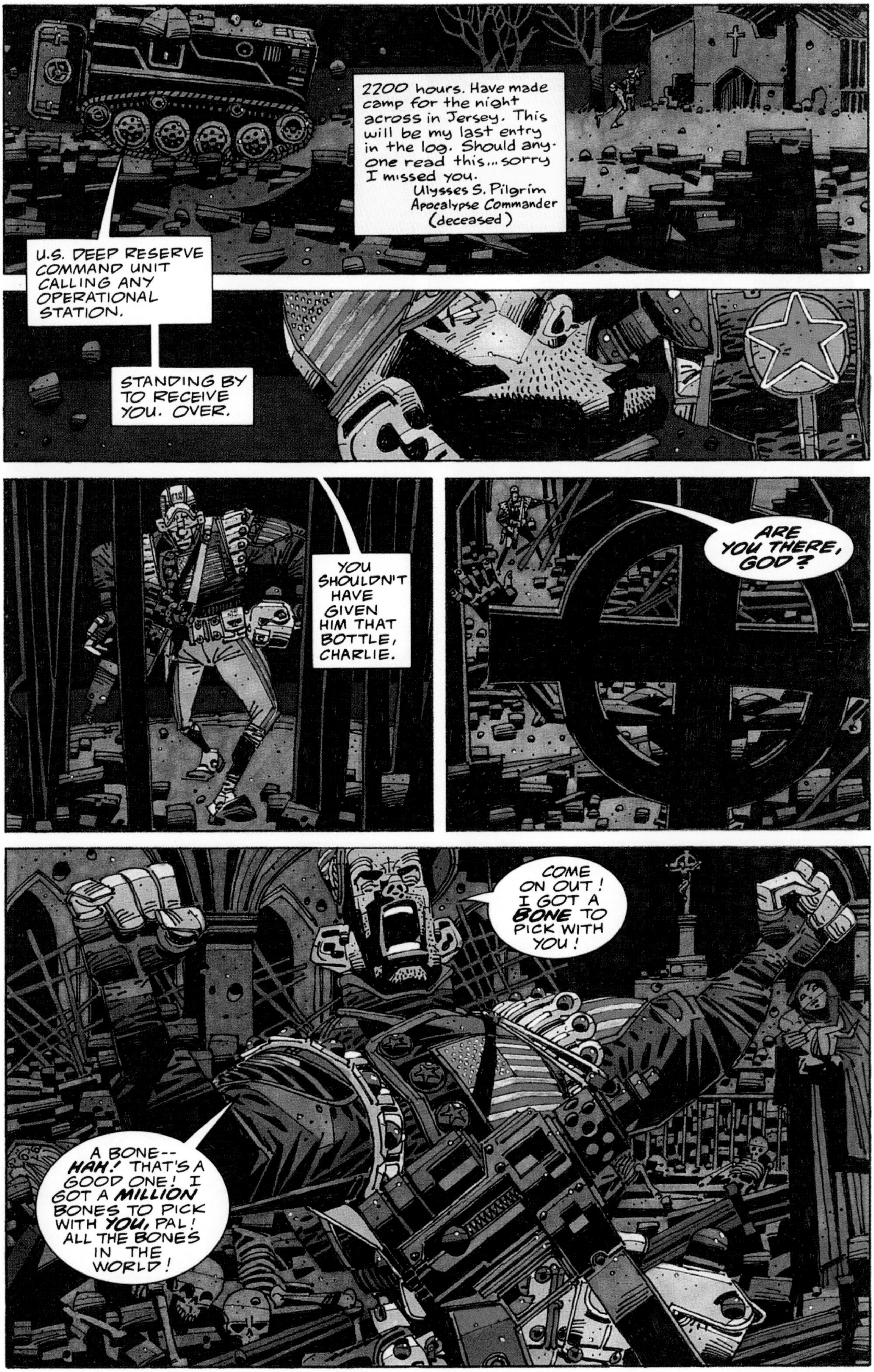
2200 hours. Have made camp for the night across in Jersey. This will be my last entry in the log. Should anyone read this... sorry I missed you.
Ulysses S. Pilgrim
Apocalypse Commander
(deceased)
U.S. DEEP RESERVE COMMAND UNIT CALLING ANY OPERATIONAL STATION.
STANDING BY TO RECEIVE YOU. OVER.
YOU SHOULDN'T HAVE GIVEN HIM THAT BOTTLE, CHARLIE.
ARE YOU THERE, GOD?
COME ON OUT! I GOT A BONE TO PICK WITH YOU!
A BONE-- HAH! THAT'S A GOOD ONE! I GOT A MILLION BONES TO PICK WITH YOU, PAL! ALL THE BONES IN THE WORLD!

THIS IS ALL *YOUR* FAULT! THAT'S RIGHT! YOU COULDA STOPPED IT-- WHY DIDN'T YOU? *EH*?

YOU'RE SO ALL-DAMN POWERFUL, WHY DIDN'T YOU *DO* SOMETHING?

HAVE YOU SEEN WHAT IT'S *LIKE* OUT THERE? *HAVE YOU?*

WELL, I'LL TELL YOU, PAL! IF THERE *IS* A GOD THEN YOU GOTTA BE ONE *TWISTED*, *EVIL SON OF A BITCH!*

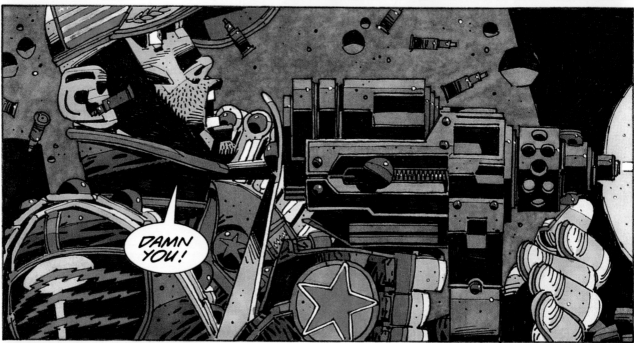

DAMN YOU!

BAKKA BAKKA

BAKKA SPZANG!

BAKKA BAKKA BAKOW!

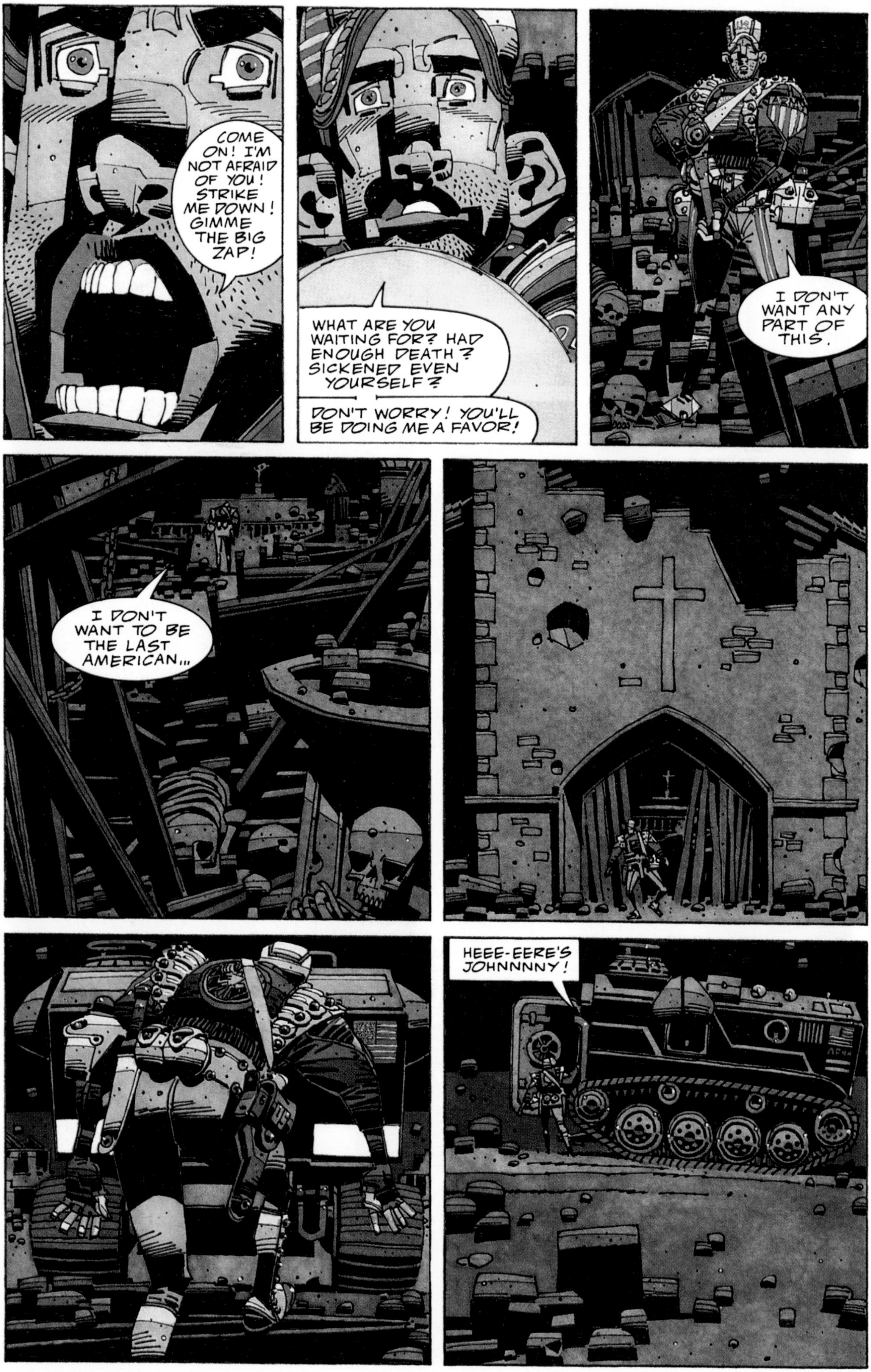
COME ON! I'M NOT AFRAID OF YOU! STRIKE ME DOWN! GIMME THE BIG ZAP!
WHAT ARE YOU WAITING FOR? HAD ENOUGH DEATH? SICKENED EVEN YOURSELF?
DON'T WORRY! YOU'LL BE DOING ME A FAVOR!
I DON'T WANT ANY PART OF THIS.
I DON'T WANT TO BE THE LAST AMERICAN...
HEEE-EERE'S JOHNNNNY!

IF THE WIND'S RIGHT WE CAN PUT A BALLOON UP TOMORROW, HAVE A LOOK AT THE COUNTRY TO THE WEST.

YOU DO THAT. JUST INCLUDE ME OUT.

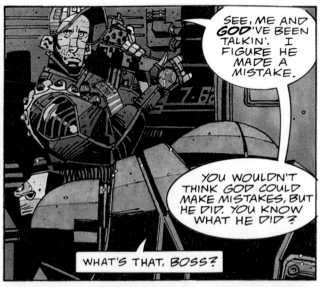

SEE, ME AND *GOD*'VE BEEN TALKIN'. I FIGURE HE MADE A MISTAKE.

YOU WOULDN'T THINK GOD COULD MAKE MISTAKES, BUT HE DID. YOU KNOW WHAT HE DID?

WHAT'S THAT, BOSS?

HE LEFT ME OUT. HE KILLED EVERYBODY ELSE AND HE LEFT ME OUT. CAN YOU BEAT THAT?

WELL, WE'LL SET THAT RIGHT--

I TOLD YA YOU SHOULDN'T HAVE LET HIM HAVE THAT BOTTLE.

PUT THE GUN DOWN, BOSS.

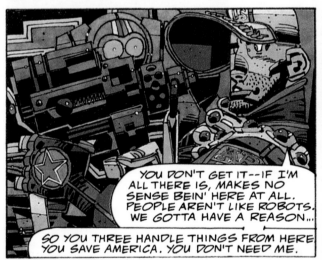

YOU DON'T GET IT--IF I'M ALL THERE IS, MAKES NO SENSE BEIN' HERE AT ALL. PEOPLE AREN'T LIKE ROBOTS. WE GOTTA HAVE A REASON...

SO YOU THREE HANDLE THINGS FROM HERE. YOU SAVE AMERICA. YOU DON'T NEED ME.

BOSS!

GOD'S WILL BE DONE, CHARLIE BOY!

VZZZT STATION FREZZZTTEST VIRGINIA CALLZZNG U.S. DzzzzKERVE UNIT... REPEAT, STAZZZIKK--zzKALLING DEEP RESERVE UNIRRRZZ...

STANDING BY TO REZZTTKVE YOU! COME IN, PLEAzzT!

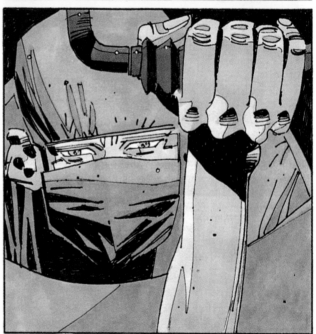

IT'S A BOY, MRS. PILGRIM!

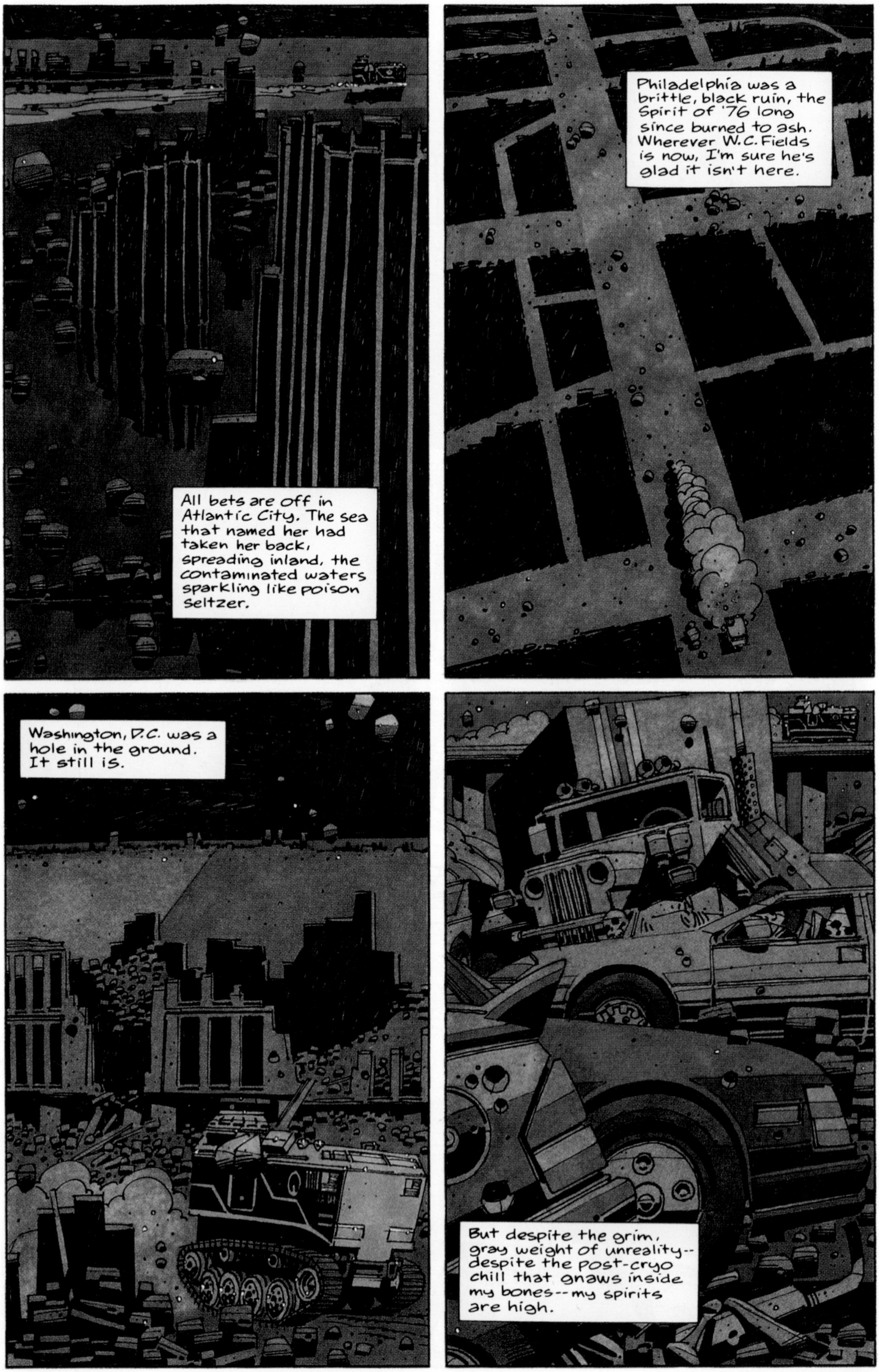
All bets are off in Atlantic City. The sea that named her had taken her back, spreading inland, the contaminated waters sparkling like poison seltzer.
Philadelphia was a brittle, black ruin, the Spirit of '76 long since burned to ash. Wherever W.C. Fields is now, I'm sure he's glad it isn't here.
Washington, D.C. was a hole in the ground. It still is.
But despite the grim, gray weight of unreality--despite the post-cryo chill that gnaws inside my bones--my spirits are high.

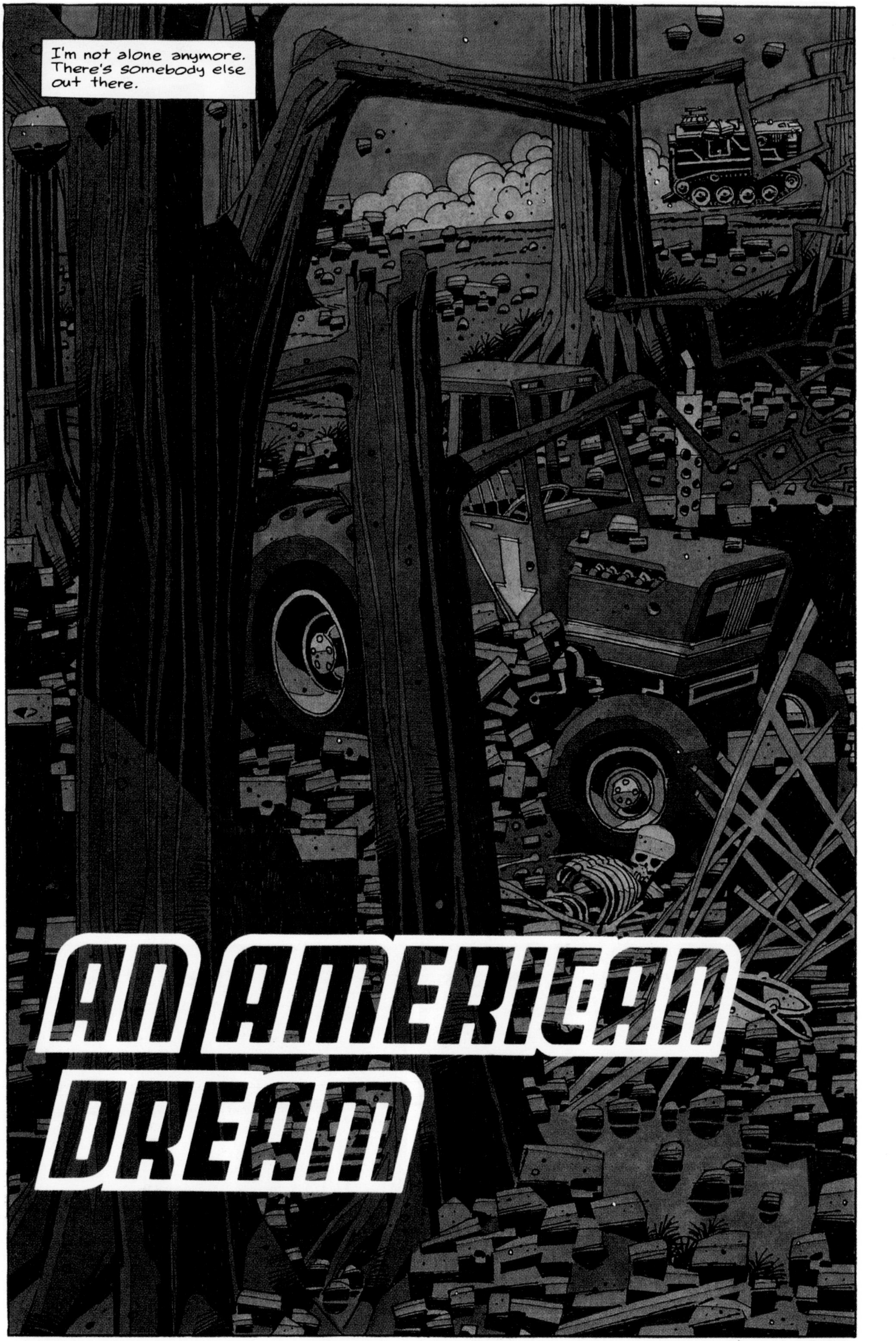
I'm not alone anymore. There's somebody else out there.
AN AMERICAN DREAM

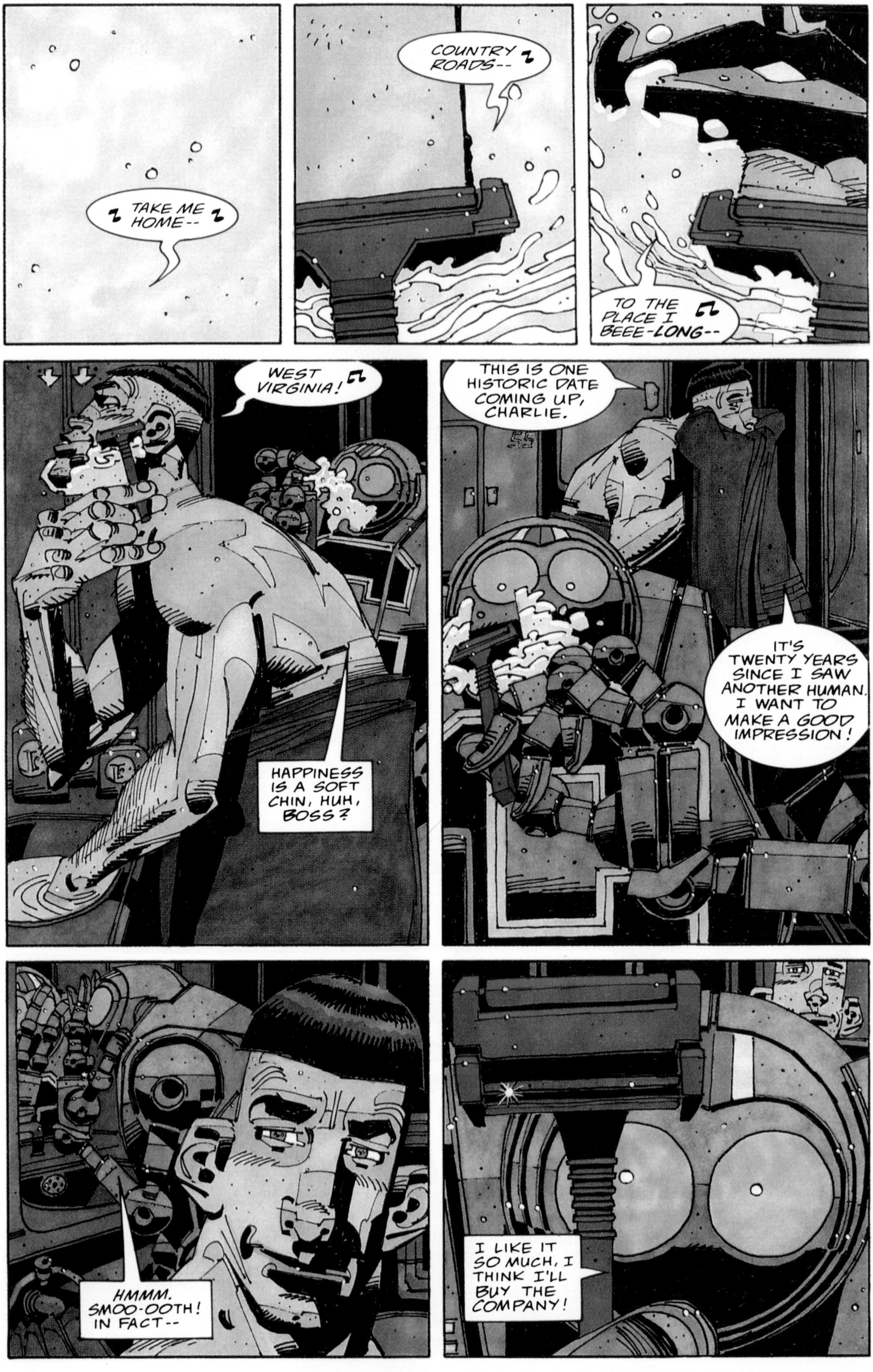
TAKE ME HOME--
COUNTRY ROADS--
TO THE PLACE I BEEE-LONG--
WEST VIRGINIA!
HAPPINESS IS A SOFT CHIN, HUH, BOSS?
THIS IS ONE HISTORIC DATE COMING UP, CHARLIE.
IT'S TWENTY YEARS SINCE I SAW ANOTHER HUMAN. I WANT TO MAKE A GOOD IMPRESSION!
HMMM. SMOO-OOTH! IN FACT--
I LIKE IT SO MUCH, I THINK I'LL BUY THE COMPANY!

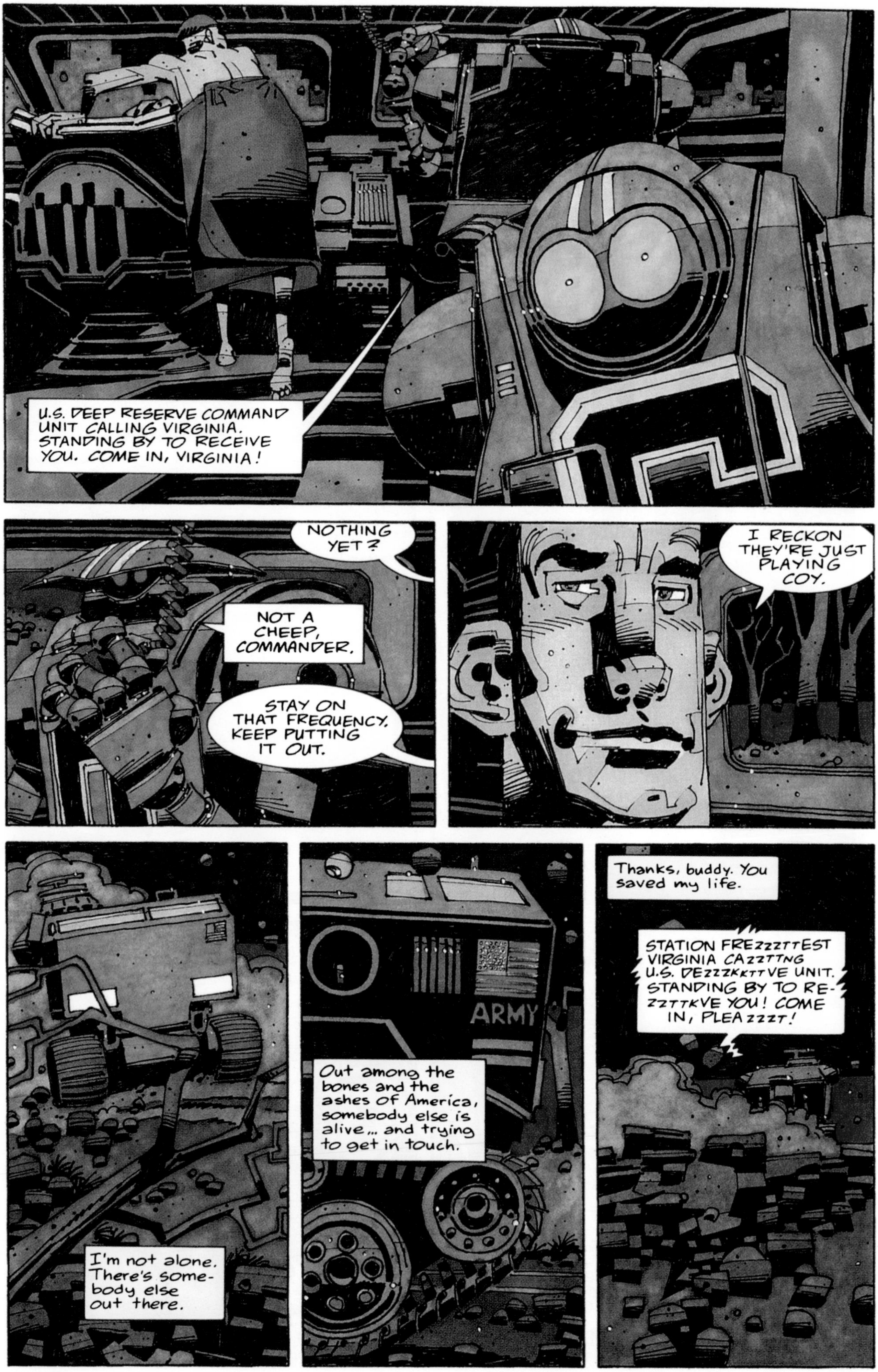
U.S. DEEP RESERVE COMMAND UNIT CALLING VIRGINIA. STANDING BY TO RECEIVE YOU. COME IN, VIRGINIA!
NOTHING YET?
NOT A CHEEP, COMMANDER.
STAY ON THAT FREQUENCY. KEEP PUTTING IT OUT.
I RECKON THEY'RE JUST PLAYING COY.
I'm not alone. There's some-body else out there.
ARMY
Out among the bones and the ashes of America, somebody else is alive... and trying to get in touch.
Thanks, buddy. You saved my life.
STATION FREzzzzTTEST VIRGINIA CAzzTTNG U.S. DEzzzzKKTTVE UNIT. STANDING BY TO RE-zzTTKVE YOU! COME IN, PLEAzzzT!

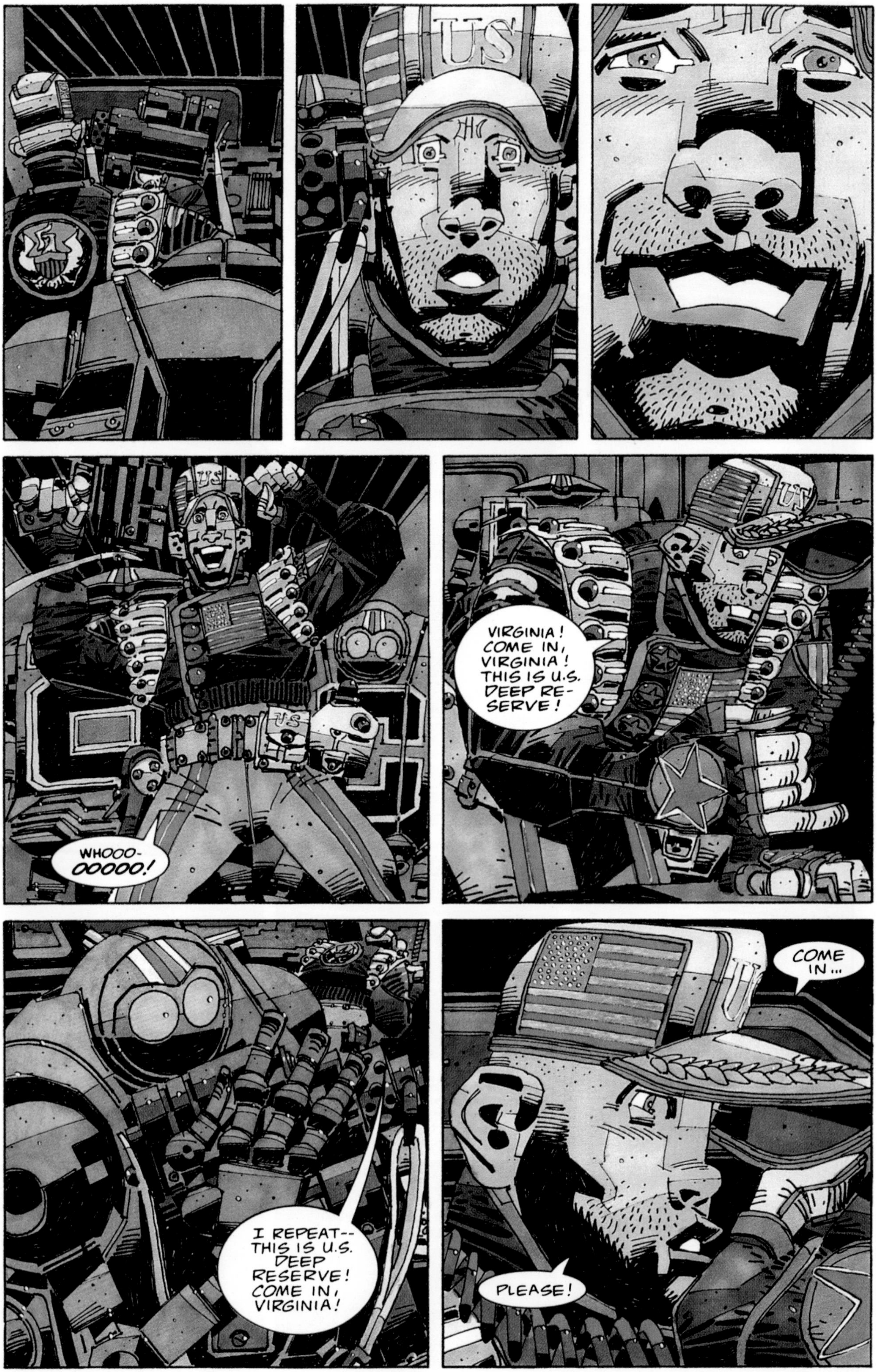
WHOOO-OOOOO!
VIRGINIA! COME IN, VIRGINIA! THIS IS U.S. DEEP RESERVE!
I REPEAT-- THIS IS U.S. DEEP RESERVE! COME IN, VIRGINIA!
COME IN...
PLEASE!

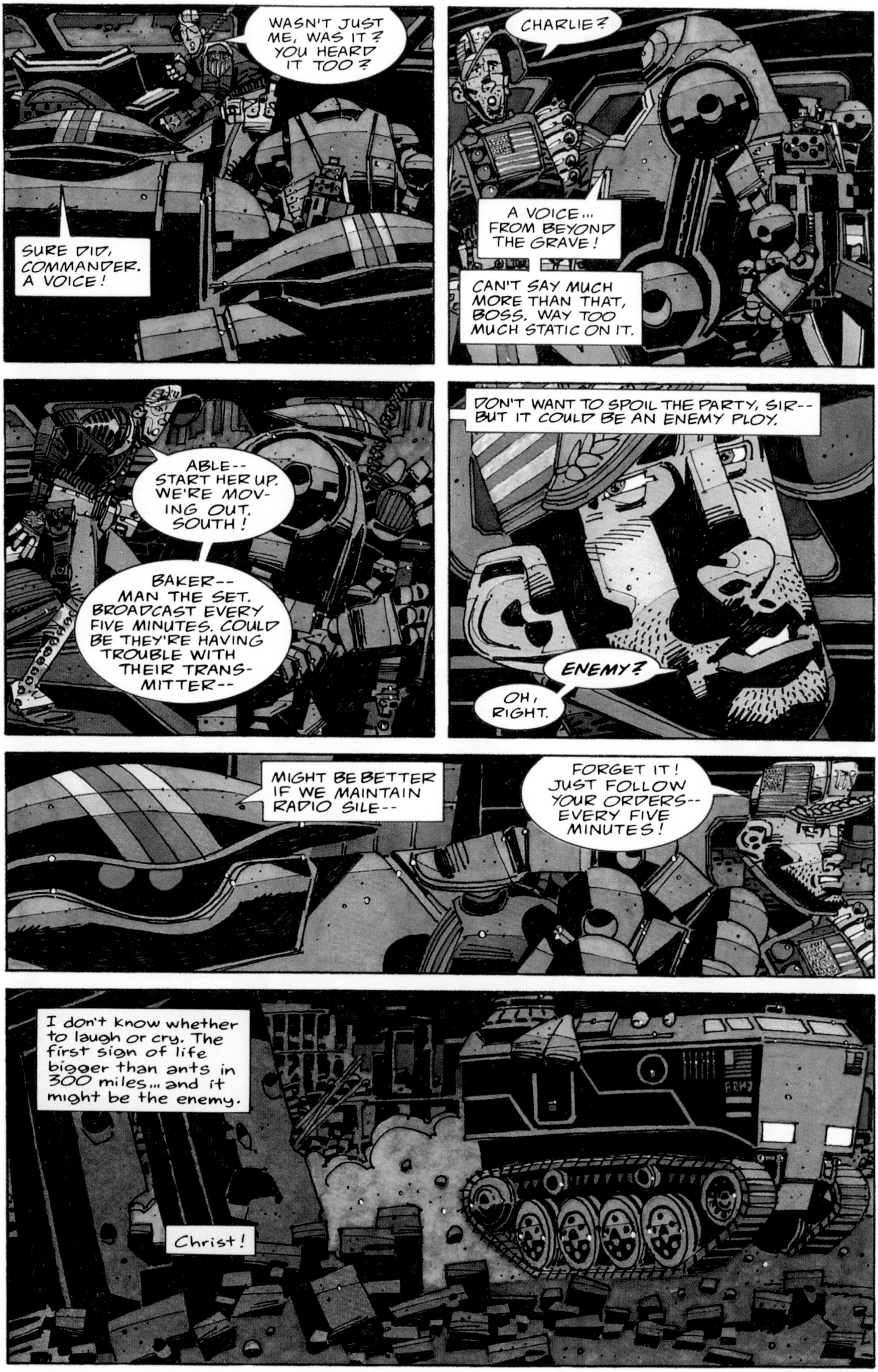
WASN'T JUST ME, WAS IT? YOU HEARD IT TOO?
SURE DID, COMMANDER. A VOICE!
CHARLIE?
A VOICE... FROM BEYOND THE GRAVE!
CAN'T SAY MUCH MORE THAN THAT, BOSS. WAY TOO MUCH STATIC ON IT.
ABLE-- START HER UP. WE'RE MOVING OUT. SOUTH!
BAKER-- MAN THE SET. BROADCAST EVERY FIVE MINUTES. COULD BE THEY'RE HAVING TROUBLE WITH THEIR TRANSMITTER--
DON'T WANT TO SPOIL THE PARTY, SIR-- BUT IT COULD BE AN ENEMY PLOY.
ENEMY?
OH, RIGHT.
MIGHT BE BETTER IF WE MAINTAIN RADIO SILE--
FORGET IT! JUST FOLLOW YOUR ORDERS-- EVERY FIVE MINUTES!
I don't know whether to laugh or cry. The first sign of life bigger than ants in 300 miles... and it might be the enemy.
Christ!

U.S. DEEP RESERVE CALLING VIRGINIA. COME IN, VIRGINIA!

It's 23 years since I made the journey south on 95. The Potomac was a couple of miles from the road back then--

The Quantico Marine Corps Reservation wasn't a bonfire site, either.

A WORD TO THE WISE, BOSS--

AS BAKER CAUTIONED, IT MIGHT NOT PAY TO BE *TOO* OPTIMISTIC.

CHARLIE, I DON'T GIVE A SHIT IF IT *IS* THE ENEMY!

I JUST WANT TO SEE *PEOPLE* AGAIN. I WANT TO SEE SOMETHING *ALIVE* IN THIS CORPSE OF A COUNTRY!

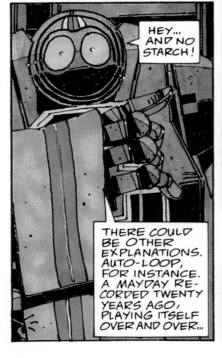

HEY... AND NO STARCH!

THERE COULD BE OTHER EXPLANATIONS. AUTO-LOOP, FOR INSTANCE. A MAYDAY RECORDED TWENTY YEARS AGO, PLAYING ITSELF OVER AND OVER...

THEY ASKED FOR US BY *NAME*, CHARLIE. DEEP RESERVE. MEANS *THEY* MUST'VE HEARD *US*.

RIGHT. OF COURSE.

I JUST DON'T WANT YOU BUILDING *YOUR* HOPES TOO HIGH, BOSS!

YOU'RE ALL HEART, PAL!

BUT EVEN IF THEY TURN OUT TO BE RUSSIAN CANNIBALS ARMED WITH I.C.B.M.s, I'M *STILL* GOING TO BE GLAD TO SEE THEM!

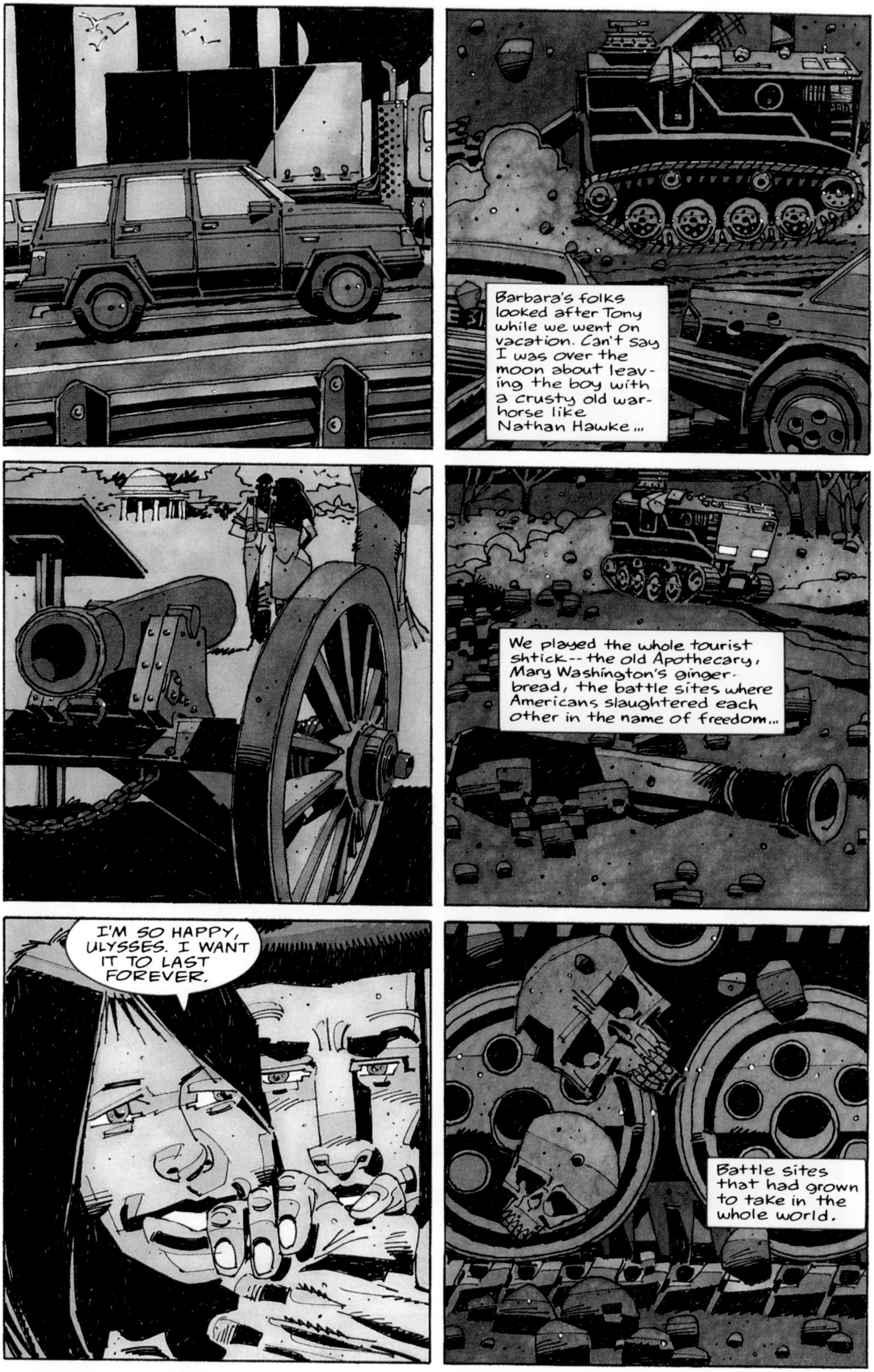
Barbara's folks looked after Tony while we went on vacation. Can't say I was over the moon about leaving the boy with a crusty old war-horse like Nathan Hawke...
We played the whole tourist shtick -- the old Apothecary, Mary Washington's ginger-bread, the battle sites where Americans slaughtered each other in the name of freedom...
I'M SO HAPPY, ULYSSES. I WANT IT TO LAST FOREVER.
Battle sites that had grown to take in the whole world.

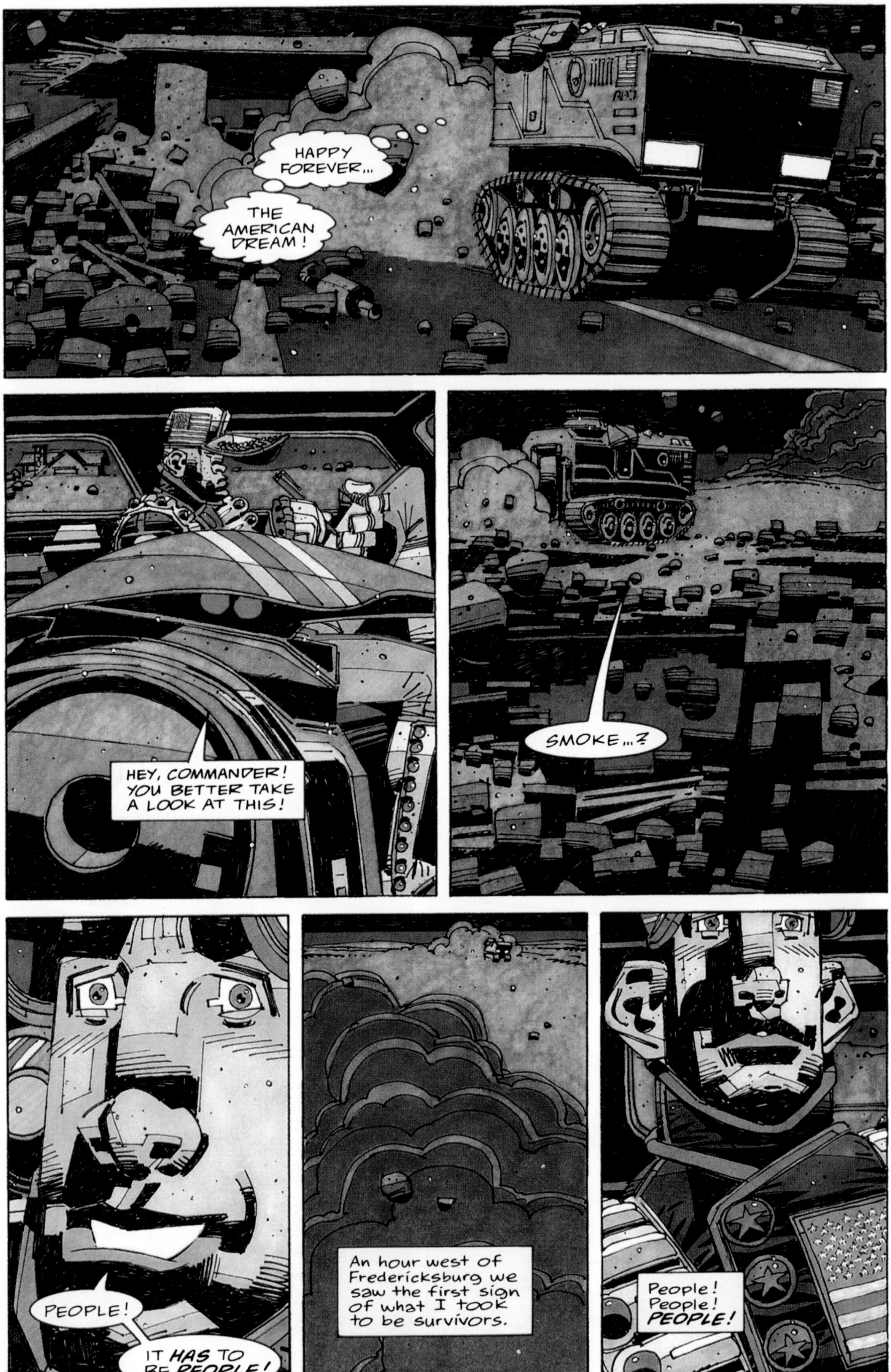
HAPPY FOREVER...
THE AMERICAN DREAM!
HEY, COMMANDER! YOU BETTER TAKE A LOOK AT THIS!
SMOKE...?
PEOPLE!
IT HAS TO BE PEOPLE!
An hour west of Fredericksburg we saw the first sign of what I took to be survivors.
People! People! PEOPLE!

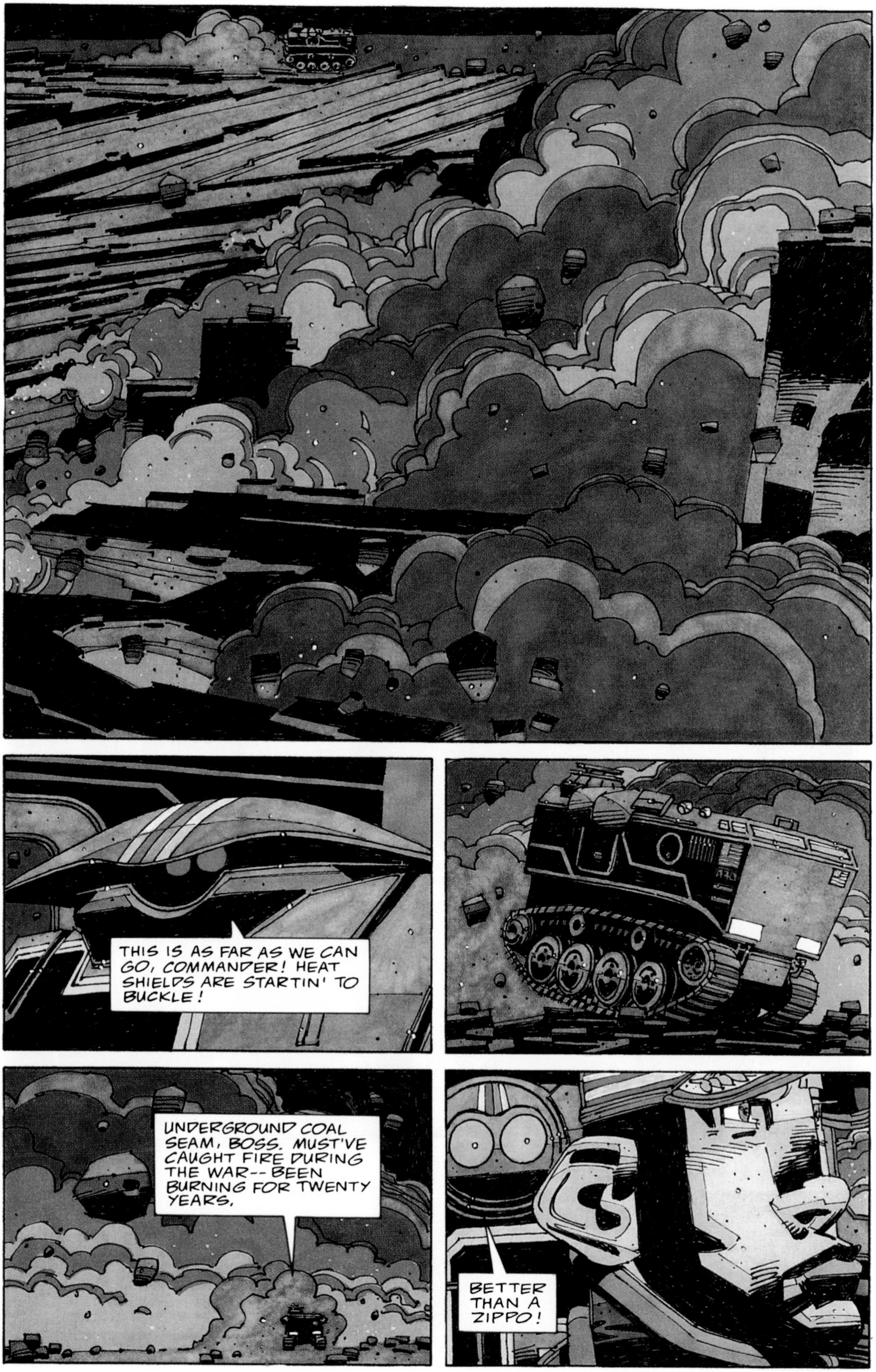
THIS IS AS FAR AS WE CAN GO, COMMANDER! HEAT SHIELDS ARE STARTIN' TO BUCKLE!
UNDERGROUND COAL SEAM, BOSS. MUST'VE CAUGHT FIRE DURING THE WAR-- BEEN BURNING FOR TWENTY YEARS.
BETTER THAN A ZIPPO!

THIS IS U.S. DEEP RESERVE. COME IN, VIRGINIA!

DAMN! WHY WON'T YOU ANSWER?

BASTARDS!

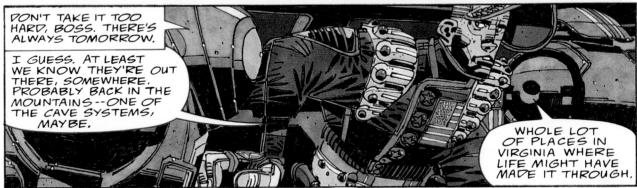

DON'T TAKE IT TOO HARD, BOSS. THERE'S ALWAYS TOMORROW.

I GUESS. AT LEAST WE KNOW THEY'RE OUT THERE, SOMEWHERE. PROBABLY BACK IN THE MOUNTAINS--ONE OF THE CAVE SYSTEMS, MAYBE.

WHOLE LOT OF PLACES IN VIRGINIA WHERE LIFE MIGHT HAVE MADE IT THROUGH.

WE JUST KEEP LOOKIN' TILL WE FIND THEM.

I'M GONNA HIT THE SACK, WAKE ME IN FOUR.

HE AIN'T SHAPIN' UP TOO WELL, IS HE CHARLIE?

IN A WORD-- NO.

HIS MOOD'S OSCILLATING FROM ONE EXTREME TO THE OTHER. I HAVE TO ADMIT, GENTLEMEN--

--I'M BEGINNING TO GET VERY WORRIED.

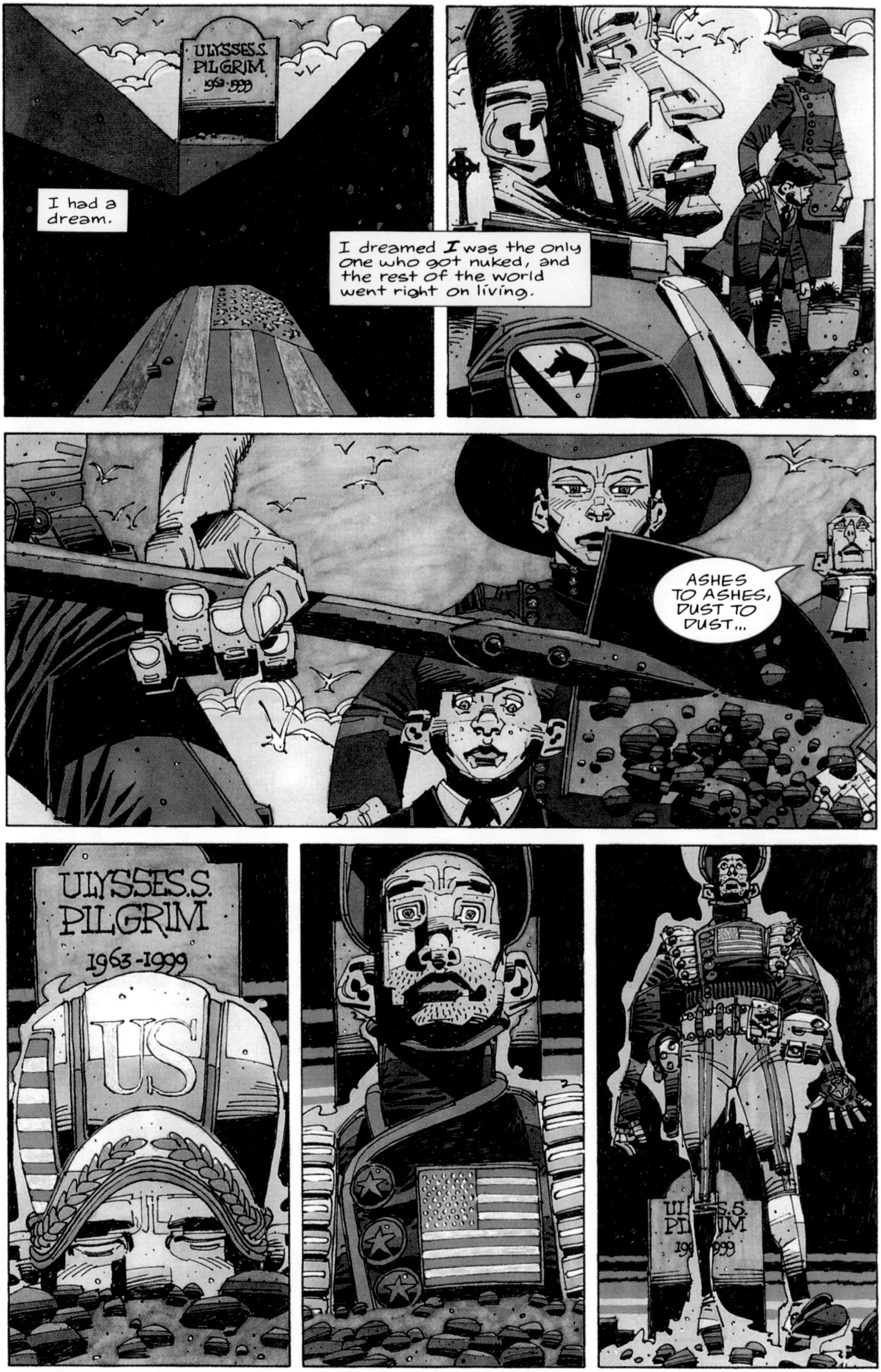

ULYSSES.S. PILGRIM 1963-1999
I had a dream.
I dreamed I was the only one who got nuked, and the rest of the world went right on living.
ASHES TO ASHES, DUST TO DUST...
ULYSSES.S. PILGRIM 1963-1999
US

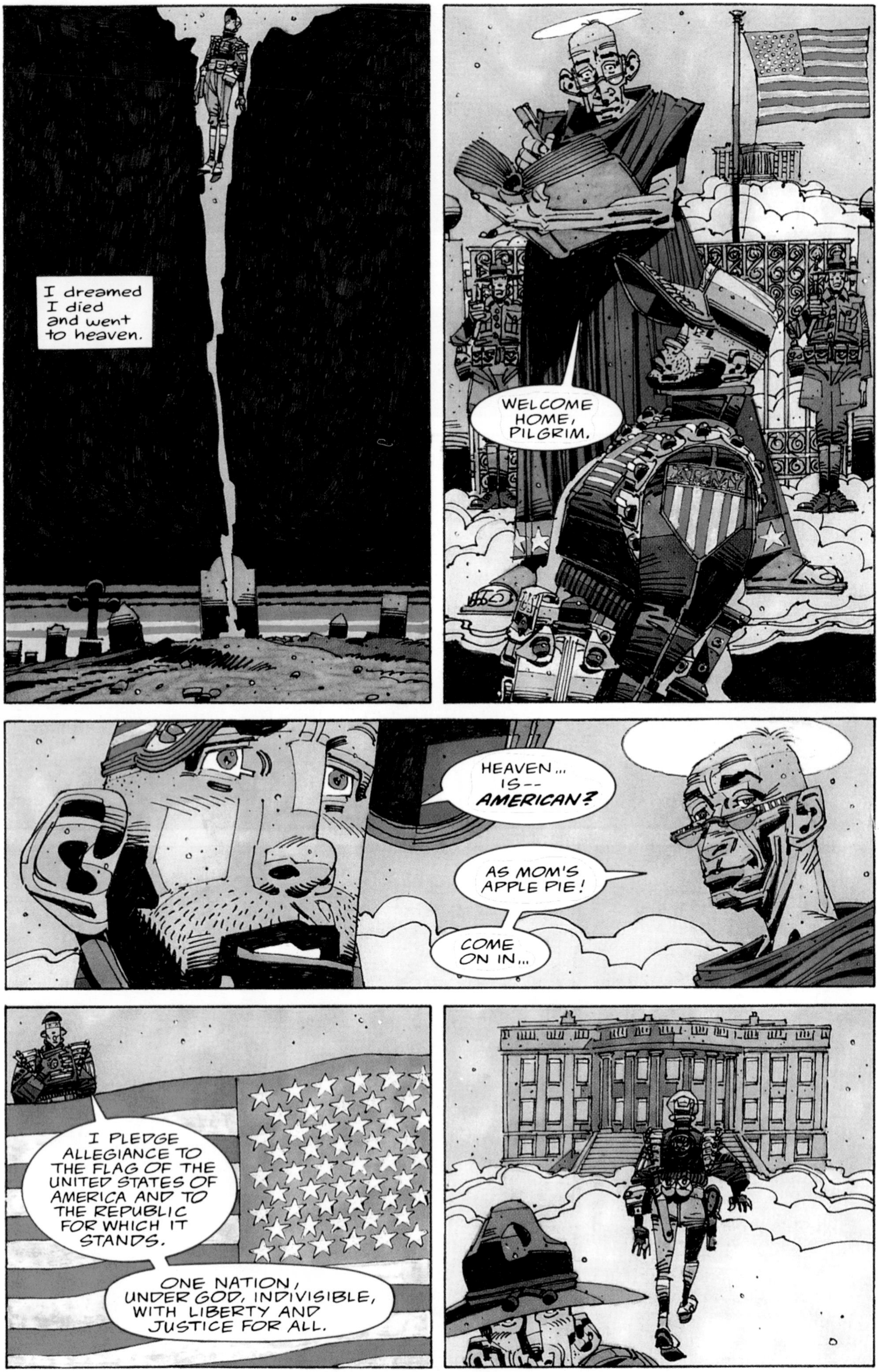
I dreamed I died and went to heaven.
WELCOME HOME, PILGRIM.
HEAVEN... IS-- AMERICAN?
AS MOM'S APPLE PIE!
COME ON IN...
I PLEDGE ALLEGIANCE TO THE FLAG OF THE UNITED STATES OF AMERICA AND TO THE REPUBLIC FOR WHICH IT STANDS.
ONE NATION, UNDER GOD, INDIVISIBLE, WITH LIBERTY AND JUSTICE FOR ALL.

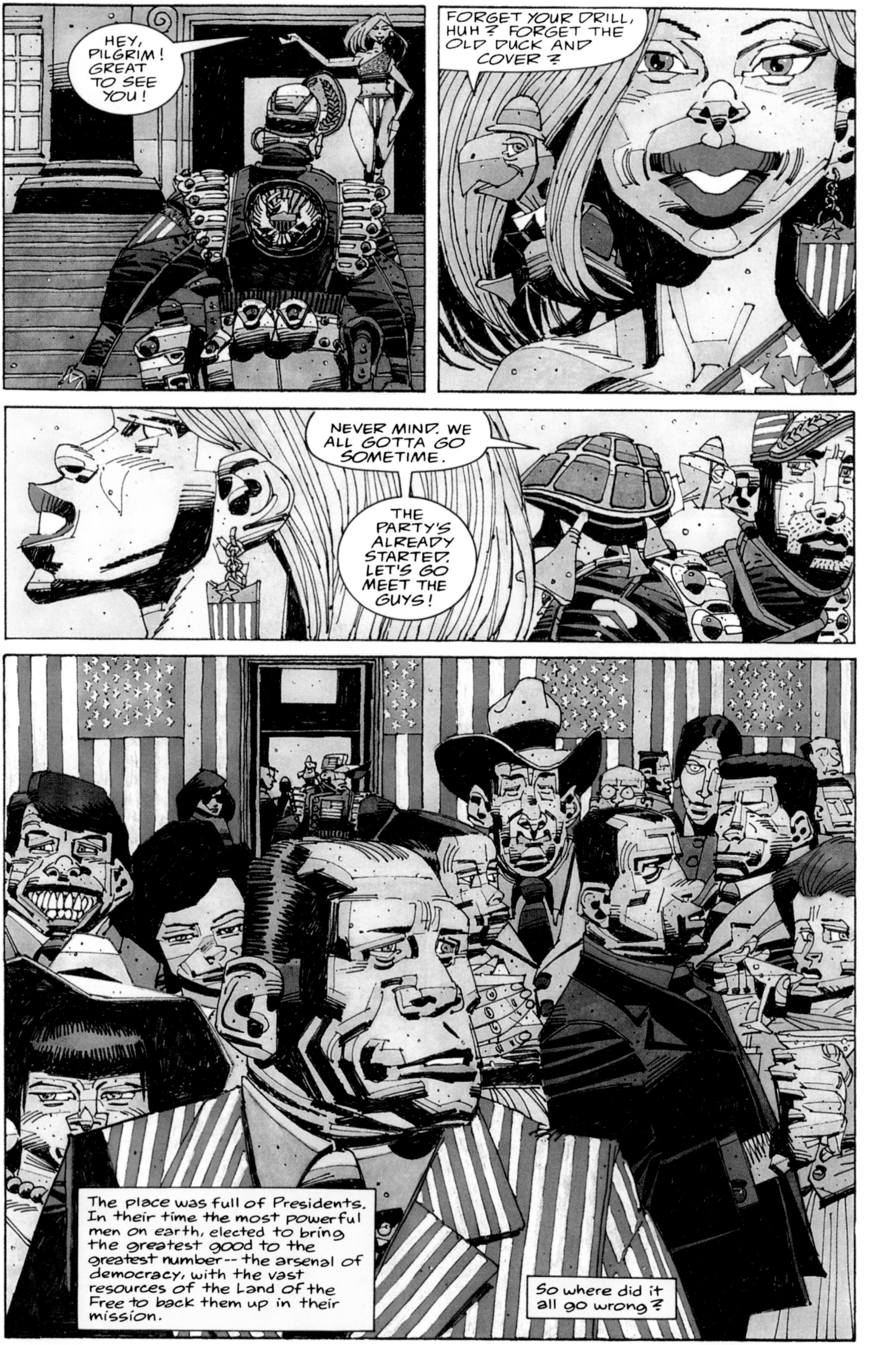
HEY, PILGRIM! GREAT TO SEE YOU!
FORGET YOUR DRILL, HUH? FORGET THE OLD DUCK AND COVER?
NEVER MIND. WE ALL GOTTA GO SOMETIME.
THE PARTY'S ALREADY STARTED. LET'S GO MEET THE GUYS!
The place was full of Presidents. In their time the most powerful men on earth, elected to bring the greatest good to the greatest number-- the arsenal of democracy, with the vast resources of the Land of the Free to back them up in their mission.
So where did it all go wrong?

ACH! ATOMIC VEAPONS HAVE CHANGED EVERYTHING-- EXCEPT THE VAY PEOPLE *THINK!*

DON'T BOTHER ME WITH YOUR CONSCIENTIOUS SCRUPLES--

AFTER ALL, THE THING'S *SUPERB* PHYSICS!

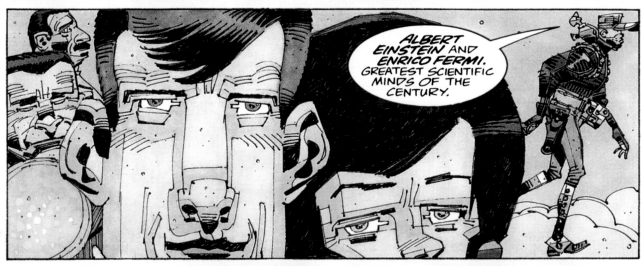

ALBERT EINSTEIN AND ENRICO FERMI. GREATEST SCIENTIFIC MINDS OF THE CENTURY.

LISSEN, PINKO--

NO POWER ON EARTH IS STRONGER THAN THE UNITED STATES OF AMERICA TODAY. NONE WILL BE STRONGER IN THE FUTURE.

THIS IS THE *ONLY* NATIONAL DEFENSE POSTURE WHICH CAN *EVER* BE ACCEPTABLE TO THE UNITED STATES!

YOU GOT THE WRONG END OF THE STICK, DICK!

IT IS NOW ONLY A MATTER OF TIME BEFORE MADNESS DESPERATION, GREED OR MISCALCULATION LET *LOOSE* THIS TERRIBLE FORCE!

WHAT DO YOU SAY, RON?

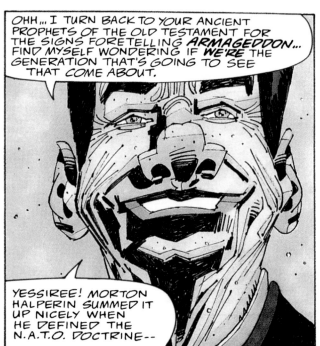

OHH... I TURN BACK TO YOUR ANCIENT PROPHETS OF THE OLD TESTAMENT FOR THE SIGNS FORETELLING *ARMAGEDDON*... FIND MYSELF WONDERING IF *WE'RE* THE GENERATION THAT'S GOING TO SEE THAT *COME ABOUT*.

YESSIREE! MORTON HALPERIN SUMMED IT UP NICELY WHEN HE DEFINED THE N.A.T.O. DOCTRINE--

"WE WILL FIGHT WITH CONVENTIONAL FORCES UNTIL WE ARE LOSING, THEN WE WILL FIGHT WITH TACTICAL NUCLEAR WEAPONS UNTIL WE ARE LOSING... AND THEN WE WILL BLOW UP THE WORLD!"

OR WAS IT NANCY SAID THAT?

HA HA HA HA HA!

They were men. Only men.

That's what went wrong. Strong men-- charismatic-- powerful.

But in the end-- only men.

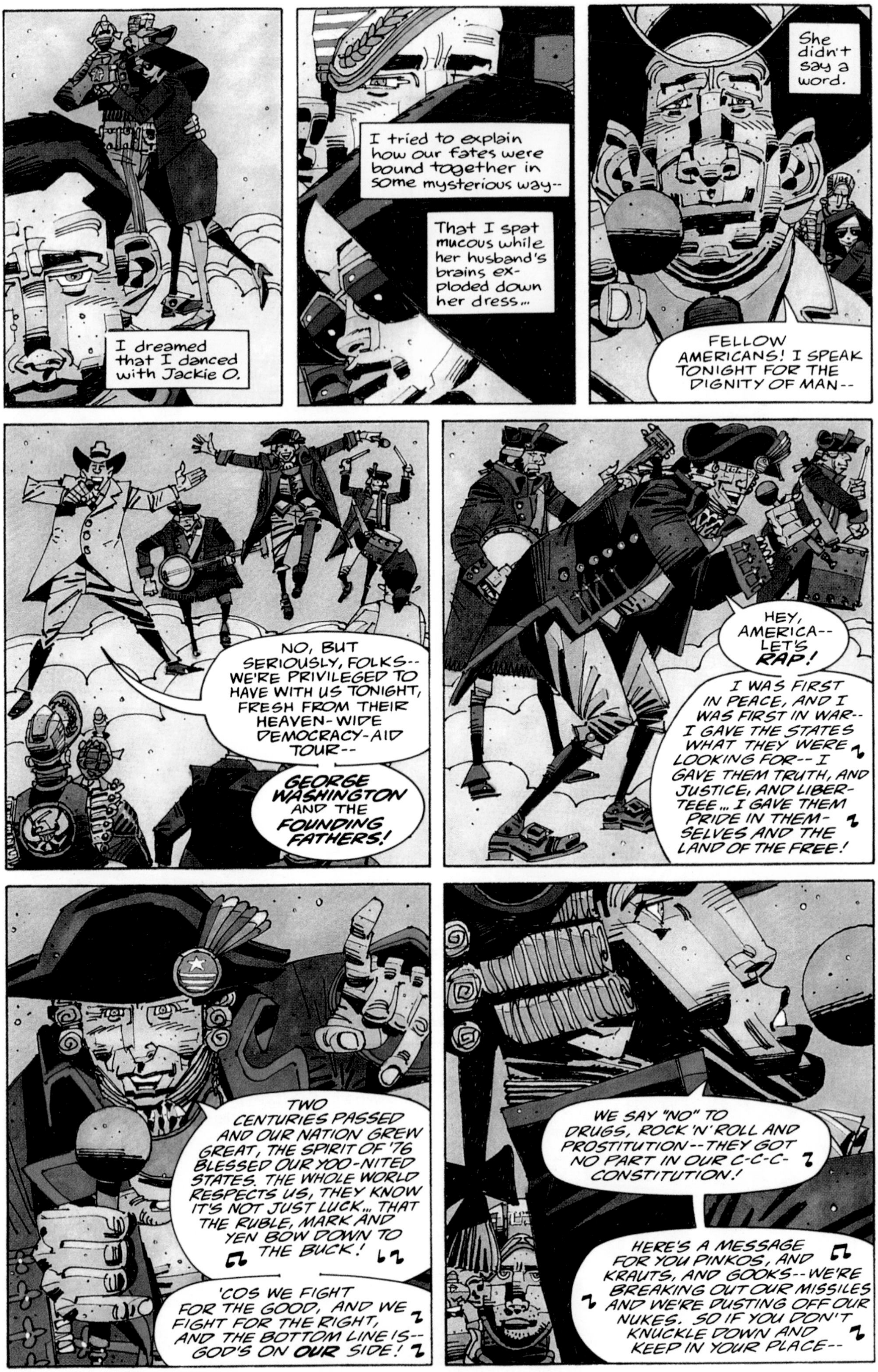
I dreamed that I danced with Jackie O.
I tried to explain how our fates were bound together in some mysterious way--
That I spat mucous while her husband's brains exploded down her dress...
She didn't say a word.
FELLOW AMERICANS! I SPEAK TONIGHT FOR THE DIGNITY OF MAN--
NO, BUT SERIOUSLY, FOLKS-- WE'RE PRIVILEGED TO HAVE WITH US TONIGHT, FRESH FROM THEIR HEAVEN-WIDE DEMOCRACY-AID TOUR--
GEORGE WASHINGTON AND THE FOUNDING FATHERS!
HEY, AMERICA-- LET'S RAP!
I WAS FIRST IN PEACE, AND I WAS FIRST IN WAR-- I GAVE THE STATES WHAT THEY WERE LOOKING FOR-- I GAVE THEM TRUTH, AND JUSTICE, AND LIBERTEEE... I GAVE THEM PRIDE IN THEMSELVES AND THE LAND OF THE FREE!
TWO CENTURIES PASSED AND OUR NATION GREW GREAT, THE SPIRIT OF '76 BLESSED OUR YOO-NITED STATES. THE WHOLE WORLD RESPECTS US, THEY KNOW IT'S NOT JUST LUCK... THAT THE RUBLE, MARK AND YEN BOW DOWN TO THE BUCK!
'COS WE FIGHT FOR THE GOOD, AND WE FIGHT FOR THE RIGHT, AND THE BOTTOM LINE IS-- GOD'S ON OUR SIDE!
WE SAY "NO" TO DRUGS, ROCK 'N' ROLL AND PROSTITUTION--THEY GOT NO PART IN OUR C-C-C-CONSTITUTION!
HERE'S A MESSAGE FOR YOU PINKOS, AND KRAUTS, AND GOOKS--WE'RE BREAKING OUT OUR MISSILES AND WE'RE DUSTING OFF OUR NUKES. SO IF YOU DON'T KNUCKLE DOWN AND KEEP IN YOUR PLACE--

YOU CAN KISS GOODBYE TO THE H-H-H-HUMAN RACE!

HECK! THEY JUST WON'T LISTEN, BERT! I'VE WARNED 'EM AND WARNED 'EM-- BUT THEY JUST WON'T LISTEN!

NO NEED TO FEEL GUILTY, JIMMY! YOU DID YOUR BEST... THAT'S ALL ANY MAN CAN DO-- EVEN AN AMERICAN.

I TOLD THEM...

MORE DESTRUCTIVE POWER THAN IN ALL OF THE SECOND WORLD WAR WILL BE UNLEASHED EVERY *SECOND* FOR THE LONG AFTERNOON IT WOULD TAKE FOR ALL THE MISSILES AND BOMBS TO FALL!

A SECOND WORLD WAR EVERY SECOND-- MORE PEOPLE *KILLED* IN THE FIRST FEW HOURS THAN IN ALL THE WARS OF HISTORY PUT TO-GETHER!

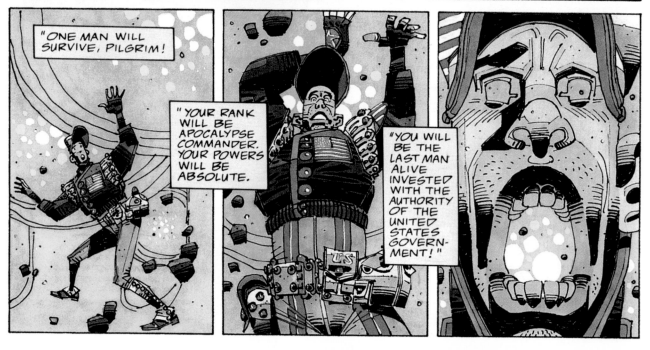

"ONE MAN WILL SURVIVE, PILGRIM!

"YOUR RANK WILL BE APOCALYPSE COMMANDER. YOUR POWERS WILL BE ABSOLUTE.

"YOU WILL BE THE LAST MAN ALIVE INVESTED WITH THE AUTHORITY OF THE UNITED STATES GOVERN-MENT!"

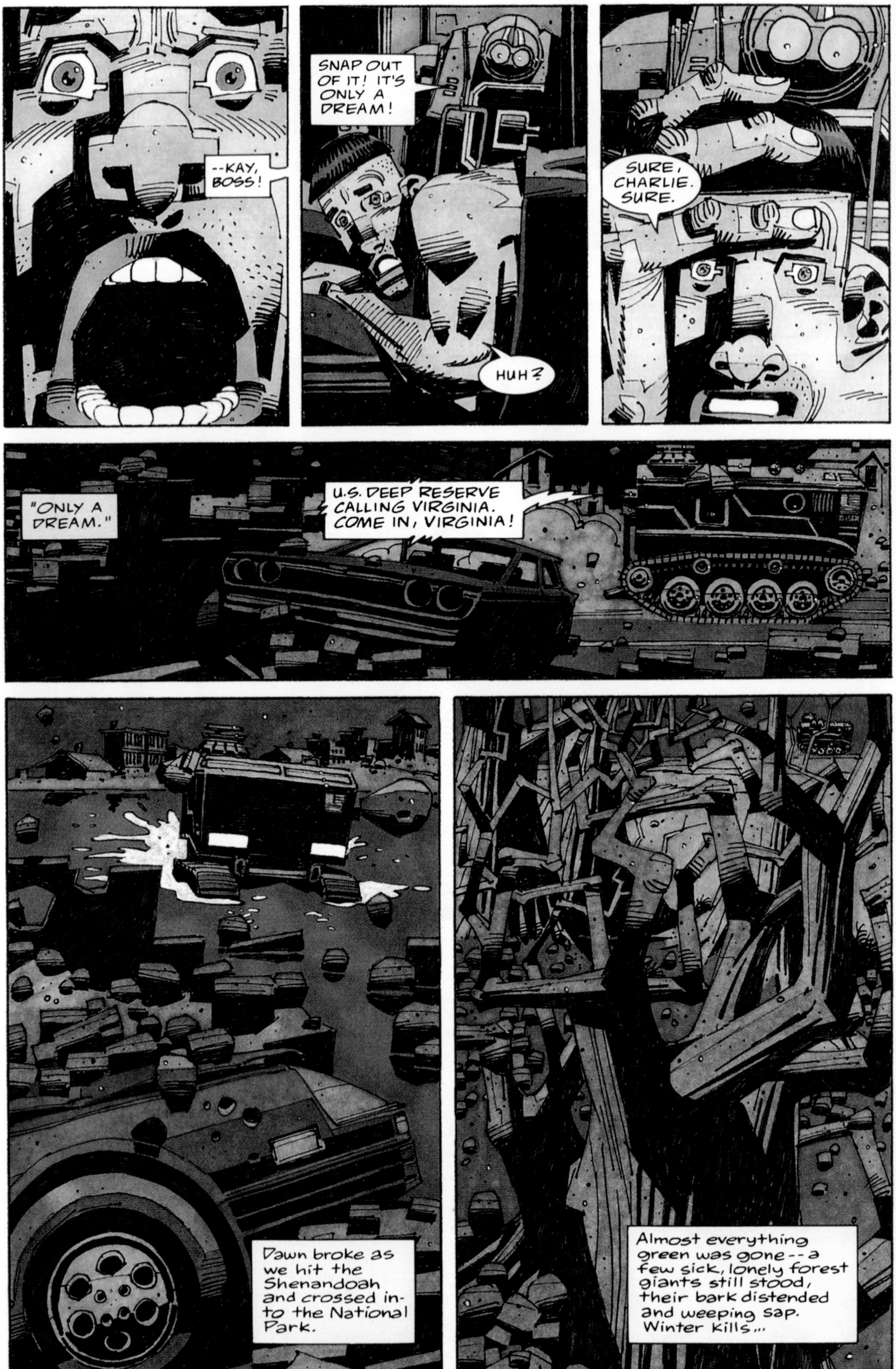
--KAY, BOSS!
SNAP OUT OF IT! IT'S ONLY A DREAM!
HUH?
SURE, CHARLIE. SURE.
"ONLY A DREAM."
U.S. DEEP RESERVE CALLING VIRGINIA. COME IN, VIRGINIA!
Dawn broke as we hit the Shenandoah and crossed in-to the National Park.
Almost everything green was gone--a few sick, lonely forest giants still stood, their bark distended and weeping sap. Winter kills...

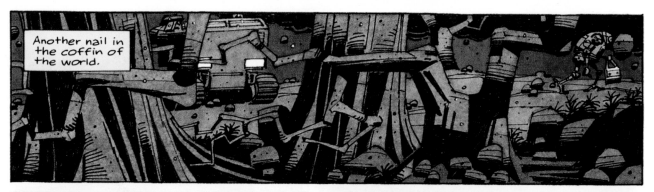

Another nail in the coffin of the world.

Charlie had a field day. He'd logged 17 different vegetative mutations before I switched off the comlink.

There was only one thing I wanted to hear--

KRAAAKZZZZT!

KRFFTZZZ! ZVZZT! FZZZKK!

IT'S THEM!

HEY!

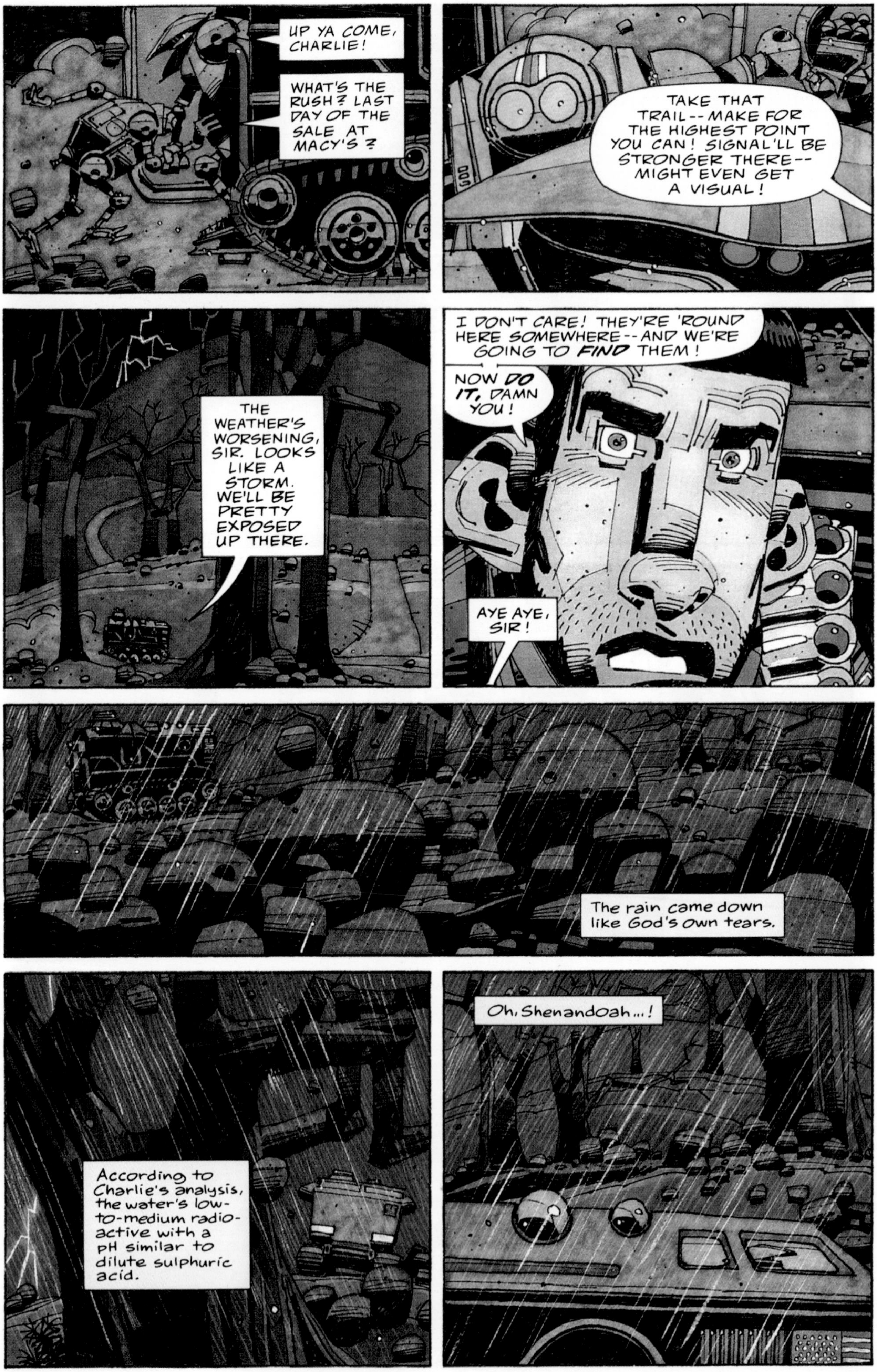

UP YA COME, CHARLIE!
WHAT'S THE RUSH? LAST DAY OF THE SALE AT MACY'S?
TAKE THAT TRAIL--MAKE FOR THE HIGHEST POINT YOU CAN! SIGNAL'LL BE STRONGER THERE--MIGHT EVEN GET A VISUAL!
THE WEATHER'S WORSENING, SIR. LOOKS LIKE A STORM. WE'LL BE PRETTY EXPOSED UP THERE.
I DON'T CARE! THEY'RE 'ROUND HERE SOMEWHERE--AND WE'RE GOING TO FIND THEM!
NOW DO IT, DAMN YOU!
AYE AYE, SIR!
The rain came down like God's own tears.
According to Charlie's analysis, the water's low-to-medium radio-active with a pH similar to dilute sulphuric acid.
Oh, Shenandoah...!

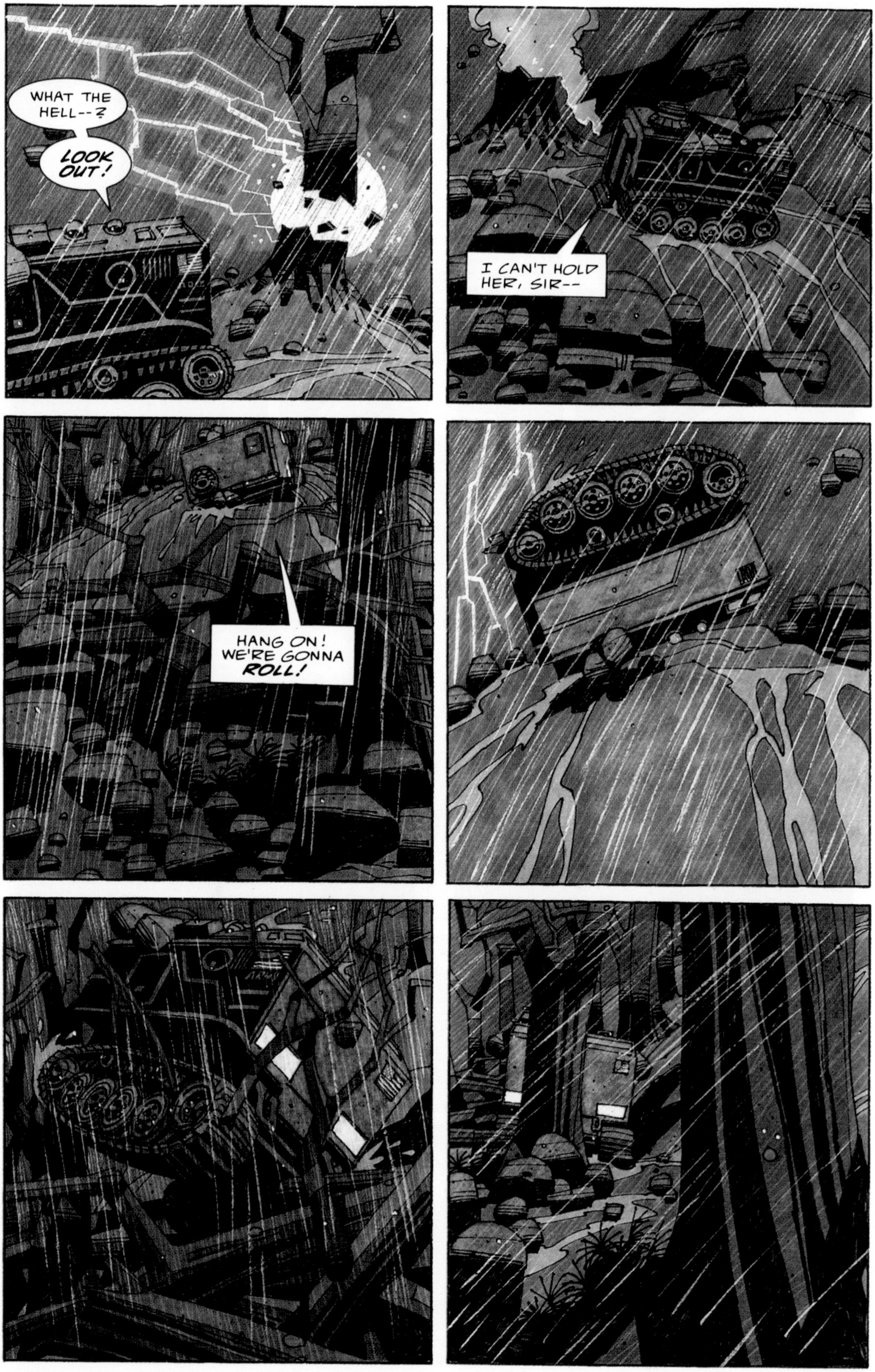
WHAT THE HELL--?
LOOK OUT!
I CAN'T HOLD HER, SIR--
HANG ON! WE'RE GONNA ROLL!

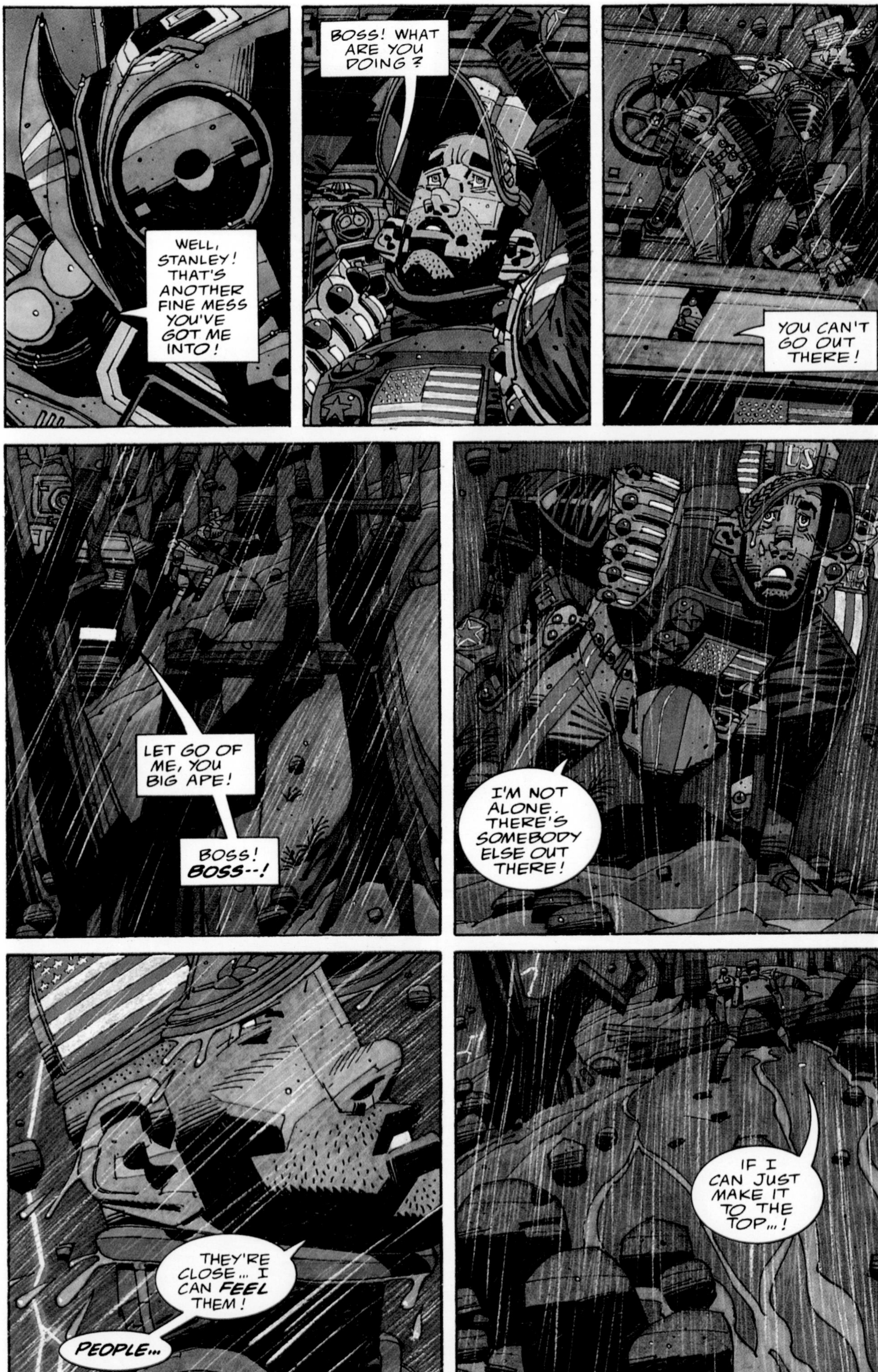
WELL, STANLEY! THAT'S ANOTHER FINE MESS YOU'VE GOT ME INTO!
BOSS! WHAT ARE YOU DOING?
YOU CAN'T GO OUT THERE!
LET GO OF ME, YOU BIG APE!
BOSS! BOSS--!
I'M NOT ALONE. THERE'S SOMEBODY ELSE OUT THERE!
THEY'RE CLOSE... I CAN FEEL THEM!
PEOPLE...
IF I CAN JUST MAKE IT TO THE TOP...!

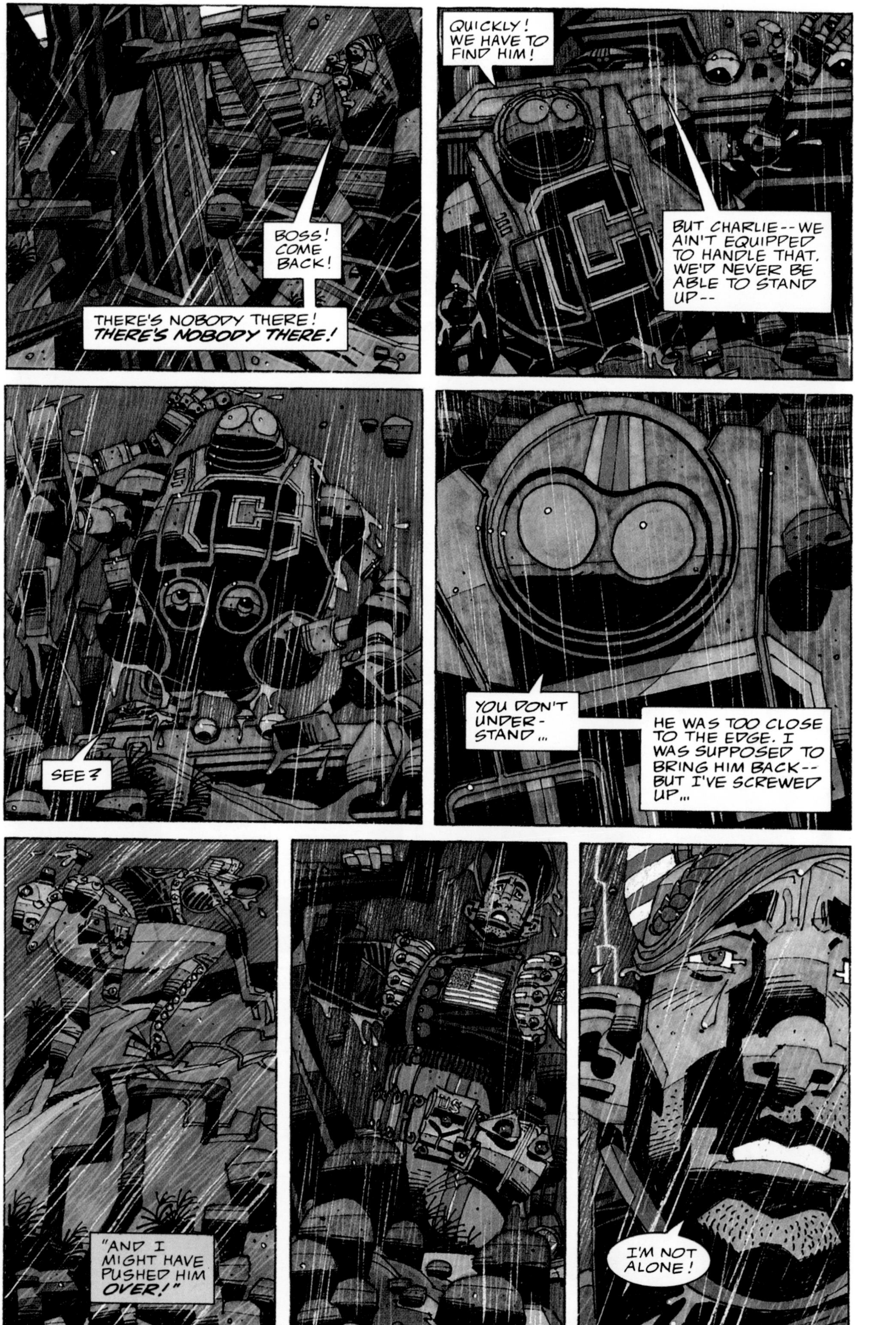
BOSS! COME BACK!
THERE'S NOBODY THERE! THERE'S NOBODY THERE!
QUICKLY! WE HAVE TO FIND HIM!
BUT CHARLIE--WE AIN'T EQUIPPED TO HANDLE THAT. WE'D NEVER BE ABLE TO STAND UP--
SEE?
YOU DON'T UNDER-STAND...
HE WAS TOO CLOSE TO THE EDGE. I WAS SUPPOSED TO BRING HIM BACK--BUT I'VE SCREWED UP...
"AND I MIGHT HAVE PUSHED HIM OVER!"
I'M NOT ALONE!

I'M NOT ALONE...

BOSS, I'M SORRY. IT WASN'T MEANT TO HAPPEN LIKE THIS.

I ... UH, I WANT TO TELL YOU THE TRUTH.

TRUTH?

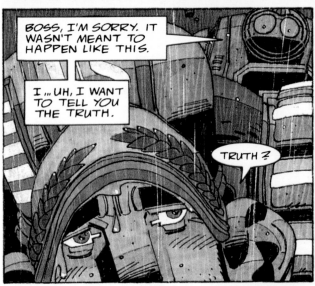

I WANT YOU TO KNOW IT WASN'T MY IDEA. I DIDN'T HAVE ANY CHOICE. MY PROGRAMMING WAS QUITE SPECIFIC--

IF YOU BECAME SUICIDAL, I WAS TO HIT YOU WITH A FAKE MESSAGE. GIVE YOU A REASON FOR GOING ON, SEE.

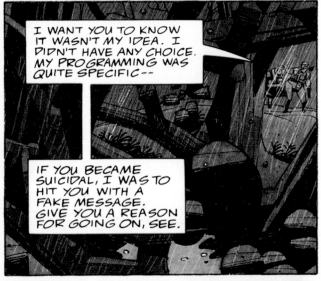

FAKE MESSAGE...?

I REALLY AM SORRY, BOSS. AND THAT'S NOT JUST PRO-GRAMMED BULLSHIT!

YOU MEAN ... THERE'S NOBODY...?

HAHAHAHAHAHAHAHA!

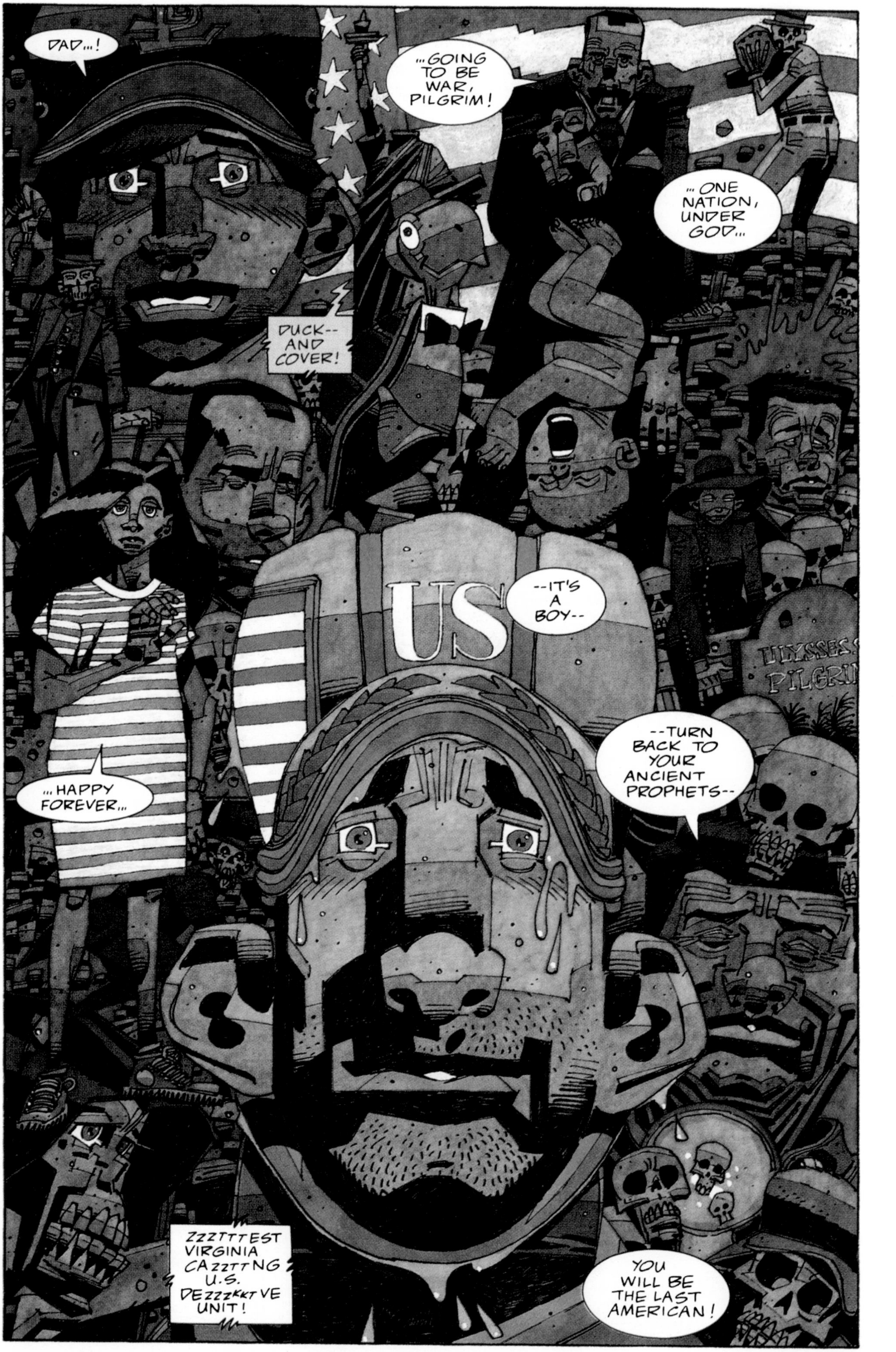
DAD...!
...GOING TO BE WAR, PILGRIM!
...ONE NATION, UNDER GOD...
DUCK--AND COVER!
--IT'S A BOY--
ULYSSES PILGRIM
...HAPPY FOREVER...
--TURN BACK TO YOUR ANCIENT PROPHETS--
ZZZTTTEST VIRGINIA CAZZTTNG U.S. DEZZZKKTVE UNIT!
YOU WILL BE THE LAST AMERICAN!

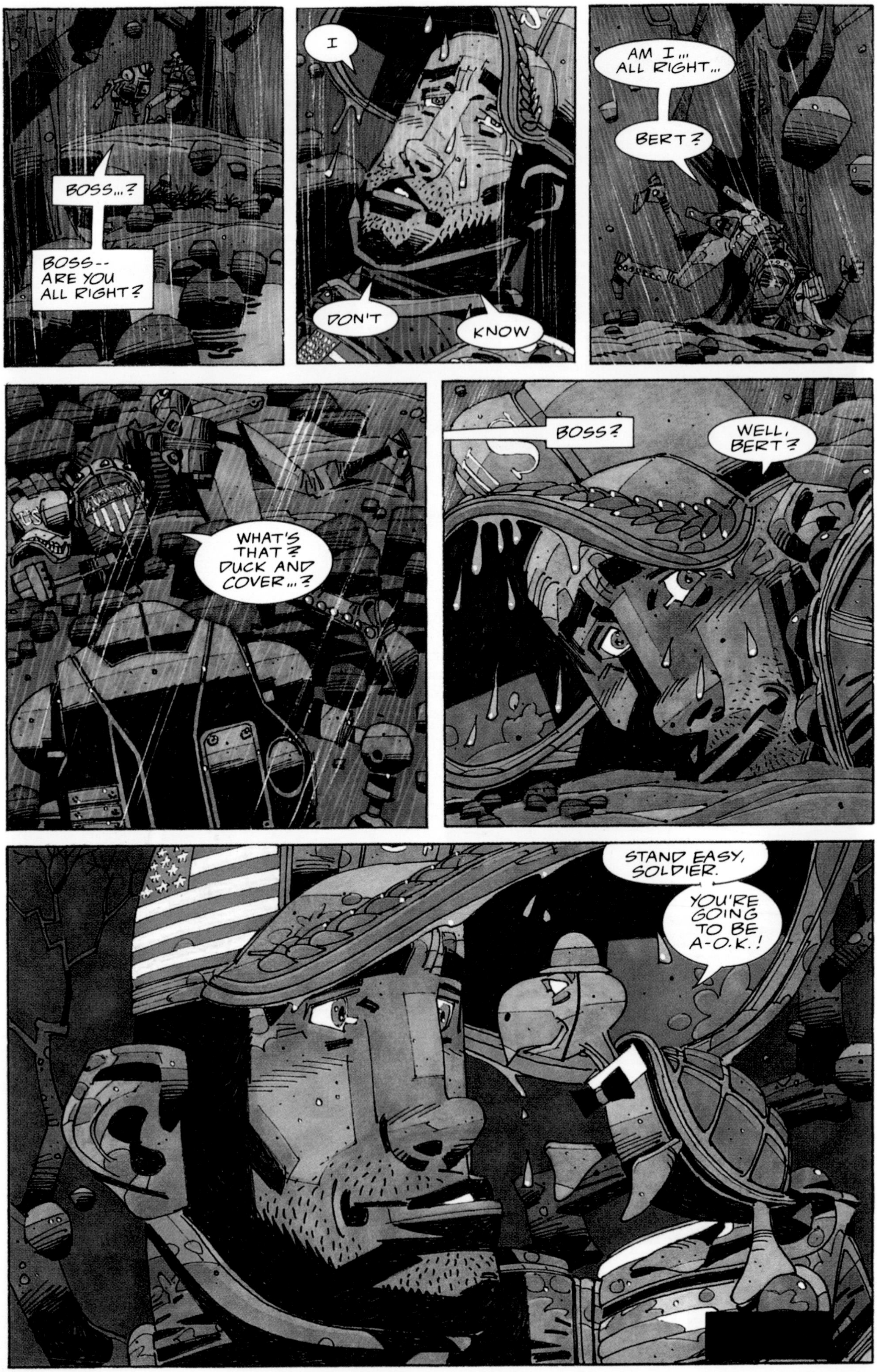
BOSS...?
BOSS-- ARE YOU ALL RIGHT?
I
DON'T
KNOW
AM I... ALL RIGHT...
BERT?
WHAT'S THAT? DUCK AND COVER...?
BOSS?
WELL, BERT?
STAND EASY, SOLDIER.
YOU'RE GOING TO BE A-O.K.!

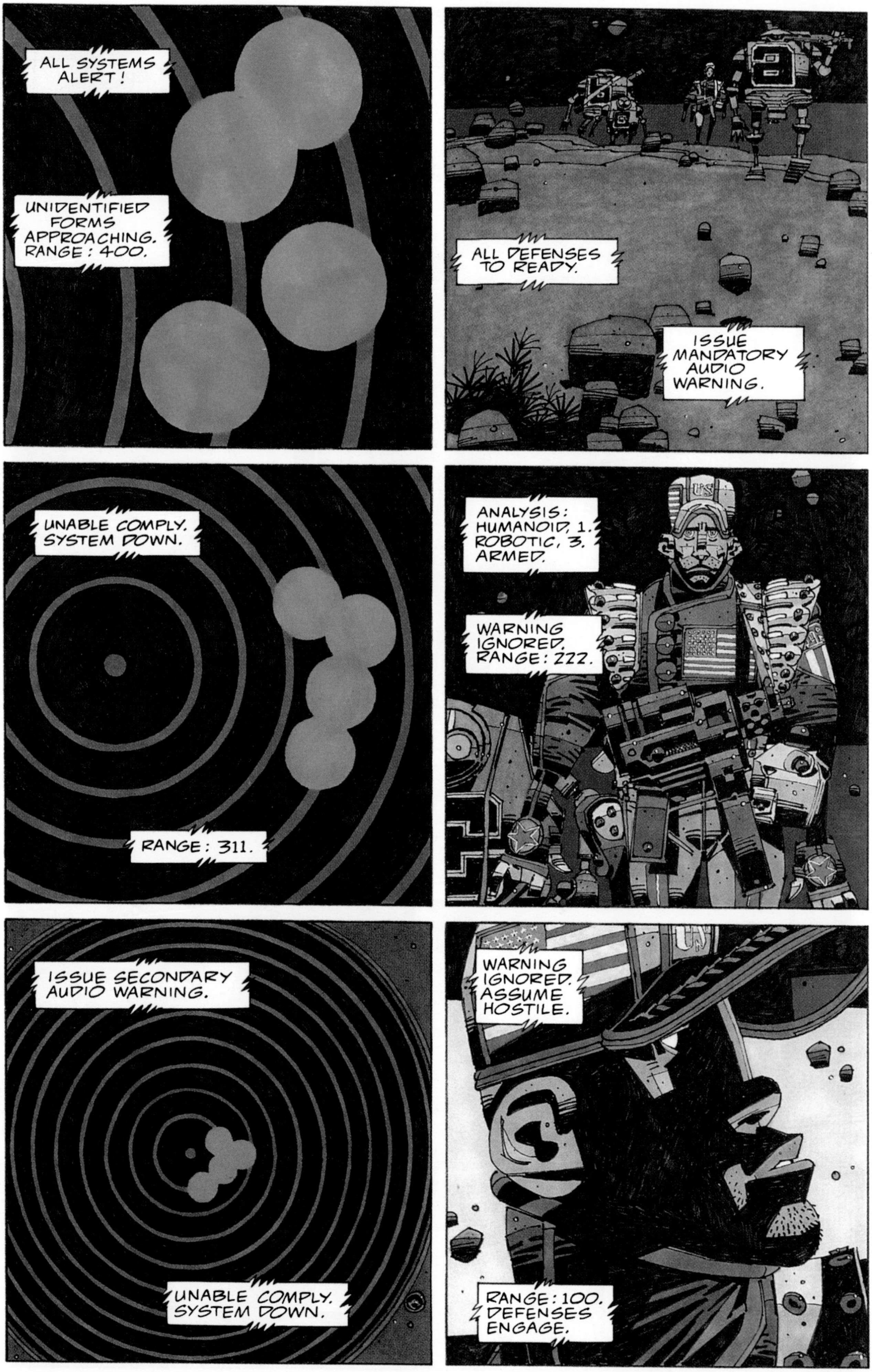
ALL SYSTEMS ALERT!
UNIDENTIFIED FORMS APPROACHING. RANGE: 400.
ALL DEFENSES TO READY.
ISSUE MANDATORY AUDIO WARNING.
UNABLE COMPLY. SYSTEM DOWN.
RANGE: 311.
ANALYSIS: HUMANOID, 1. ROBOTIC, 3. ARMED.
WARNING IGNORED. RANGE: 222.
ISSUE SECONDARY AUDIO WARNING.
UNABLE COMPLY. SYSTEM DOWN.
WARNING IGNORED. ASSUME HOSTILE.
RANGE: 100. DEFENSES ENGAGE.

July 23, 2019. Shenandoah National Park. It's 25 years since I heard the angry chatter of bullets with my name on them -- since I smelled the harshness of burned air, the sick-sweet stench of my own fear...

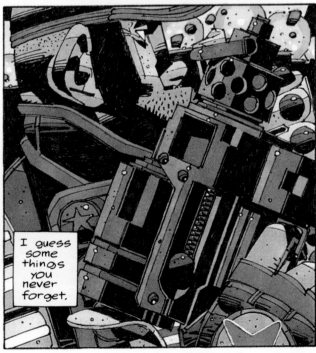

I guess some things you never forget.

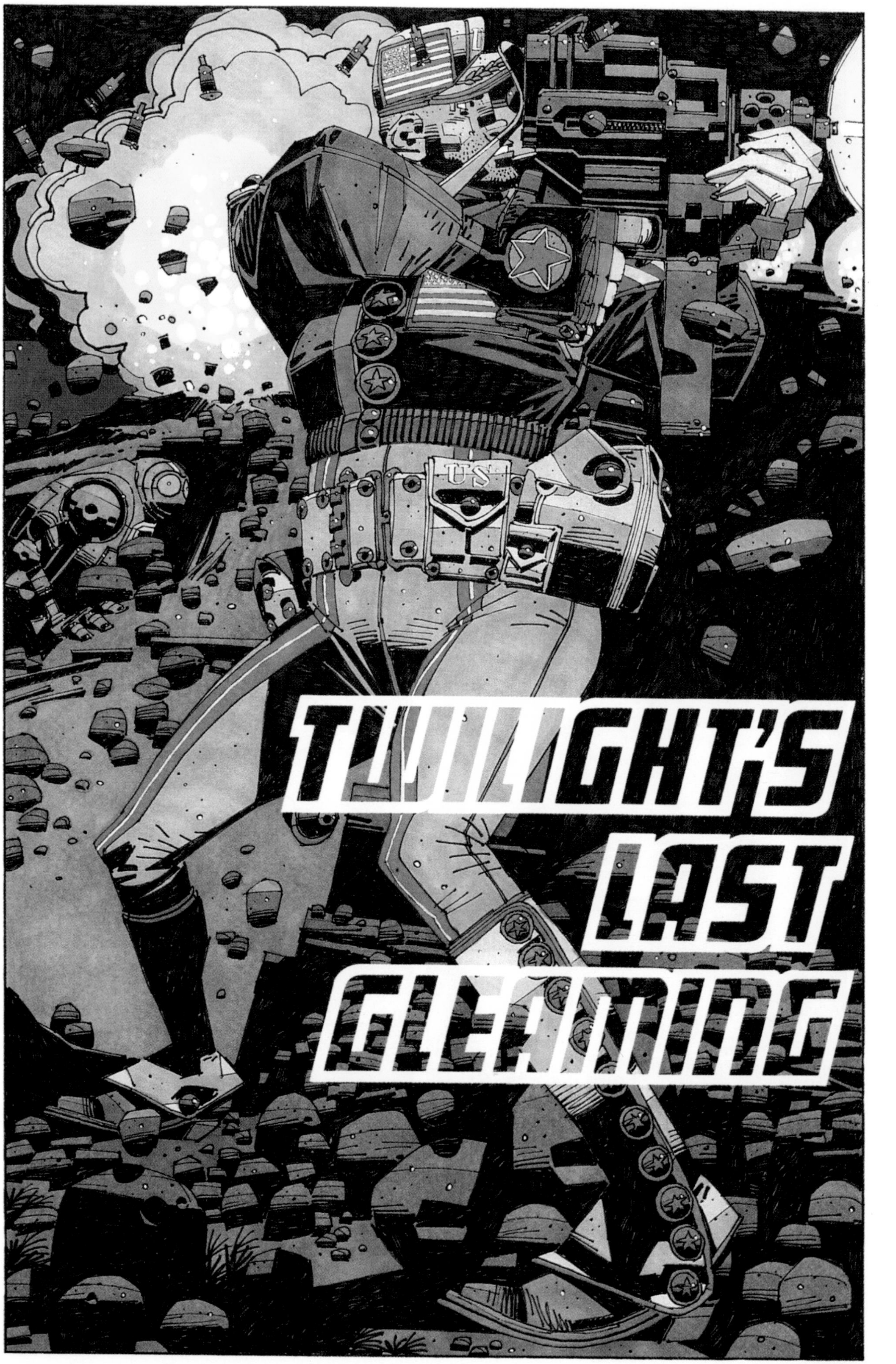
TWILIGHT'S
LAST
GLEAMING
US

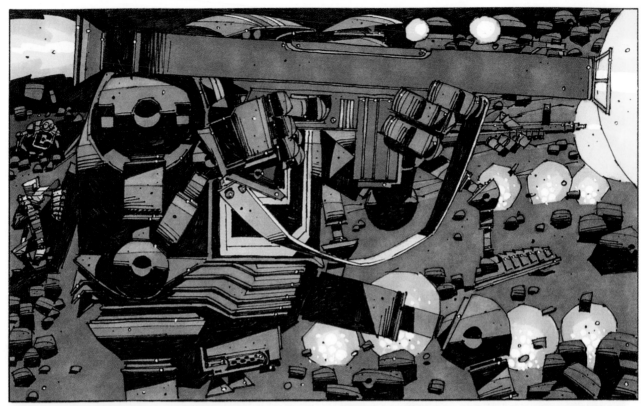

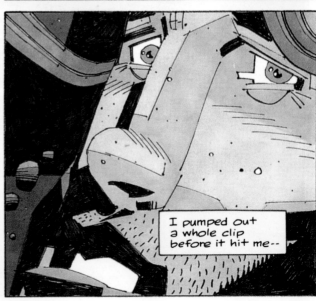

I pumped out
a whole clip
before it hit me--

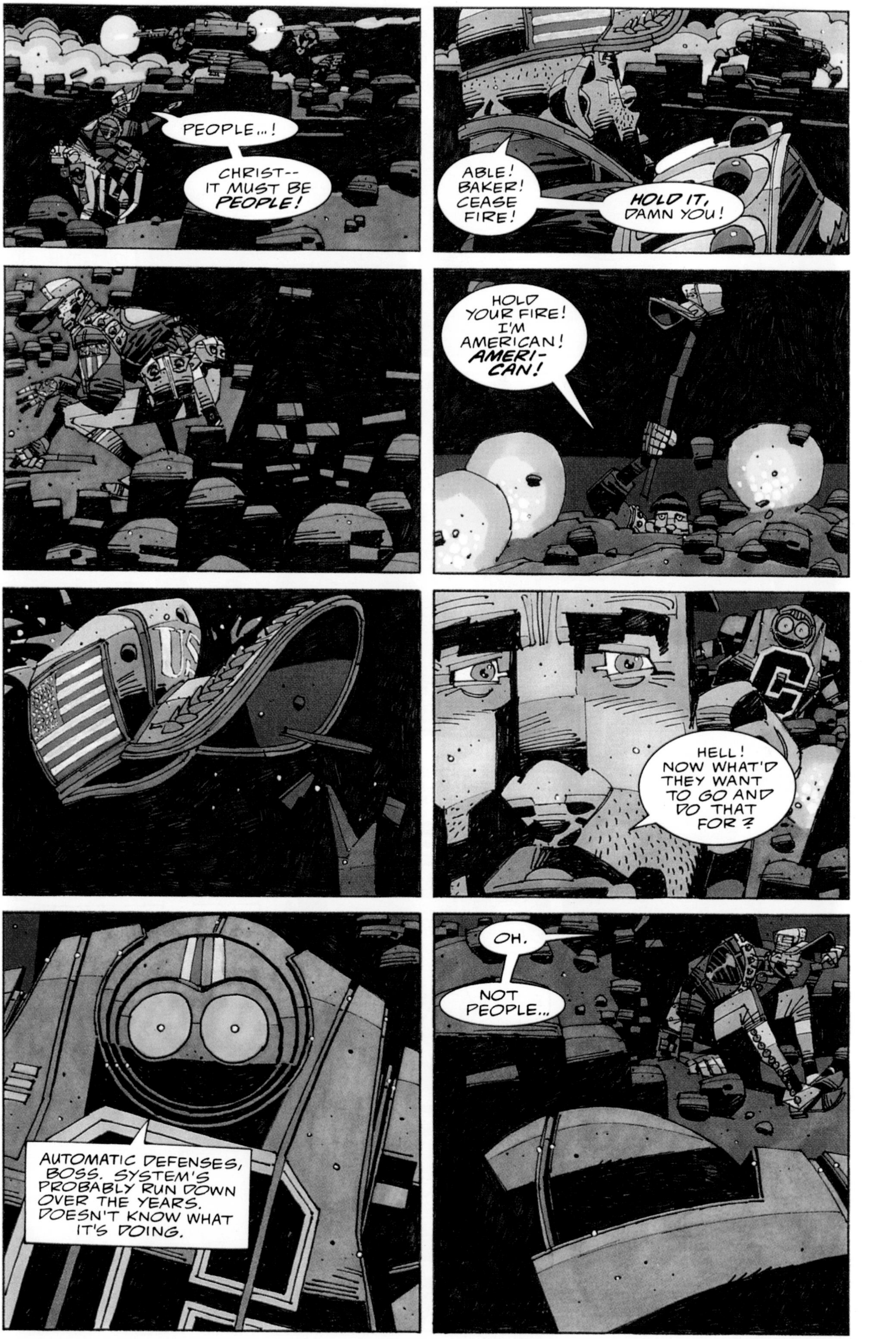
PEOPLE...!
CHRIST-- IT MUST BE PEOPLE!
ABLE! BAKER! CEASE FIRE!
HOLD IT, DAMN YOU!
HOLD YOUR FIRE! I'M AMERICAN! AMERI-CAN!
HELL! NOW WHAT'D THEY WANT TO GO AND DO THAT FOR?
AUTOMATIC DEFENSES, BOSS. SYSTEM'S PROBABLY RUN DOWN OVER THE YEARS. DOESN'T KNOW WHAT IT'S DOING.
OH.
NOT PEOPLE...

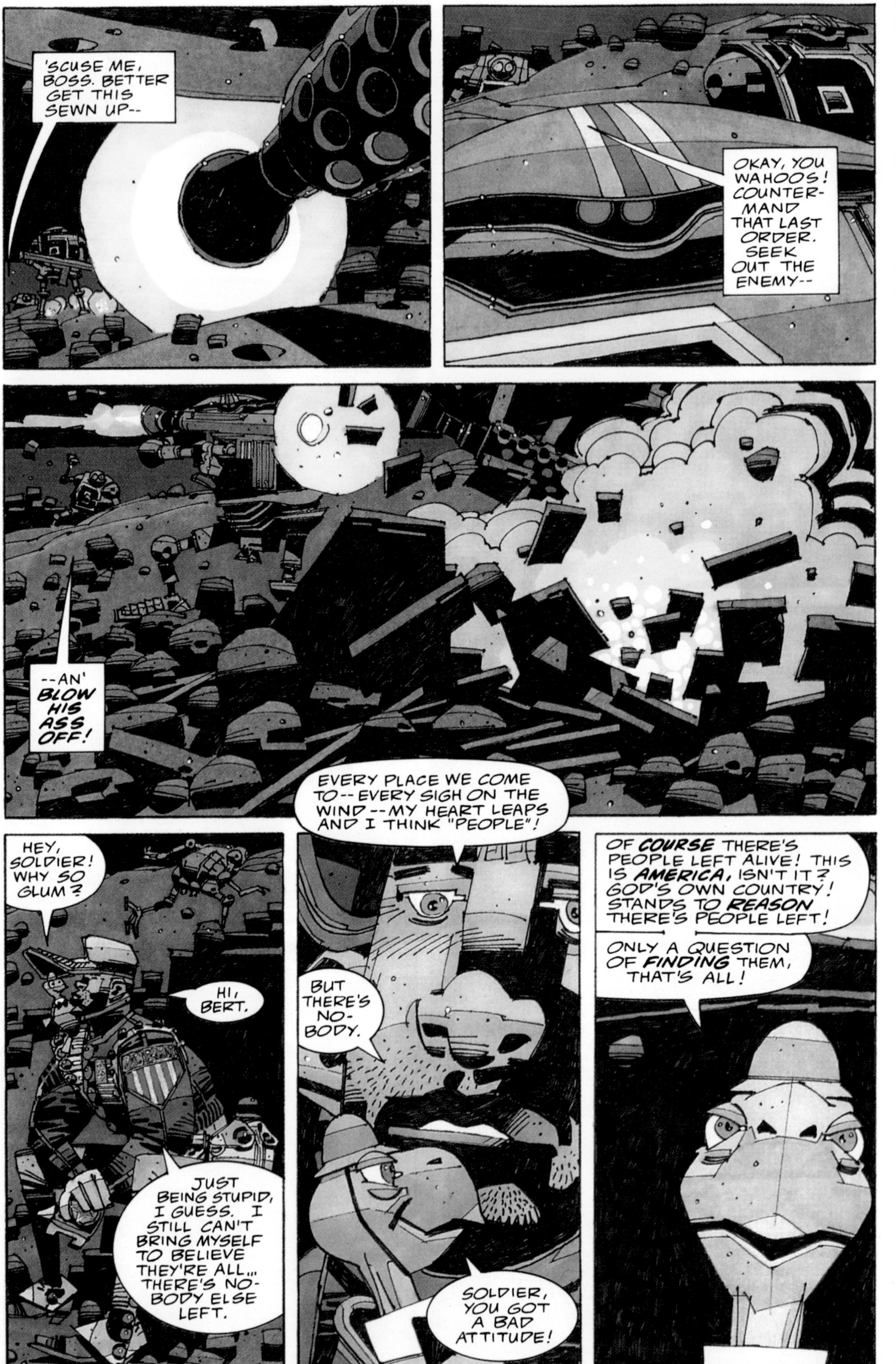

'SCUSE ME, BOSS. BETTER GET THIS SEWN UP--
OKAY, YOU WAHOOS! COUNTER-MAND THAT LAST ORDER. SEEK OUT THE ENEMY--
--AN' BLOW HIS ASS OFF!
HEY, SOLDIER! WHY SO GLUM?
HI, BERT.
JUST BEING STUPID, I GUESS. I STILL CAN'T BRING MYSELF TO BELIEVE THEY'RE ALL... THERE'S NO-BODY ELSE LEFT.
EVERY PLACE WE COME TO-- EVERY SIGH ON THE WIND--MY HEART LEAPS AND I THINK "PEOPLE"!
BUT THERE'S NO-BODY.
SOLDIER, YOU GOT A BAD ATTITUDE!
OF COURSE THERE'S PEOPLE LEFT ALIVE! THIS IS AMERICA, ISN'T IT? GOD'S OWN COUNTRY! STANDS TO REASON THERE'S PEOPLE LEFT!
ONLY A QUESTION OF FINDING THEM, THAT'S ALL!

THAT'S THE LAST, CHARLIE. APPROACH IS CLEAR.
UH... IS THE COMMANDER OKAY?
IN A WORD-- NO.
HE'S TALKING TO HIS IMAGINARY TURTLE AGAIN.
DAMN! I WISH I'D NEVER LET HIM WATCH THAT MOVIE!
NOT YOUR FAULT, CHARLIE. YOU WASN'T TO KNOW.
I THOUGHT THEY PROGRAMMED YOU TO STOP HIM GOING CRAZY?
THEY DID THEIR BEST...
UNFORTUNATELY, THERE WASN'T MUCH DATA ON THE "LAST MAN IN THE WORLD SYNDROME"... TILL NOW!
US
ENTRY'S CLEAR, COM-MANDER. WE'RE GOIN' IN!

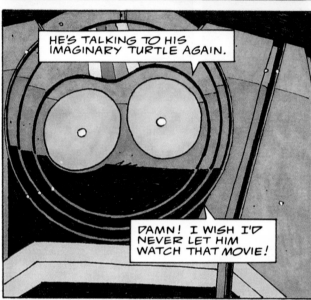

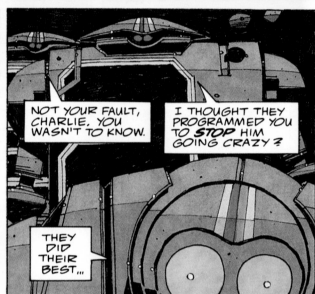

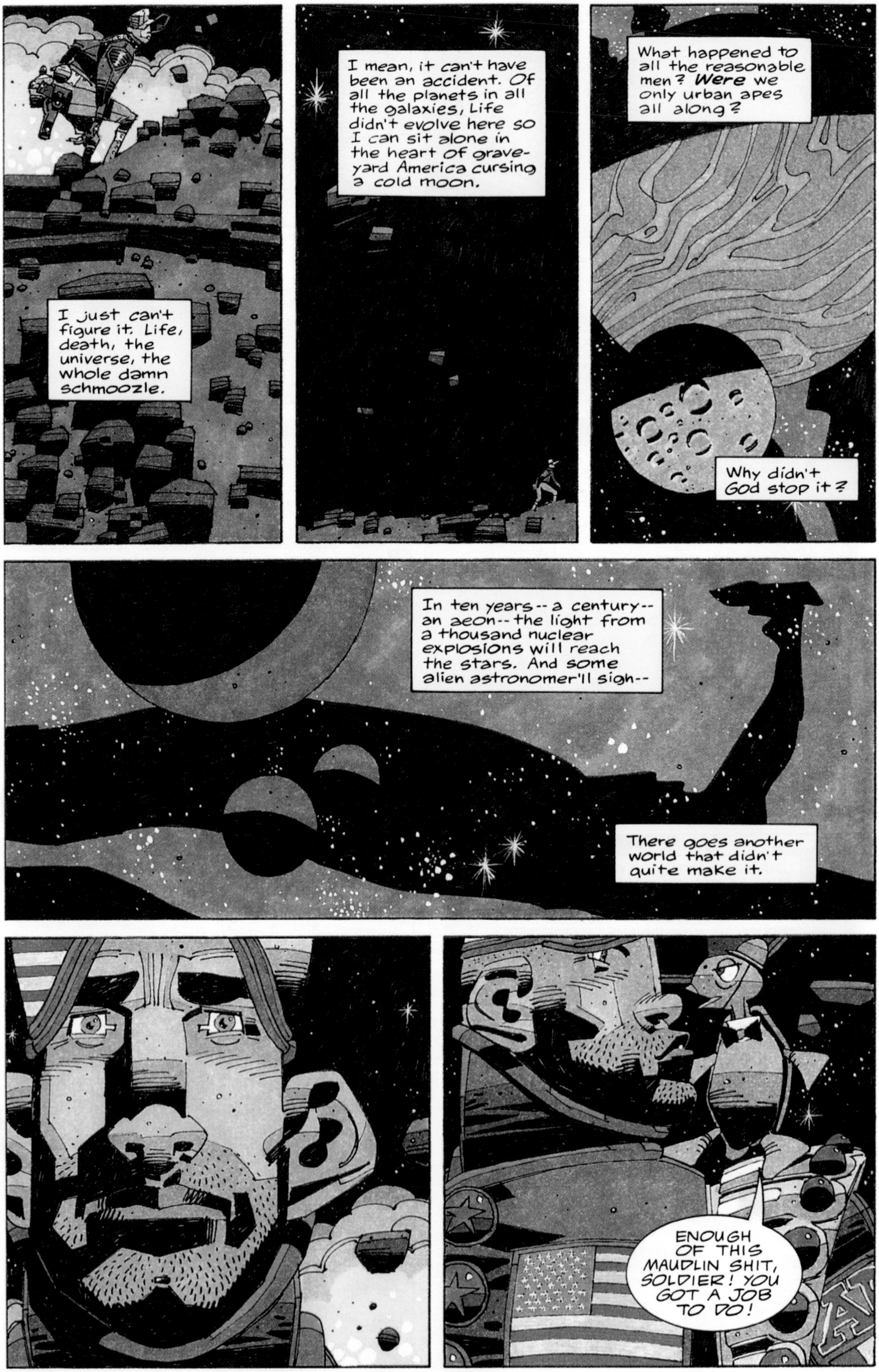
I just can't figure it. Life, death, the universe, the whole damn schmoozle.
I mean, it can't have been an accident. Of all the planets in all the galaxies, Life didn't evolve here so I can sit alone in the heart of graveyard America cursing a cold moon.
What happened to all the reasonable men? *Were* we only urban apes all along?
Why didn't God stop it?
In ten years -- a century -- an aeon -- the light from a thousand nuclear explosions will reach the stars. And some alien astronomer'll sigh --
There goes another world that didn't quite make it.
ENOUGH OF THIS MAUDLIN SHIT, SOLDIER! YOU GOT A JOB TO DO!

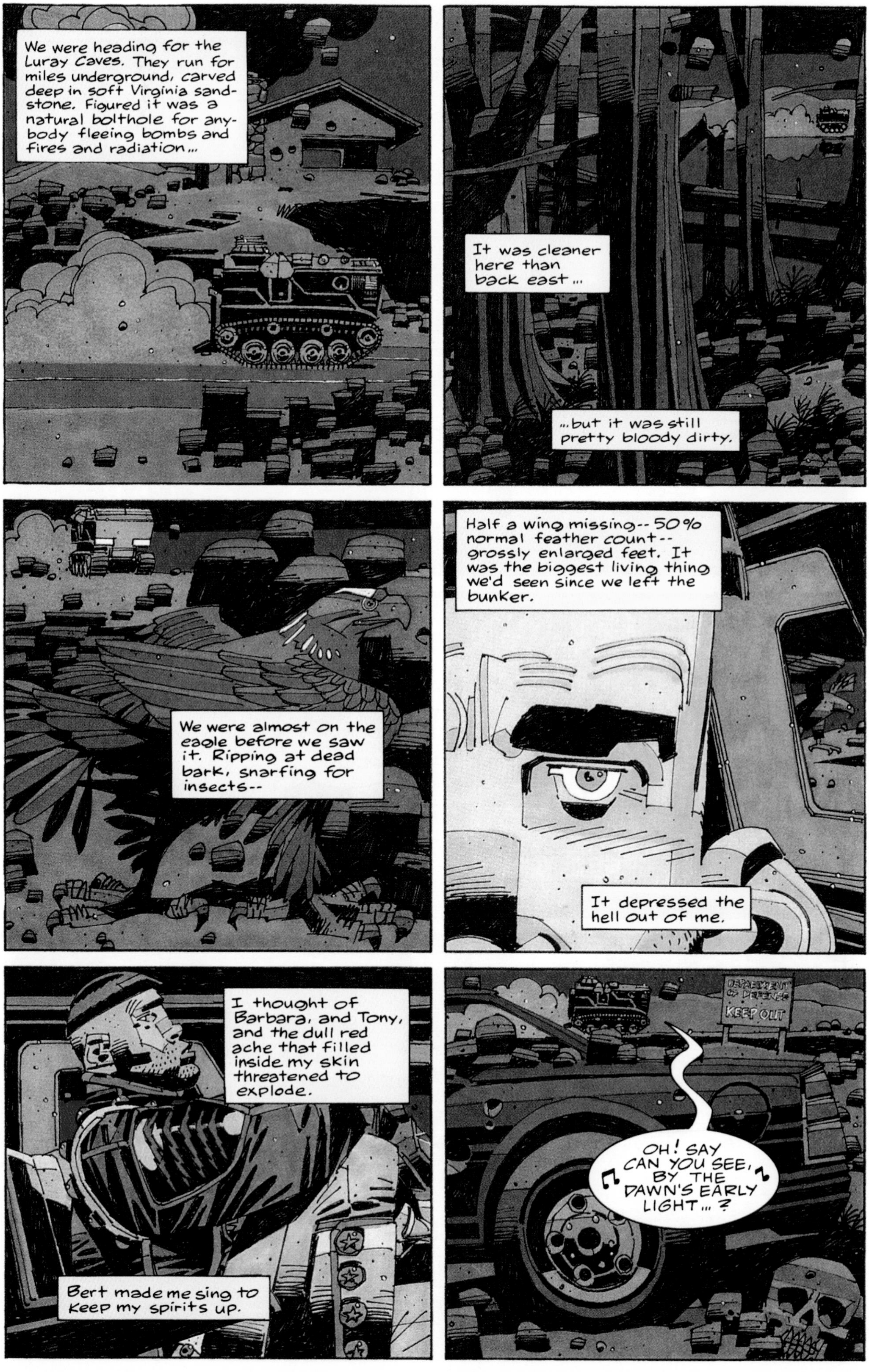
We were heading for the Luray Caves. They run for miles underground, carved deep in soft Virginia sandstone. Figured it was a natural bolthole for anybody fleeing bombs and fires and radiation...
It was cleaner here than back east...
...but it was still pretty bloody dirty.
We were almost on the eagle before we saw it. Ripping at dead bark, snarfing for insects--
Half a wing missing-- 50% normal feather count-- grossly enlarged feet. It was the biggest living thing we'd seen since we left the bunker.
It depressed the hell out of me.
I thought of Barbara, and Tony, and the dull red ache that filled inside my skin threatened to explode.
Bert made me sing to keep my spirits up.
KEEP OUT
OH! SAY CAN YOU SEE, BY THE DAWN'S EARLY LIGHT...?

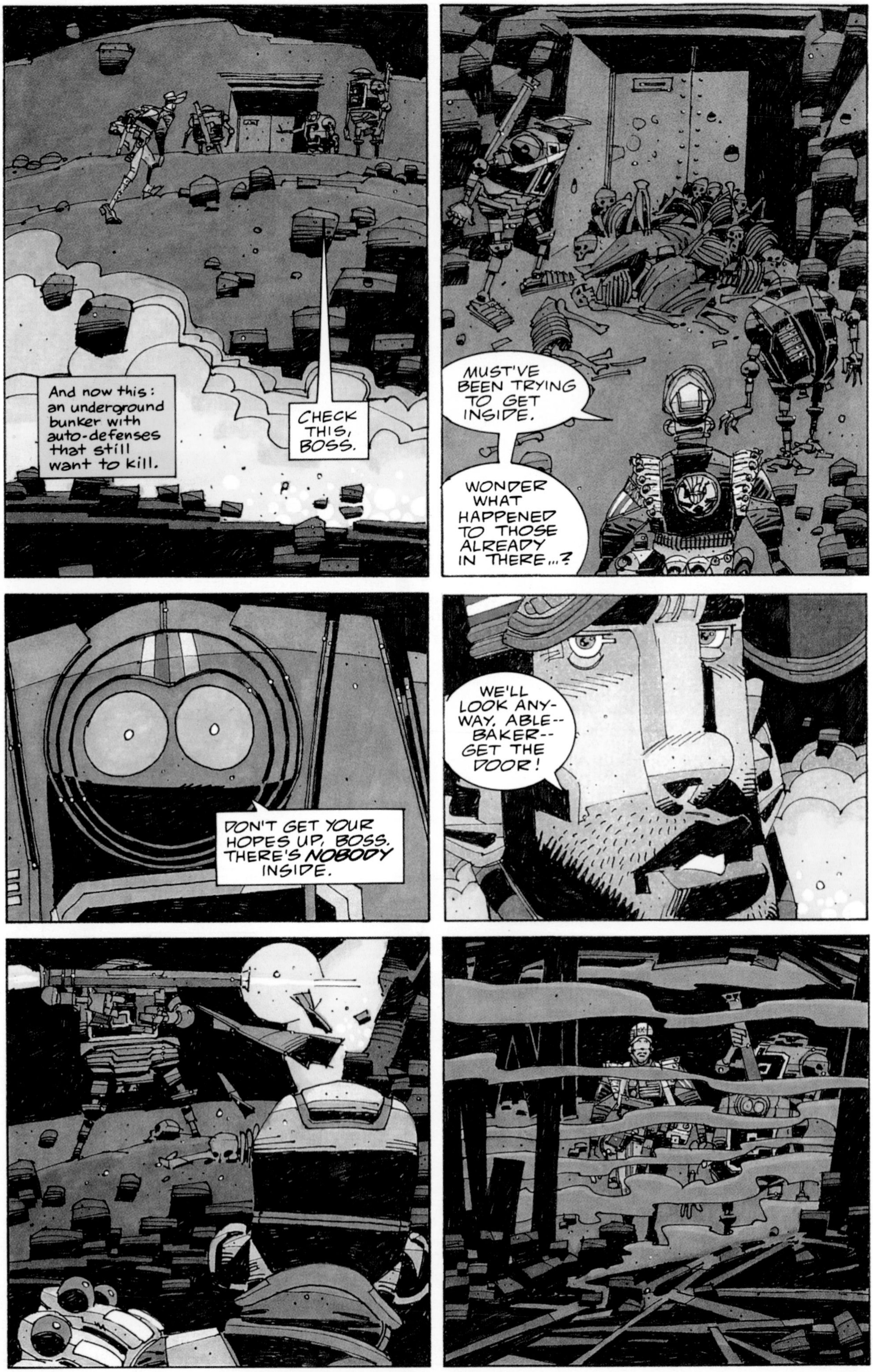
And now this: an underground bunker with auto-defenses that still want to kill.
CHECK THIS, BOSS.
MUST'VE BEEN TRYING TO GET INSIDE.
WONDER WHAT HAPPENED TO THOSE ALREADY IN THERE...?
DON'T GET YOUR HOPES UP, BOSS. THERE'S NOBODY INSIDE.
WE'LL LOOK ANYWAY. ABLE-- BAKER-- GET THE DOOR!

It was like a tomb in there. Only it wasn't-- else why would they have been clamoring to get in?

Just one reason: because inside, underground, life could maybe go on.

OVER HERE!

ELEVATORS TO THE LOWER LEVELS. OUT OF ACTION--POWER MUST HAVE BEEN RESERVED FOR THE DEFENSES.

EXIT

DOOR'S RUSTED SHUT.

OPEN IT!

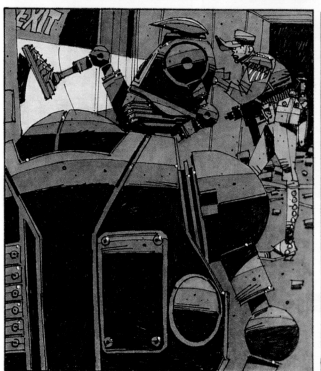

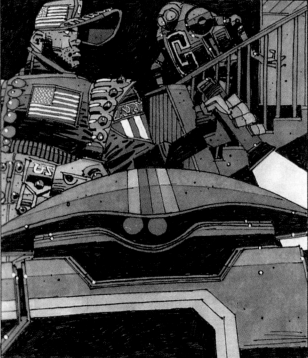

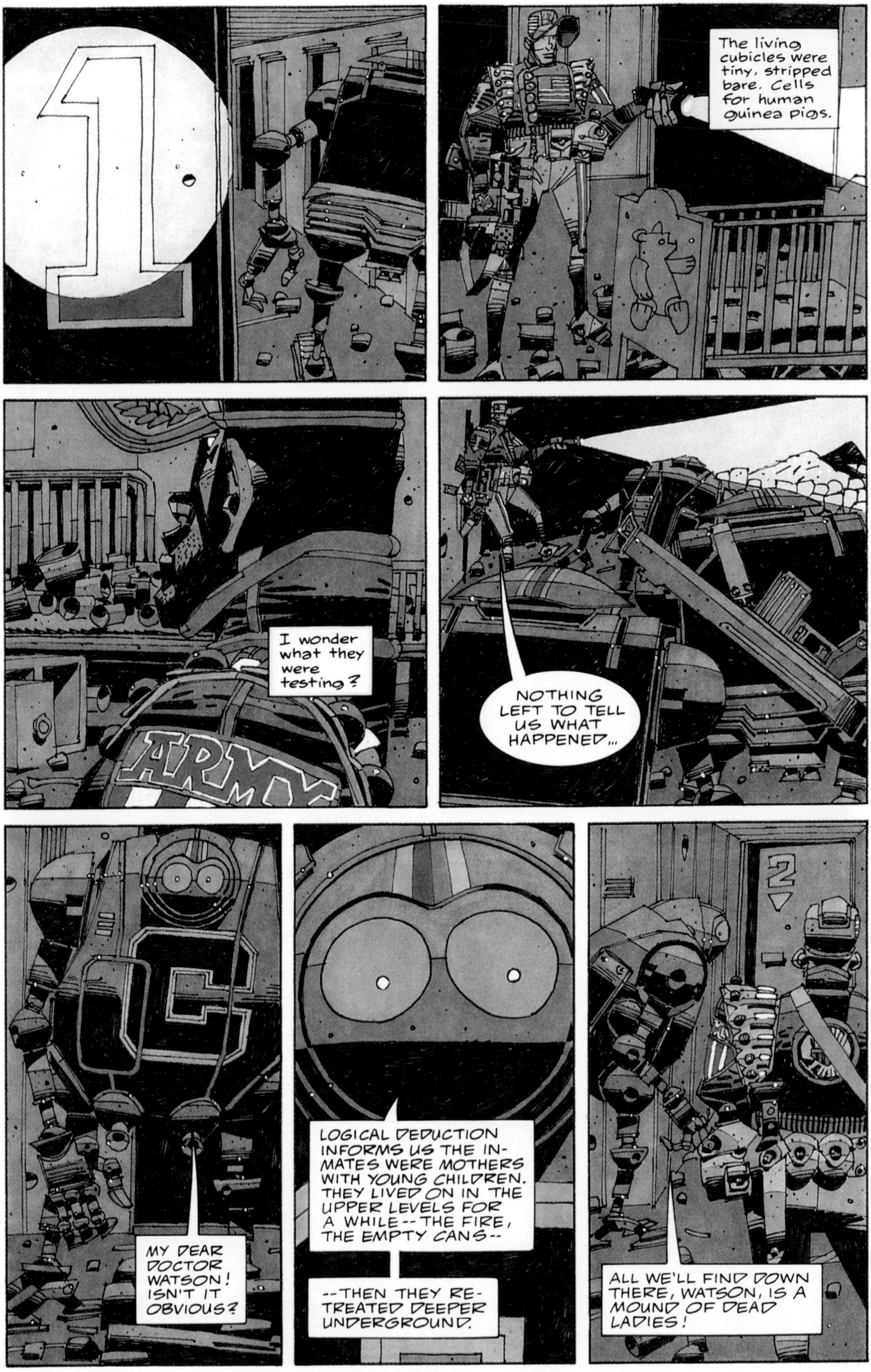
1
The living cubicles were tiny, stripped bare. Cells for human guinea pigs.
ARMY
I wonder what they were testing?
NOTHING LEFT TO TELL US WHAT HAPPENED...
MY DEAR DOCTOR WATSON! ISN'T IT OBVIOUS?
LOGICAL DEDUCTION INFORMS US THE IN- MATES WERE MOTHERS WITH YOUNG CHILDREN. THEY LIVED ON IN THE UPPER LEVELS FOR A WHILE -- THE FIRE, THE EMPTY CANS --
-- THEN THEY RE- TREATED DEEPER UNDERGROUND.
2
ALL WE'LL FIND DOWN THERE, WATSON, IS A MOUND OF DEAD LADIES!

X-RAY EQUIPMENT, RADIATION DETECTORS, DANGEROUS, WHATEVER THEY WERE DOING.

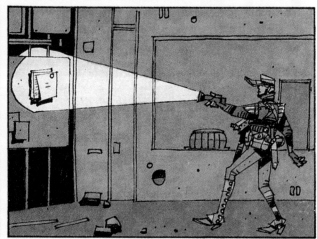

My diary

Hello somebody. I am Melinda. The doctors called me alpha delta 99 017. but that was before. Now I hear th scrabling and they

"...WON'T GO AWAY. THERE WERE 20 OF US, FROM ALL OVER. I CAME ON A BUS FROM BROOKLIN. LANA CAME FROM KANSAS. SHE WAS 99/013.

"EVERYBODY WAS HAVING BABIES.

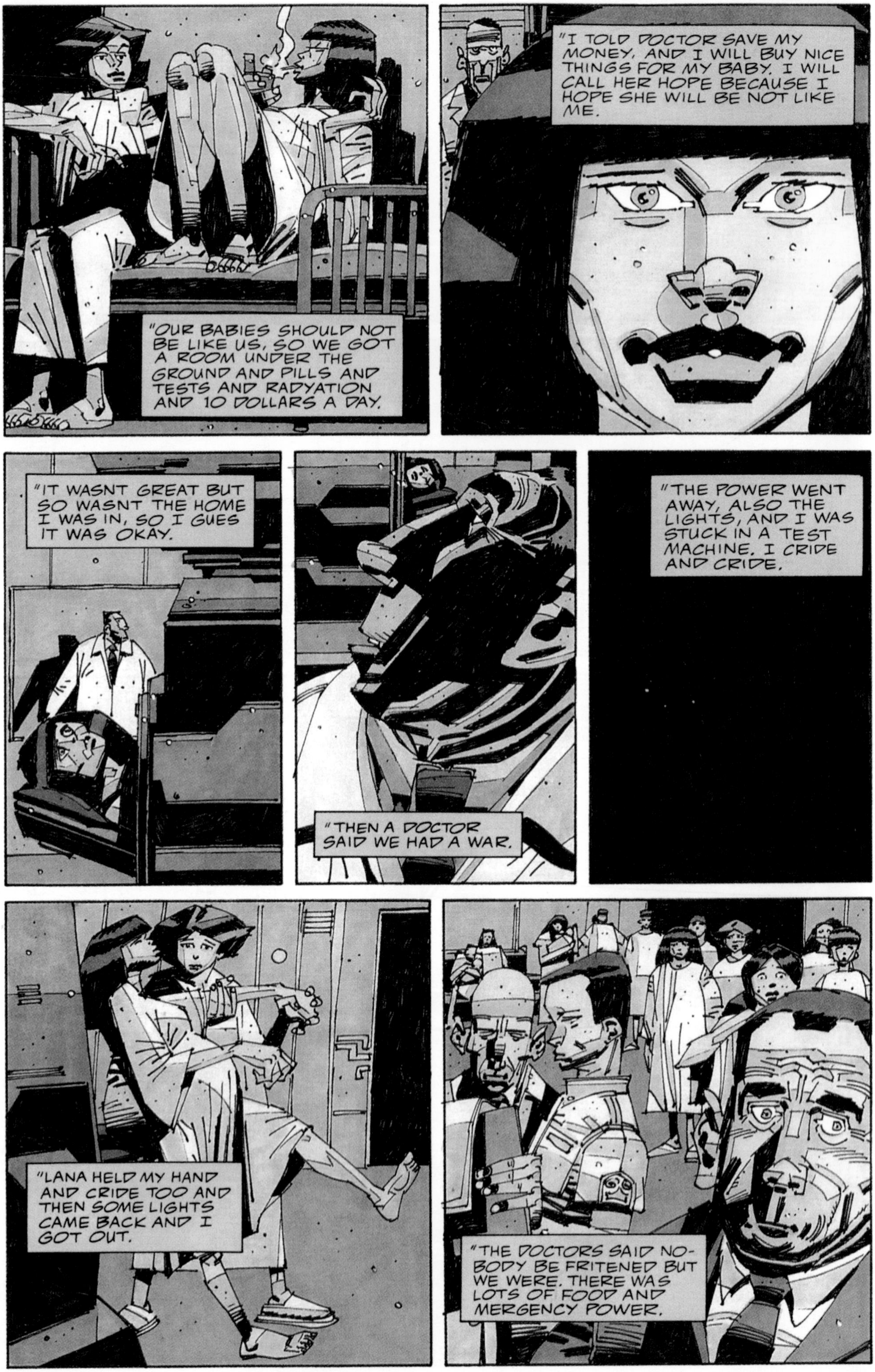
"OUR BABIES SHOULD NOT BE LIKE US, SO WE GOT A ROOM UNDER THE GROUND AND PILLS AND TESTS AND RADYATION AND 10 DOLLARS A DAY.
"I TOLD DOCTOR SAVE MY MONEY, AND I WILL BUY NICE THINGS FOR MY BABY. I WILL CALL HER HOPE BECAUSE I HOPE SHE WILL BE NOT LIKE ME.
"IT WASNT GREAT BUT SO WASNT THE HOME I WAS IN, SO I GUES IT WAS OKAY.
"THEN A DOCTOR SAID WE HAD A WAR.
"THE POWER WENT AWAY, ALSO THE LIGHTS, AND I WAS STUCK IN A TEST MACHINE. I CRIDE AND CRIDE.
"LANA HELD MY HAND AND CRIDE TOO AND THEN SOME LIGHTS CAME BACK AND I GOT OUT.
"THE DOCTORS SAID NO-BODY BE FRITENED BUT WE WERE. THERE WAS LOTS OF FOOD AND MERGENCY POWER.

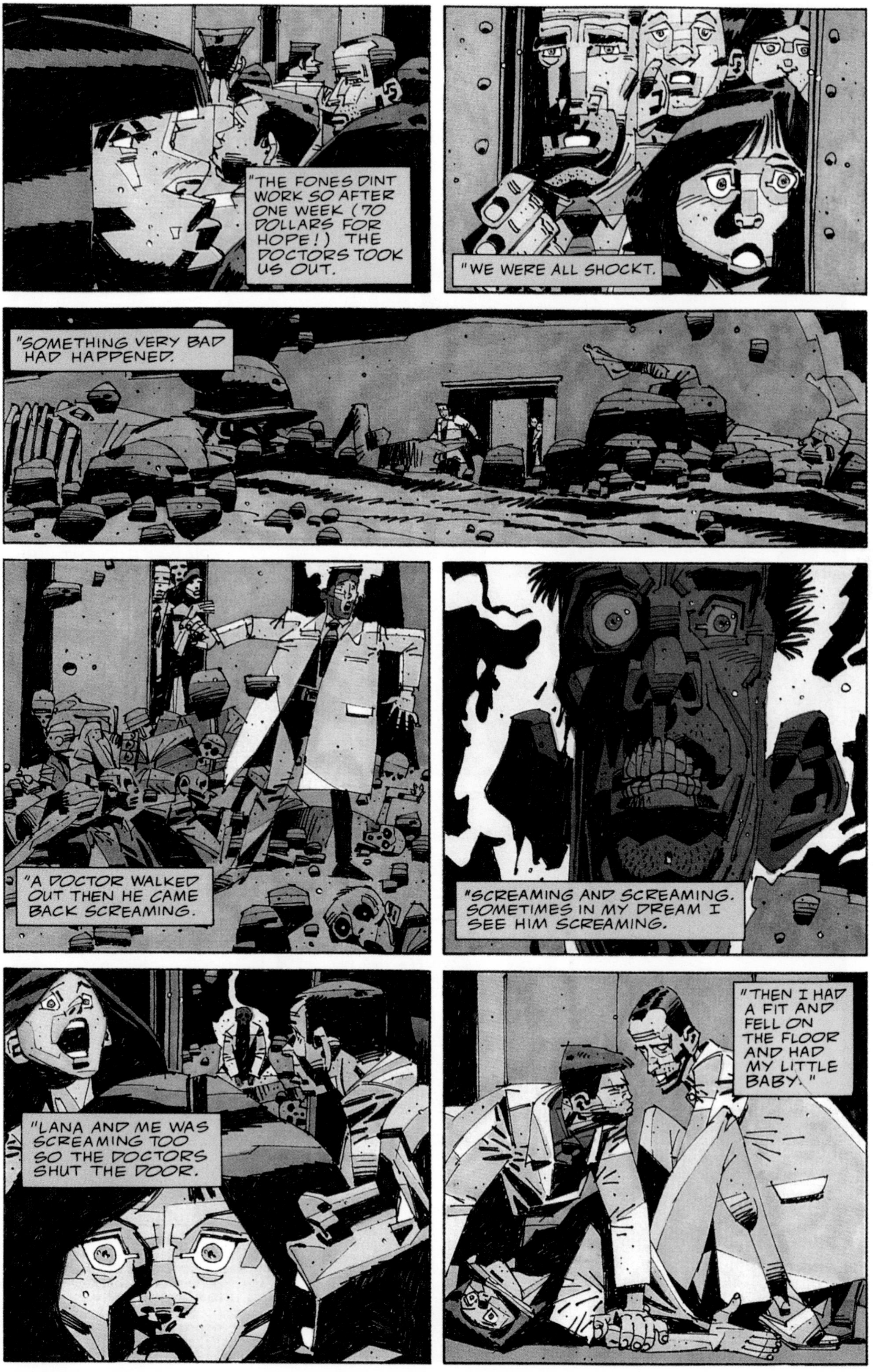
"THE FONES DINT WORK SO AFTER ONE WEEK (70 DOLLARS FOR HOPE!) THE DOCTORS TOOK US OUT.
"WE WERE ALL SHOCKT.
"SOMETHING VERY BAD HAD HAPPENED.
"A DOCTOR WALKED OUT THEN HE CAME BACK SCREAMING.
"SCREAMING AND SCREAMING. SOMETIMES IN MY DREAM I SEE HIM SCREAMING.
"LANA AND ME WAS SCREAMING TOO SO THE DOCTORS SHUT THE DOOR.
"THEN I HAD A FIT AND FELL ON THE FLOOR AND HAD MY LITTLE BABY."

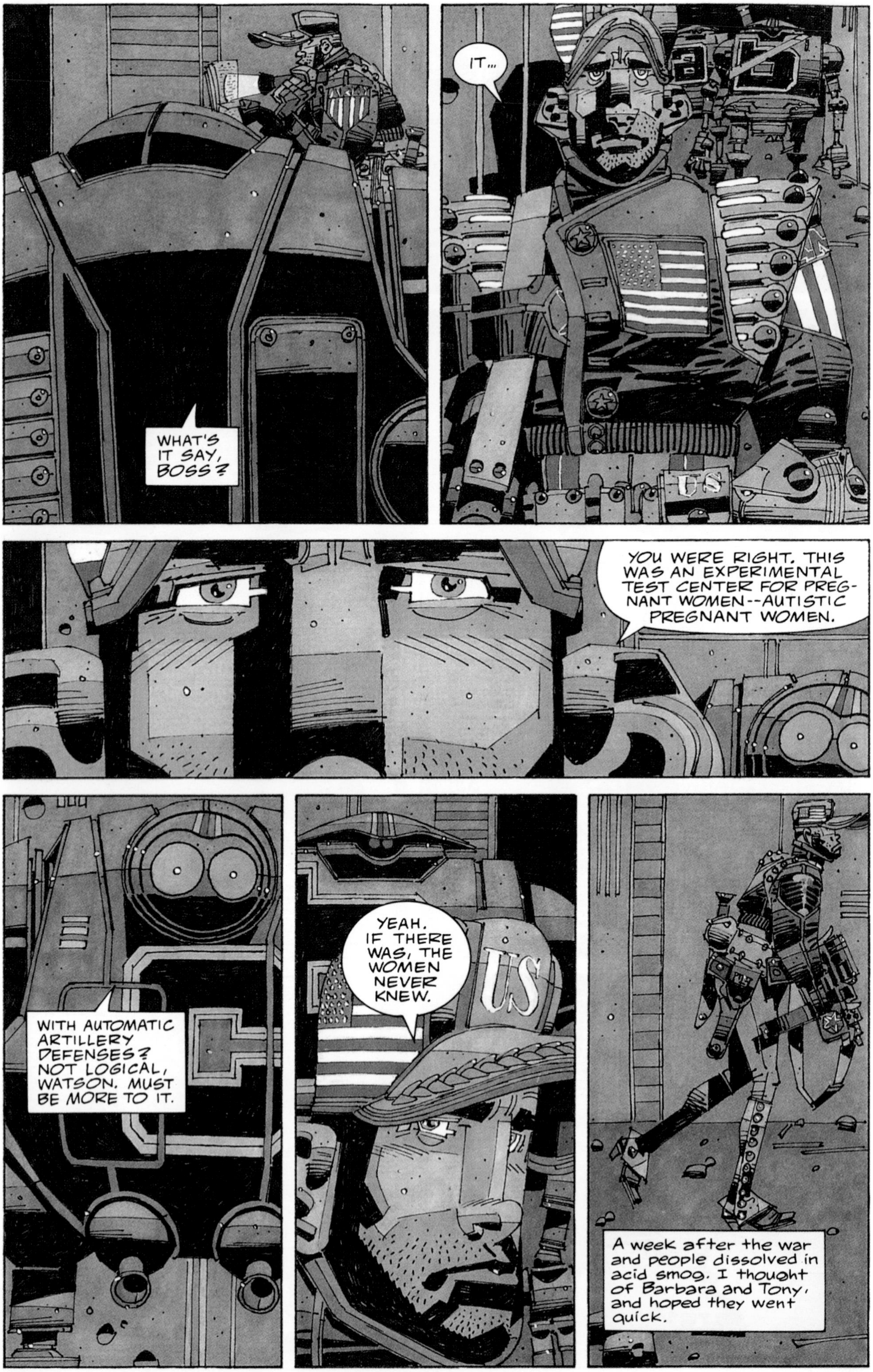
WHAT'S IT SAY, BOSS?
IT...
YOU WERE RIGHT. THIS WAS AN EXPERIMENTAL TEST CENTER FOR PREGNANT WOMEN--AUTISTIC PREGNANT WOMEN.
WITH AUTOMATIC ARTILLERY DEFENSES? NOT LOGICAL, WATSON. MUST BE MORE TO IT.
YEAH. IF THERE WAS, THE WOMEN NEVER KNEW.
A week after the war and people dissolved in acid smog. I thought of Barbara and Tony, and hoped they went quick.

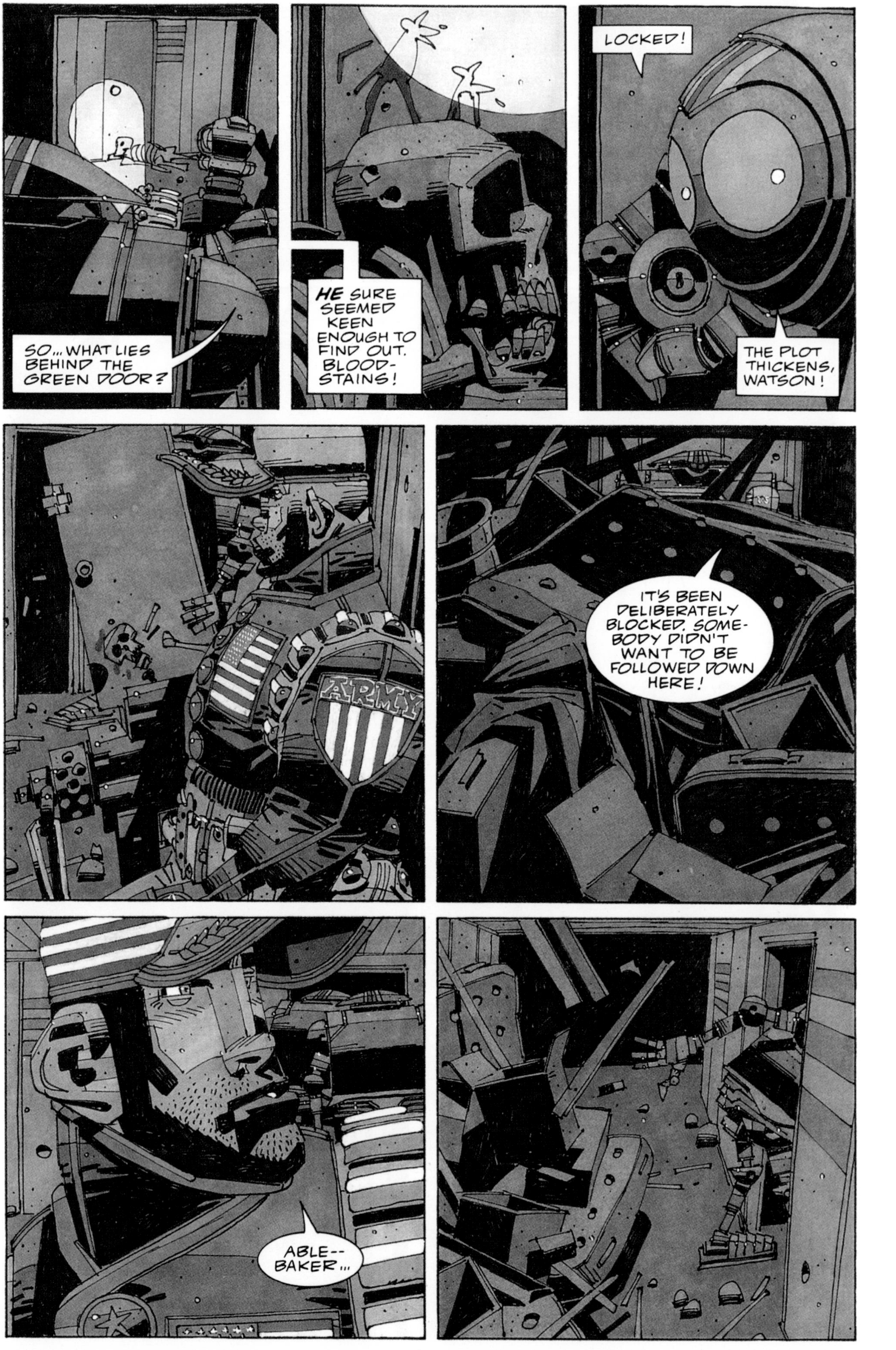
SO... WHAT LIES BEHIND THE GREEN DOOR?
HE SURE SEEMED KEEN ENOUGH TO FIND OUT. BLOOD-STAINS!
LOCKED!
THE PLOT THICKENS, WATSON!
ARMY
IT'S BEEN DELIBERATELY BLOCKED. SOME-BODY DIDN'T WANT TO BE FOLLOWED DOWN HERE!
ABLE-- BAKER...

THE WOMEN ...

...THE BABIES.

WATER-- SEEPING IN FROM THE ROCK BEYOND. THEY COULD HAVE LIVED HERE QUITE A WHILE.

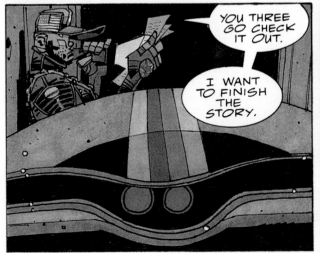

YOU THREE GO CHECK IT OUT.

I WANT TO FINISH THE STORY.

I dint call her Hope. The doctors said the worst had happened and all hope was gone. They said it was the twilight of the world.

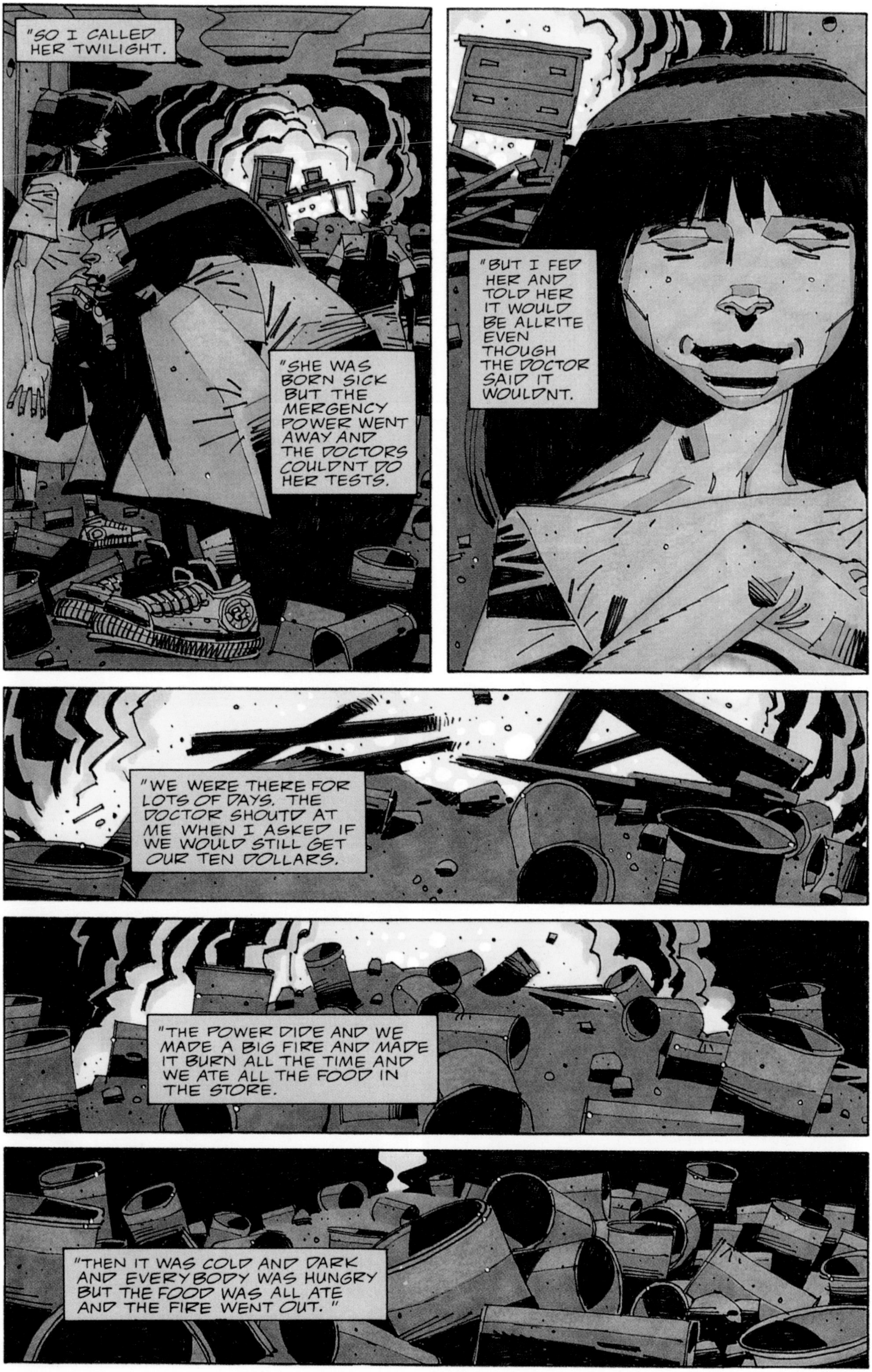
"SO I CALLED HER TWILIGHT.
"SHE WAS BORN SICK BUT THE MERGENCY POWER WENT AWAY AND THE DOCTORS COULDN'T DO HER TESTS.
"BUT I FED HER AND TOLD HER IT WOULD BE ALLRITE EVEN THOUGH THE DOCTOR SAID IT WOULDN'T.
"WE WERE THERE FOR LOTS OF DAYS. THE DOCTOR SHOUTD AT ME WHEN I ASKED IF WE WOULD STILL GET OUR TEN DOLLARS.
"THE POWER DIDE AND WE MADE A BIG FIRE AND MADE IT BURN ALL THE TIME AND WE ATE ALL THE FOOD IN THE STORE.
"THEN IT WAS COLD AND DARK AND EVERYBODY WAS HUNGRY BUT THE FOOD WAS ALL ATE AND THE FIRE WENT OUT."

OH, JESUS...!

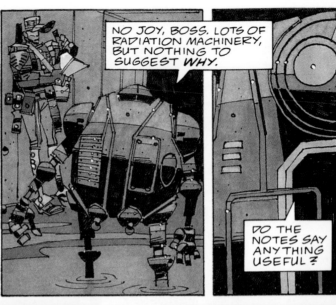

NO JOY, BOSS. LOTS OF RADIATION MACHINERY, BUT NOTHING TO SUGGEST *WHY*.

DO THE NOTES SAY ANYTHING USEFUL?

USEFUL? NO.

TRAGIC. STORY OF A GIRL WHO CALLED HER BABY "TWILIGHT"...

"THERE WAS SCREAMING IN THE DARK AND I SNATCHT UP TWILIGHT AND TRIDE TO RUN AWAY BUT I BUMPT INTO SOMETHING AND IT WAS LANA. SHE SAID THE DOCTORS HAD STOLE A BABY TO EAT IT AND I DINT BELIEVE HER. DOCTORS WOULDNT DO THAT.

"BUT ANOTHER GIRL SAID IT WAS TRUE SO WE USED MY ZIPPO TO STAY TOGETHER AND FOUND THE STEPS DOWN AND WENT AND HID.

"WE LOCKT THE DOOR BUT WE COULD HEAR THEM SCRABLING AT IT AND SOMETIMES OTHER SCREAMS AND WE WERE ALL CRYING AND THE BABIES TOO.

"BUT THE DOOR STARTED TO BREAK AND WE HAD TO FIND THE WAY DOWN AND I KNEW WE WERE GOING TO DIE BUT I MUST LOOK AFTER MY BABY.

"SO WE CAME TO THE BOTTOM AND WE BLOCKED THE STEPS AND LANA FOUND SOME WATER ON A WALL BUT MY BABY DIED SLEEPING AND MY ZIPPO IS GOING ..."

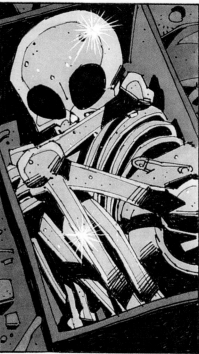

TWILIGHT'S LAST GLEAMING, HUH?

HA ...

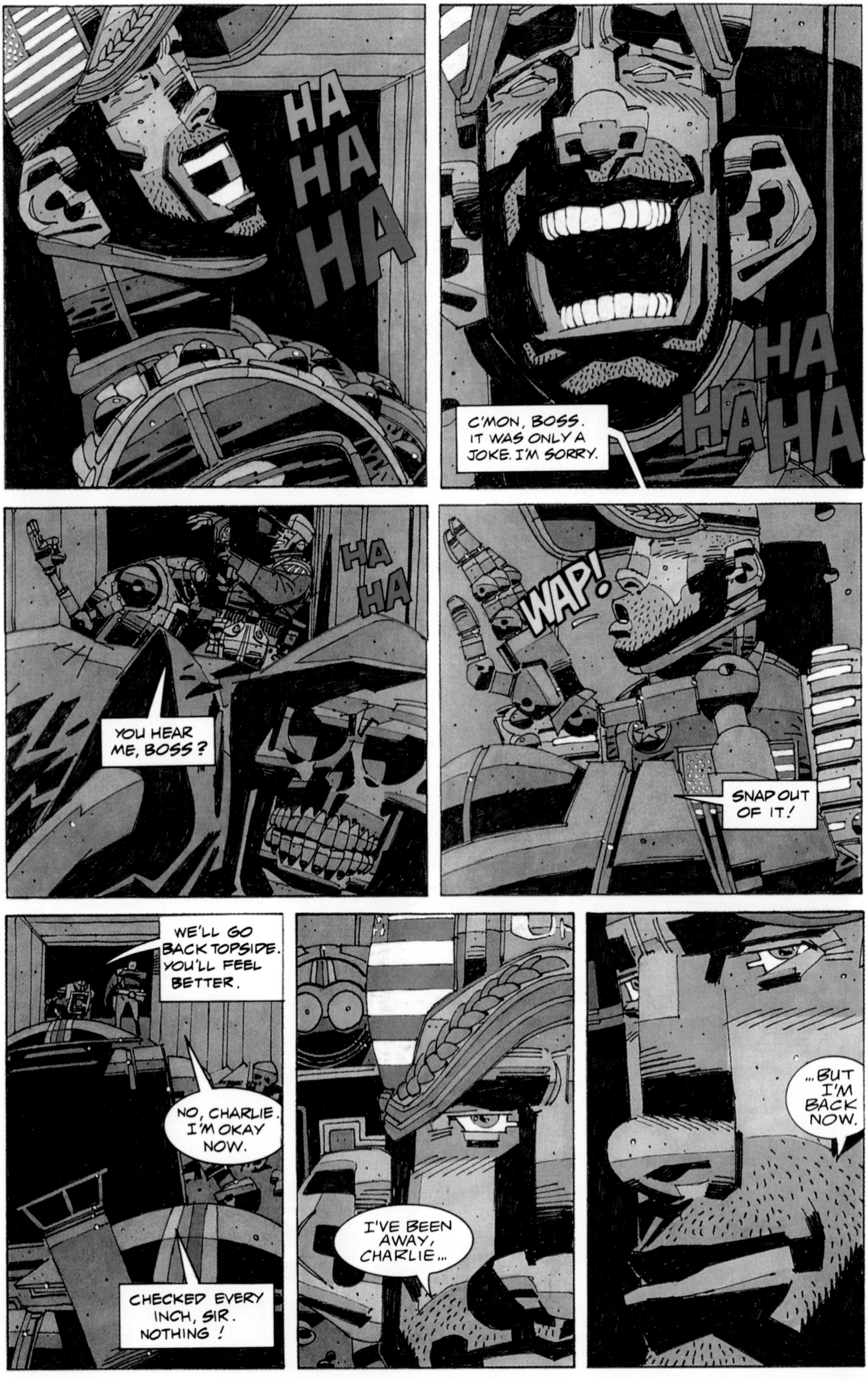
HA HA HA
HA HAHAHA
C'MON, BOSS. IT WAS ONLY A JOKE. I'M SORRY.
HA HA
YOU HEAR ME, BOSS?
WAP!
SNAP OUT OF IT!
WE'LL GO BACK TOPSIDE. YOU'LL FEEL BETTER.
NO, CHARLIE. I'M OKAY NOW.
CHECKED EVERY INCH, SIR. NOTHING!
I'VE BEEN AWAY, CHARLIE...
...BUT I'M BACK NOW.

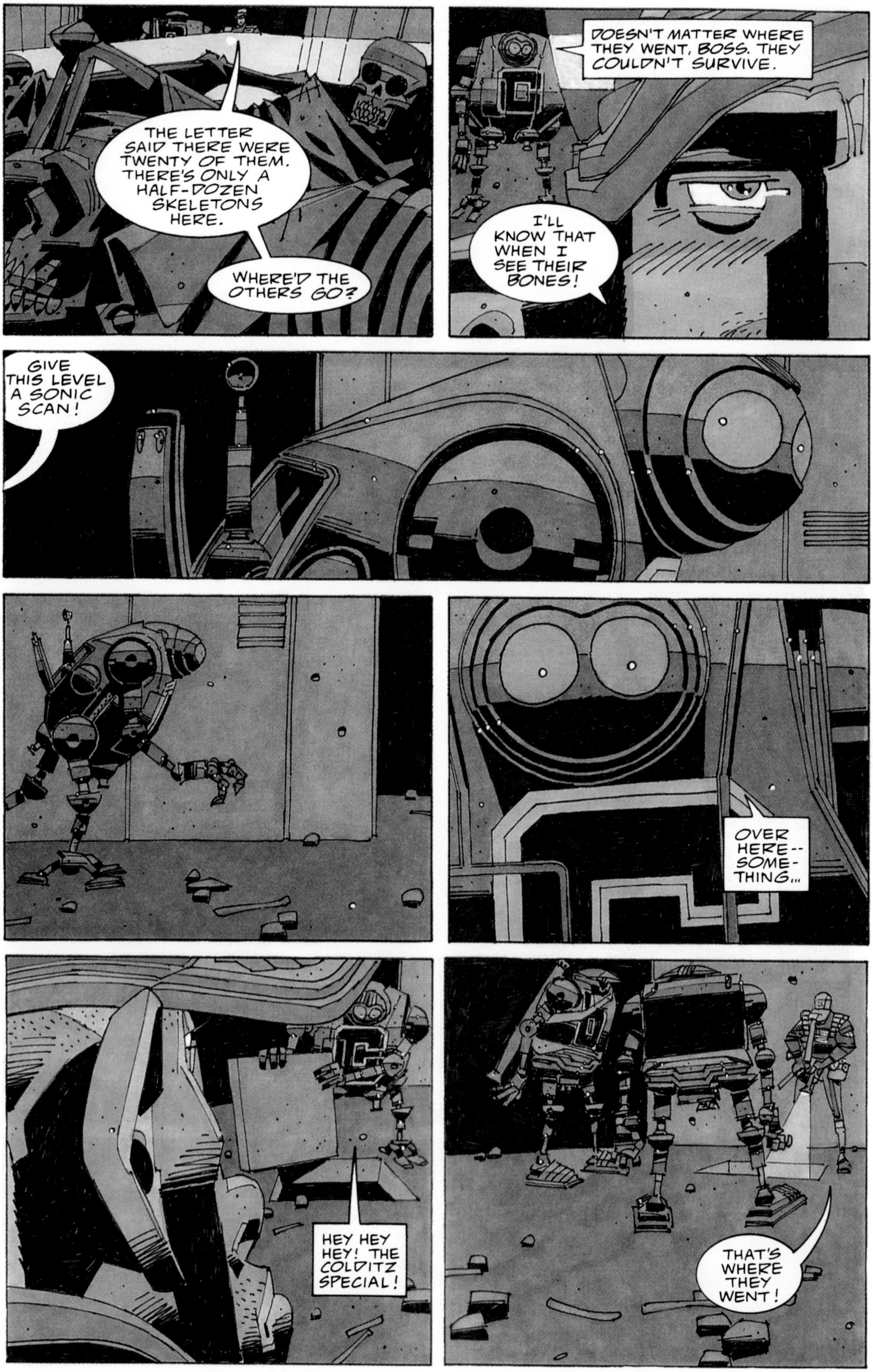
THE LETTER SAID THERE WERE TWENTY OF THEM. THERE'S ONLY A HALF-DOZEN SKELETONS HERE.
WHERE'D THE OTHERS GO?
DOESN'T MATTER WHERE THEY WENT, BOSS. THEY COULDN'T SURVIVE.
I'LL KNOW THAT WHEN I SEE THEIR BONES!
GIVE THIS LEVEL A SONIC SCAN!
OVER HERE-- SOME-THING...
HEY HEY HEY! THE COLDITZ SPECIAL!
THAT'S WHERE THEY WENT!

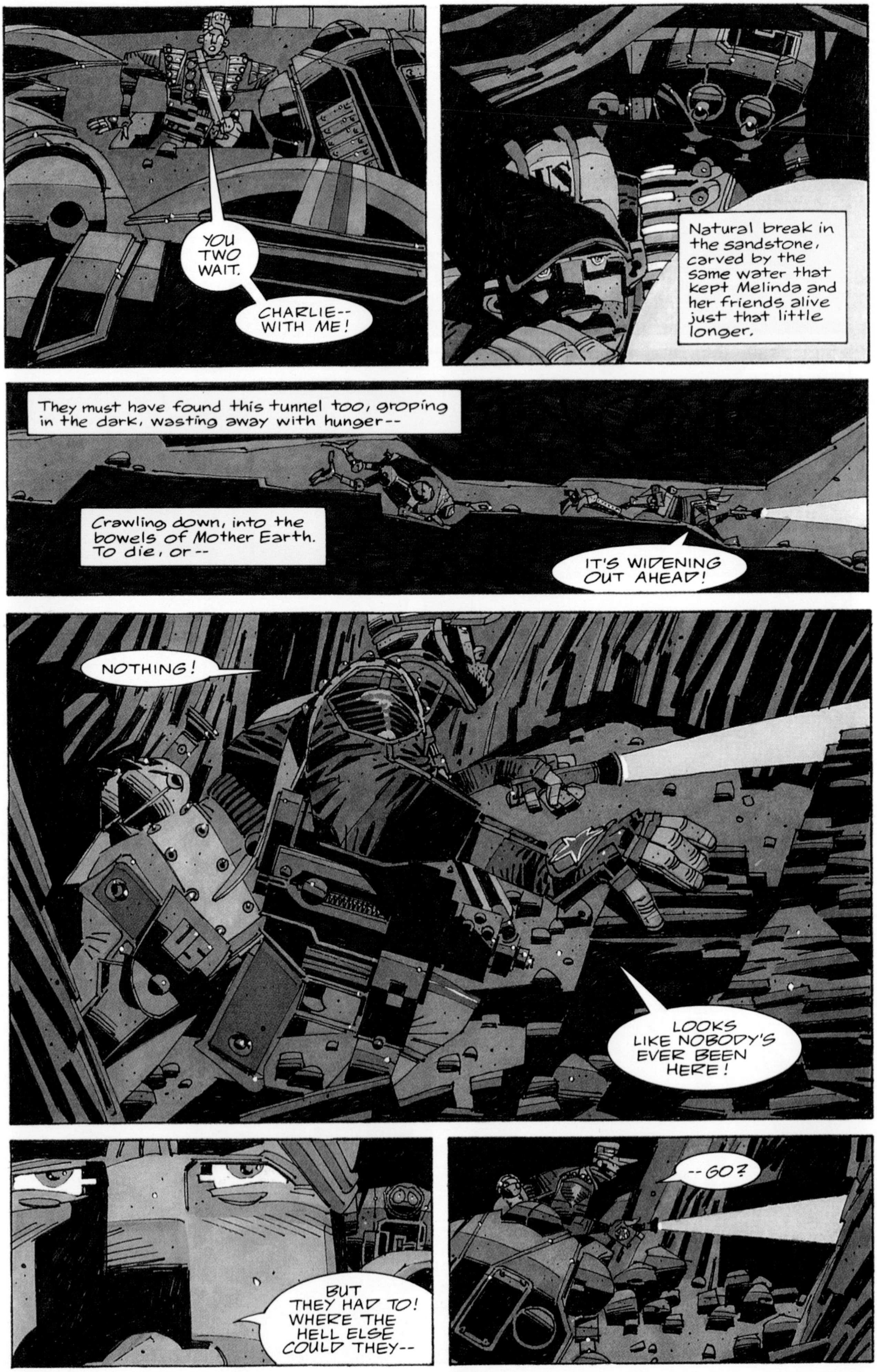

YOU TWO WAIT.
CHARLIE-- WITH ME!
Natural break in the sandstone, carved by the same water that kept Melinda and her friends alive just that little longer.
They must have found this tunnel too, groping in the dark, wasting away with hunger--
Crawling down, into the bowels of Mother Earth. To die, or--
IT'S WIDENING OUT AHEAD!
NOTHING!
LOOKS LIKE NOBODY'S EVER BEEN HERE!
BUT THEY HAD TO! WHERE THE HELL ELSE COULD THEY--
--GO?

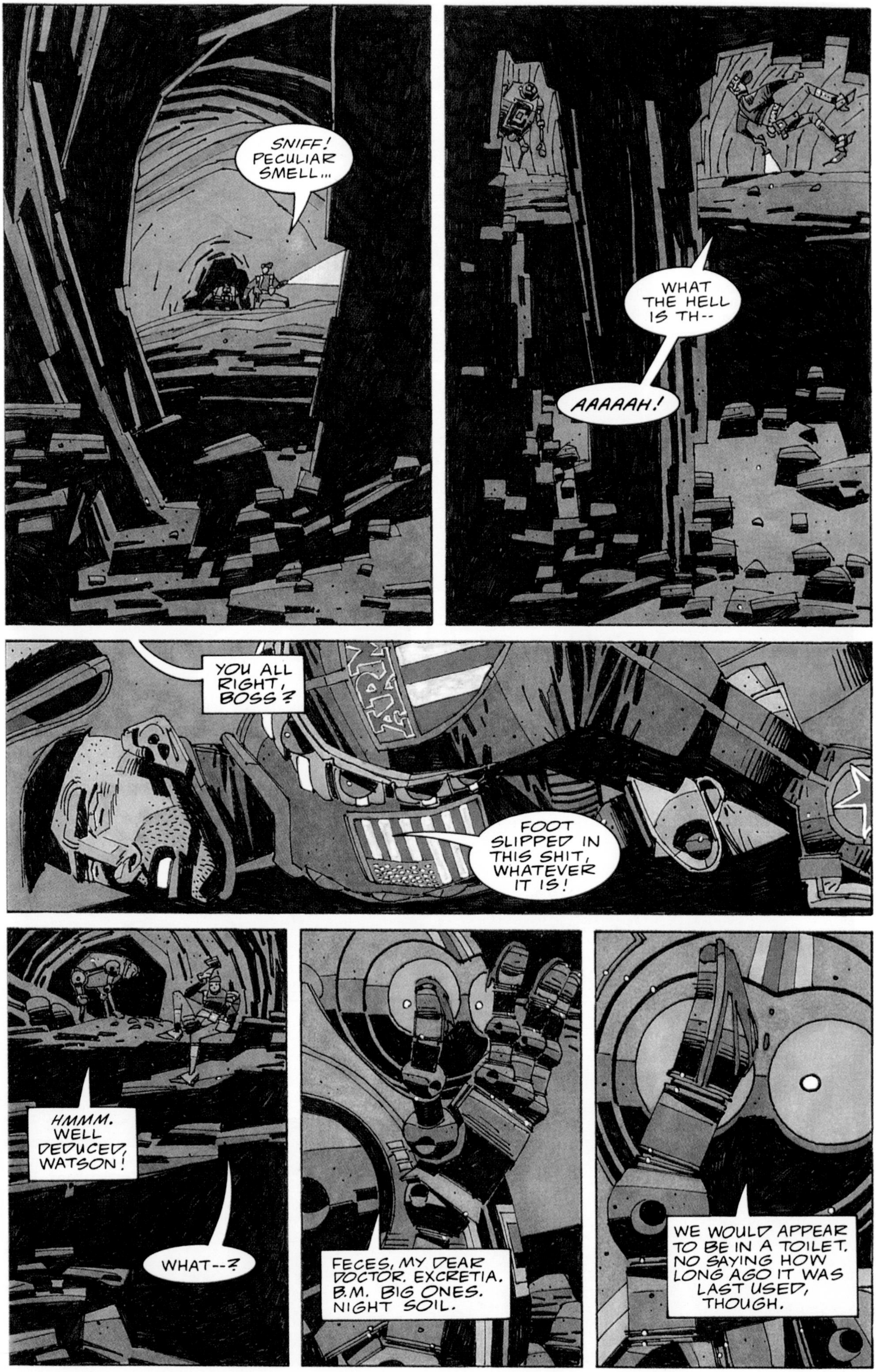
SNIFF! PECULIAR SMELL...
WHAT THE HELL IS TH--
AAAAAH!
YOU ALL RIGHT, BOSS?
FOOT SLIPPED IN THIS SHIT, WHATEVER IT IS!
HMMM. WELL DEDUCED, WATSON!
WHAT--?
FECES, MY DEAR DOCTOR. EXCRETIA. B.M. BIG ONES. NIGHT SOIL.
WE WOULD APPEAR TO BE IN A TOILET. NO SAYING HOW LONG AGO IT WAS LAST USED, THOUGH.

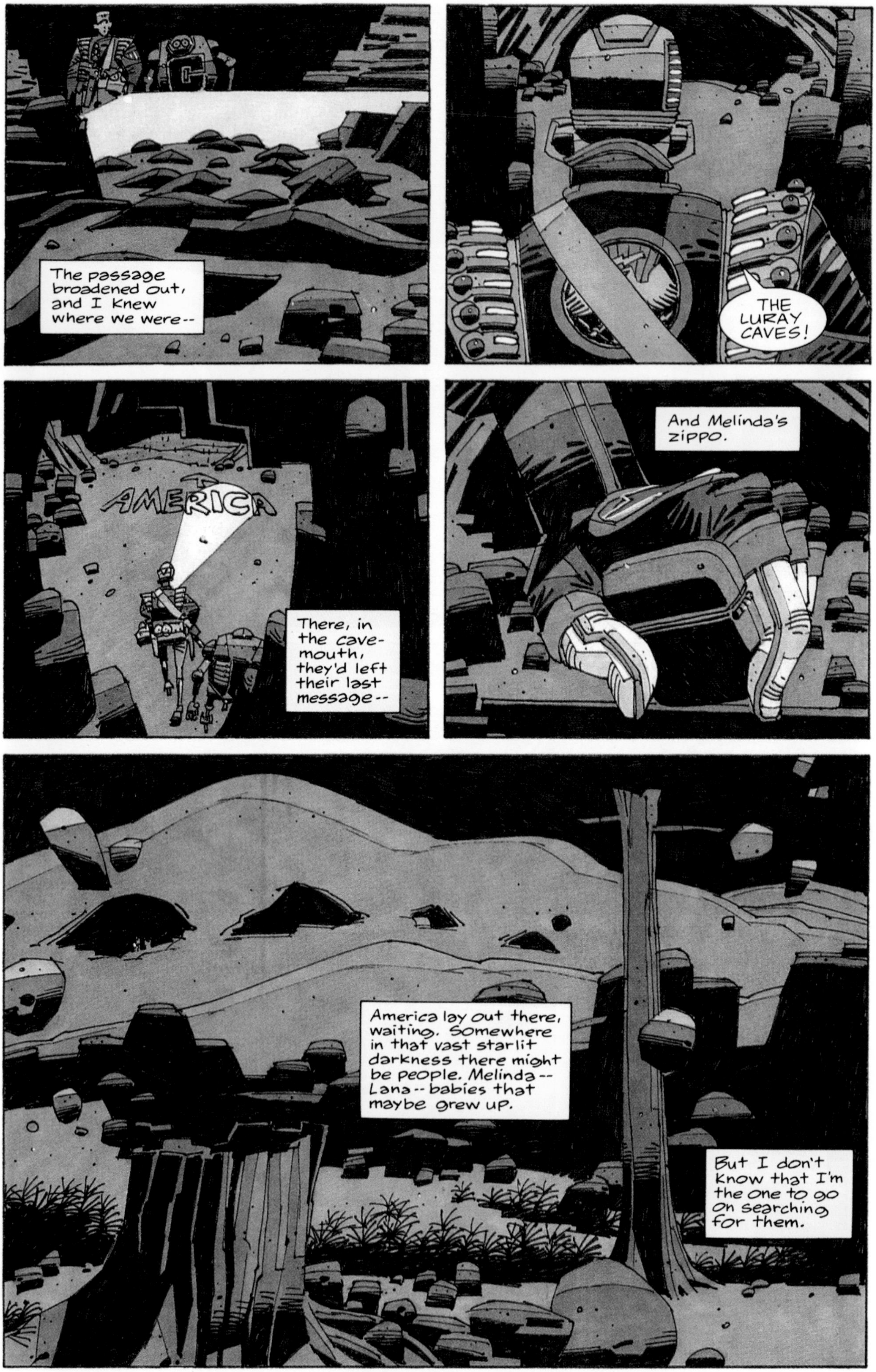
The passage broadened out, and I knew where we were--
THE LURAY CAVES!
AMERICA
There, in the cave-mouth, they'd left their last message--
And Melinda's zippo.
America lay out there, waiting. Somewhere in that vast starlit darkness there might be people. Melinda--Lana--babies that maybe grew up.
But I don't know that I'm the one to go on searching for them.

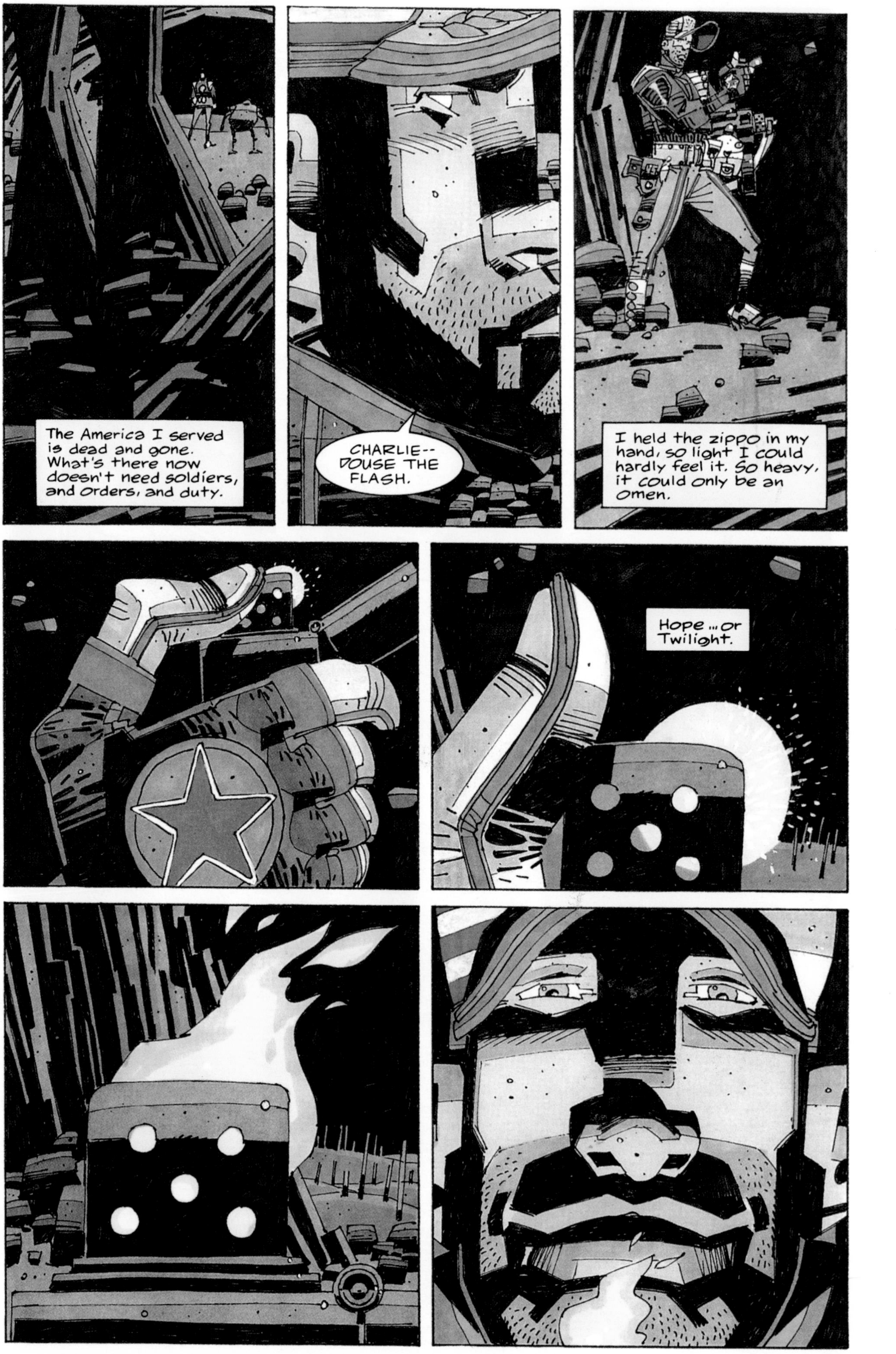

The America I served is dead and gone. What's there now doesn't need soldiers, and orders, and duty.
CHARLIE-- DOUSE THE FLASH.
I held the zippo in my hand, so light I could hardly feel it. So heavy, it could only be an omen.
Hope ... or Twilight.

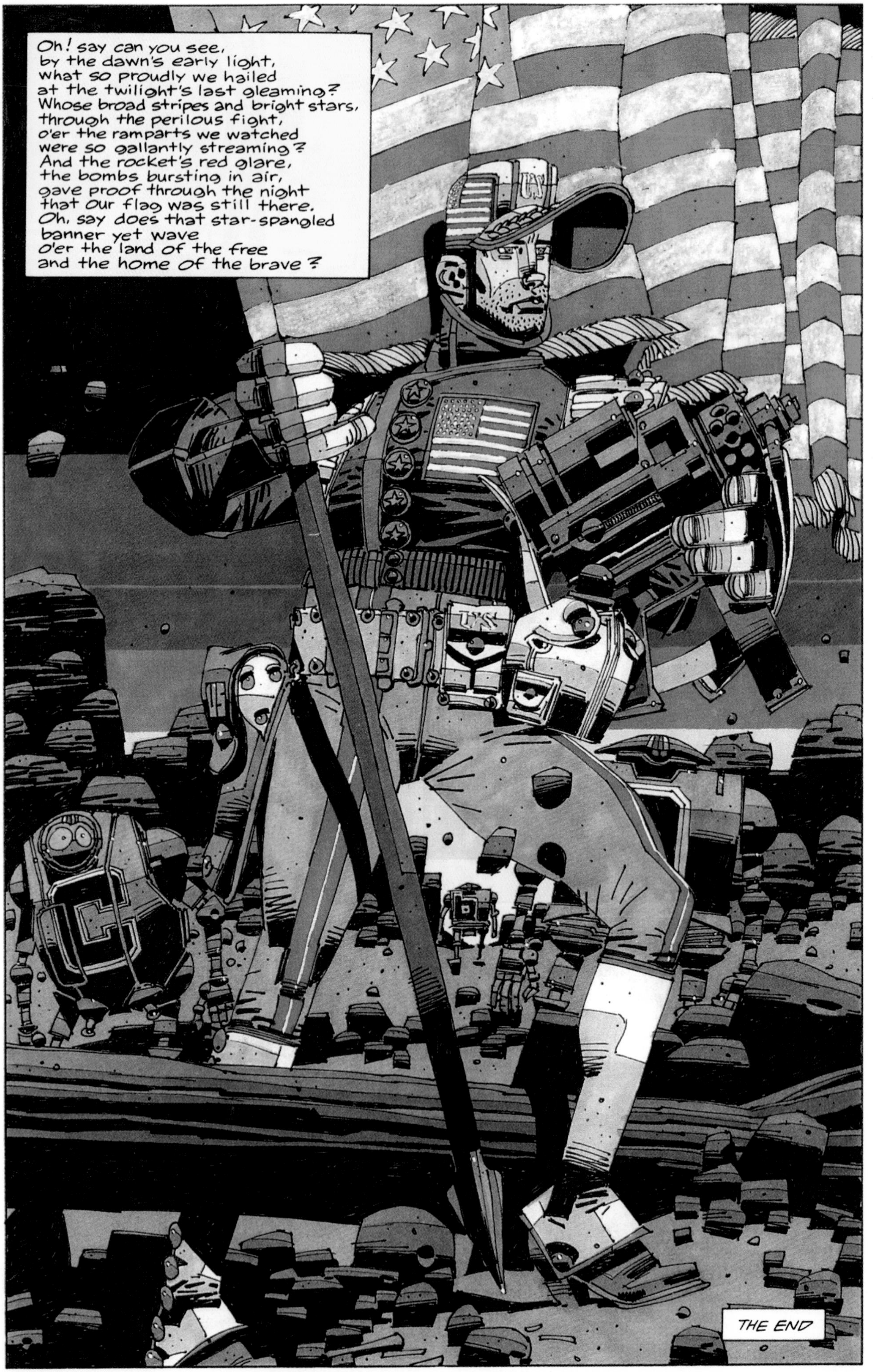
Oh! say can you see,
by the dawn's early light,
what so proudly we hailed
at the twilight's last gleaming?
Whose broad stripes and bright stars,
through the perilous fight,
o'er the ramparts we watched
were so gallantly streaming?
And the rocket's red glare,
the bombs bursting in air,
gave proof through the night
that our flag was still there.
Oh, say does that star-spangled
banner yet wave
o'er the land of the free
and the home of the brave?
THE END

GALLERY

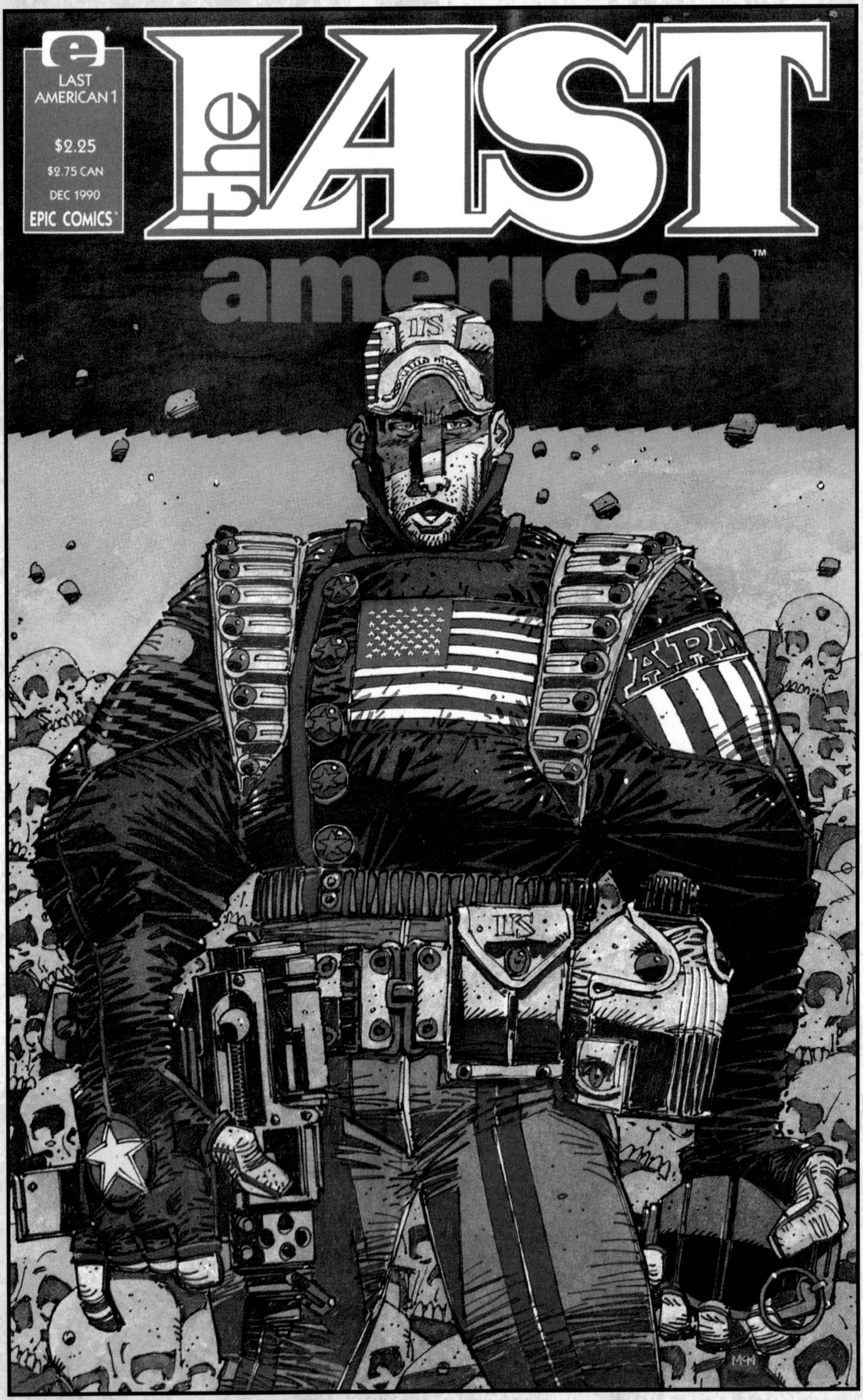
LAST
AMERICAN 1
$2.25
$2.75 CAN
DEC 1990
EPIC COMICS
the LAST
american™
US
ARM
US
McN

Epic cover 1 by **Mick McMahon**

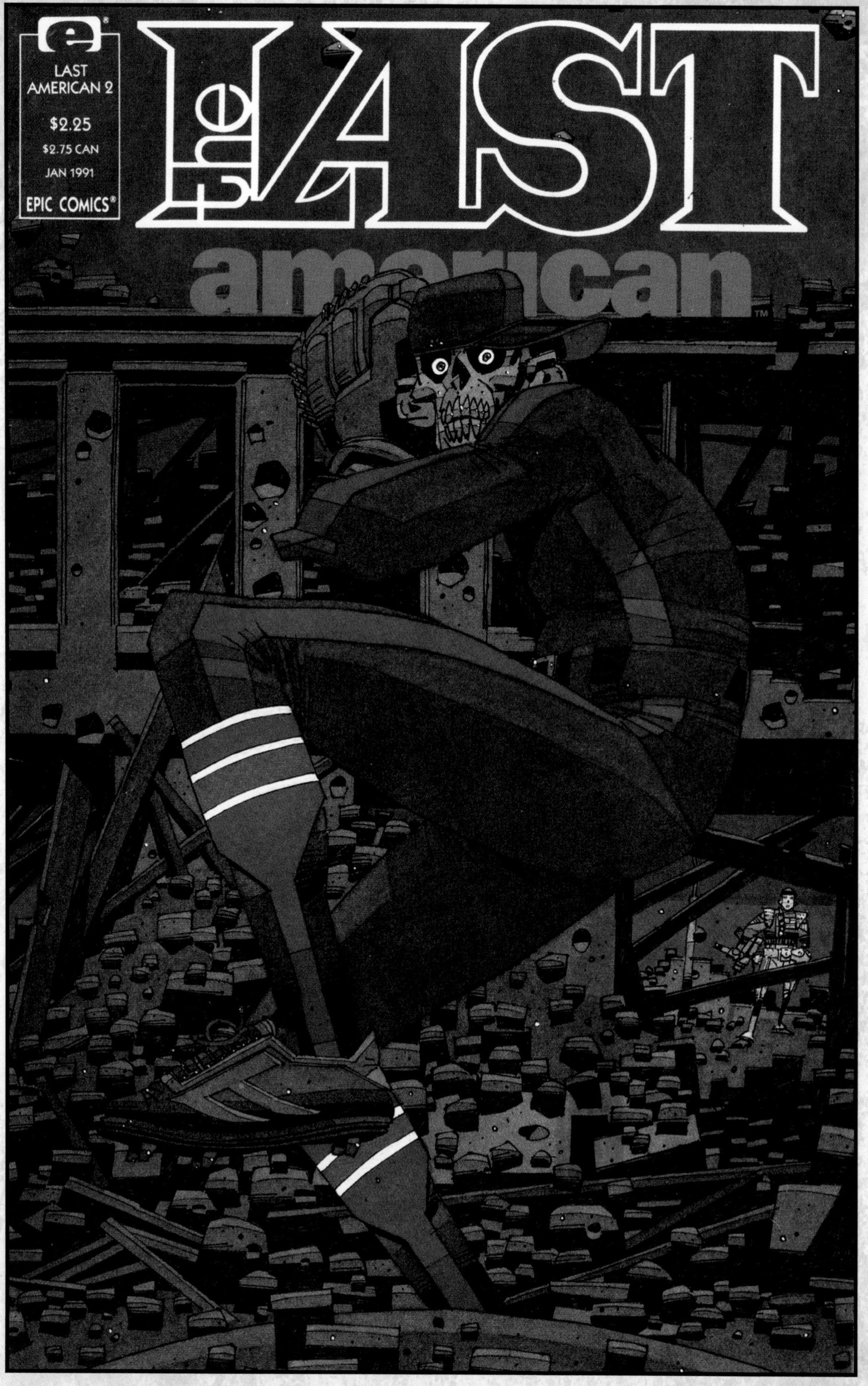
LAST
AMERICAN 2
$2.25
$2.75 CAN
JAN 1991
EPIC COMICS®
the LAST
american
TM

Epic cover 2 by **Mick McMahon**

LAST AMERICAN 3

$2.25
$2.75 CAN
FEB 1991

EPIC COMICS®

THE LAST american ™

Epic cover 3 by **Mick McMahon**

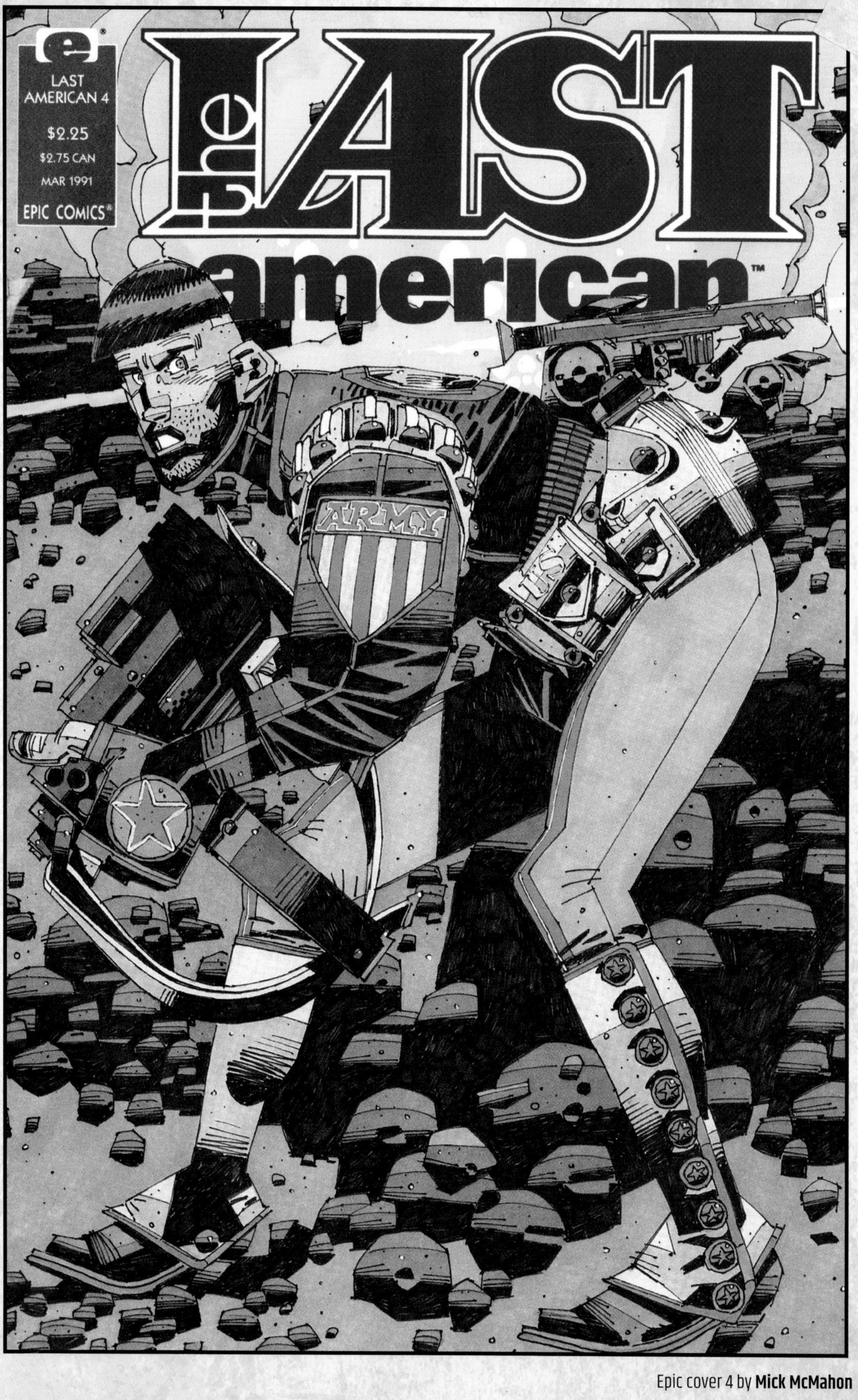
LAST AMERICAN 4
$2.25
$2.75 CAN
MAR 1991
EPIC COMICS
the LAST american
ARMY

Epic cover 4 by **Mick McMahon**

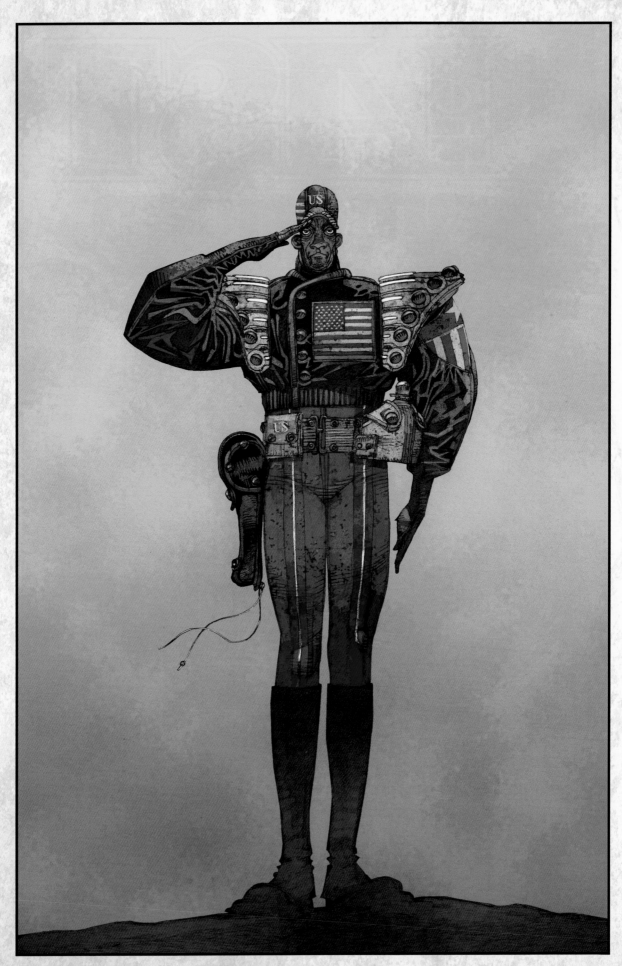

COM.X cover by **Mick McMahon**

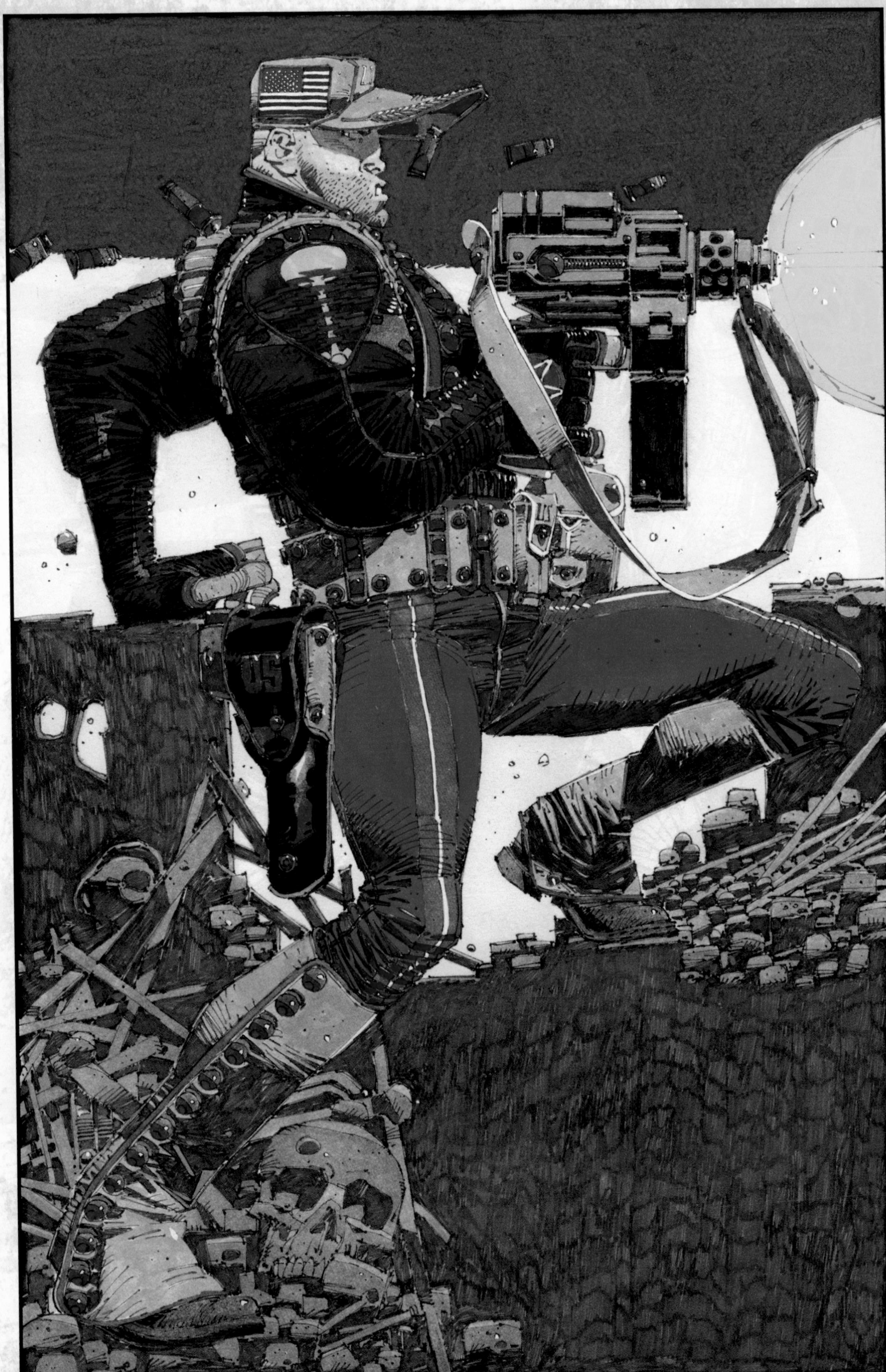

Cover by **Mick McMahon**

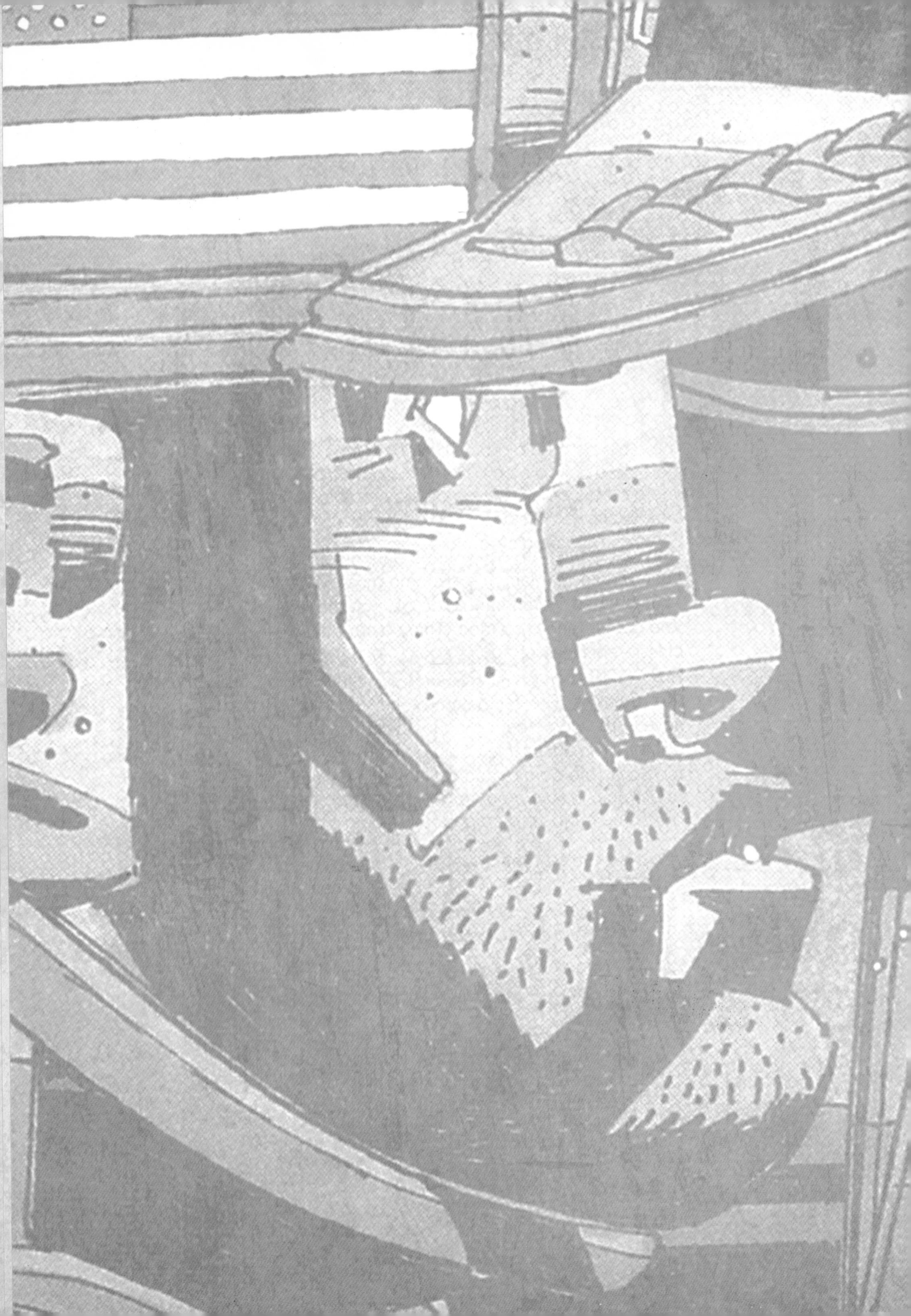